Fodor's InFocus
SINGAPORE

T0054218

Welcome to Singapore

Singapore may be a small city-state, but this gem is packed with attractions and experiences that defy its diminutive size. On one hand, it is a modern metropolis with impressive skyscrapers and an astonishingly efficient network of public transportation; on the other, it is as verdant as an urban hub could possibly be, with some of the most impressive gardens in the world and beautiful white-sand beaches. And the city's acclaimed hawkers, restaurants, and bars will keep you so well fed, watered, and entertained, you might just find it difficult to leave. As you plan your trip to Singapore, please confirm that places are still open and let us know when we need to make updates by writing to editors@fodors.com.

TOP REASONS TO GO

★ **Modern Marvels:** Sky-high pools, futuristic Supertrees, an indoor waterfall.

★ **Global Cuisine:** Singapore's local food shines especially bright amid global offerings.

★ **Outdoor Adventures:** Take a city break at one of the many manicured gardens, nature reserves, and beaches.

★ **World-Class Shopping:** Splurge at the renowned megamalls and boutiques on Orchard Road.

★ **Buzzing Nightlife:** From Chinatown speakeasies to Marina Bay bars.

Contents

MAPS

Chapter 1

EXPERIENCE
SINGAPORE

15 ULTIMATE EXPERIENCES

Singapore offers terrific experiences that should be on every traveler's list. Here are Fodor's top picks for a memorable trip.

1 | Futuristic Gardens

The extraordinary, 250-acre Gardens by the Bay has three waterfront gardens, air-conditioned conservatories, and a cluster of "Supertrees" linked by suspended walkways that soar up to 165 feet. *(Ch. 3)*

2 Mosques and Murals

Kampong Glam, Singapore's Malay center, is home to the golden-domed Sultan Mosque, colorful murals, Malay eateries and hip cafés, and stores crammed with beautiful batik fabric. *(Ch. 5)*

3 Action-Packed Beaches

Sentosa, a beachy paradise just off the coast of Singapore, has theme parks, resorts, and activities galore. Bungee jump or zip-line on Siloso Beach or throw frisbees and order cocktails at Tanjong Beach Club. *(Ch. 9)*

4 Singapore Sling

You can order a legendary Singapore Sling at just about any bar, but nothing beats sipping the coral-hued cocktail where it was first created—the Long Bar at Raffles Singapore. *(Ch. 3)*

5 Chinatown

Red lanterns and ornate architecture mix with trendy restaurants, chic bars, and superlative hawker fare in this historic neighborhood. *(Ch. 4)*

6 The World's Highest Infinity Pool

Marina Bay Sands's expansive swimming pool—the world's largest and highest at 650 feet above ground—offers a million-dollar view that blurs the line between sky and cityscape. *(Ch. 3)*

7 A Stunning Waterfall ... at the Airport

Changi International Airport isn't any ordinary airport. In its Jewel complex, the world's tallest indoor waterfall tumbles 130 feet from an oculus the size of a truck and is framed by a lush garden. *(Ch. 7)*

8 Museum Hopping

Singapore's finest museums and monuments are housed in grand colonial buildings in the Civic District. The Asian Civilisations Museum and National Gallery Singapore are must-sees. *(Ch. 3)*

9 Hawker Centers

No need to splurge for a taste of award-winning food. Hawker centers offer quick, delicious meals at low prices, making it easy to eat exceptionally well. *(Ch. 4)*

10 The Singapore Botanic Gardens

This 184-acre oasis of calm, a UNESCO World Heritage Site, is threaded with landscaped gardens; swaths of rain forest; a tranquil lake; and a ravishing collection of orchids. *(Ch. 6)*

11 Shopping on Orchard Road

Roam one of the world's most famous shopping streets, where glitzy megamalls are linked by underground tunnels so you don't have to duck traffic or brave the tropical swelter outside. *(Ch. 6)*

12 Peranakan Culture

Joo Chiat is the seat of Peranakan (a mix of local Chinese and Indonesian/Malay) culture, dotted with well-preserved shophouses, businesses, street art, and beloved eateries and bars. *(Ch. 7)*

13 Kopi Break in Tiong Bahru

Take a *kopi* (coffee) and cupcake break at Plain Vanilla or browse children's books at Woods in the Books in one of Singapore's oldest residential neighborhoods turned hipster haven *(Ch. 4)*

14 Bumboat Ride on Singapore River

Float by Merlion Park and the warehouses of Clarke's Quay on the tranquil Singapore River, where hundreds of bumboats once transported goods daily. *(Ch. 3)*

15 Little India's Markets and Temples

You could spend an entire day getting lost in Little India's warren of colorful streets and alleys, taking in temples, markets, and endless food stalls. *(Ch. 5)*

WHAT'S WHERE

1 **Civic District and Marina Bay.** The colonial-era buildings and museums of the Civic District contrast with the futuristic look of Marina Bay.

2 **Chinatown, Tanjong Pagar, and the CBD.** The temples, parks, and creative buzz of Chinatown's streets flow into the space-age skyscrapers of the CBD.

3 **Tiong Bahru, Singapore River, and River Valley.** The bends of the Singapore River are home to some of the city's hippest cafés, boutiques, and art galleries.

4 **Little India and Kampong Glam.** Colorful temples, the gleaming Sultan Mosque, and hipster haunts and street art.

5 **Orchard Road.** Where shopping malls share space with posh hotels and restaurants.

6 **Eastern Districts.** Changi, the world's best airport; Joo Chiat, a Peranakan enclave; and Geylang Serai, with a thriving market.

7 **Western Districts.** The West has nature reserves, the Singapore Zoo; and posh neighborhoods like Dempsey Hill.

8 **Sentosa Island.** Beach resorts and theme parks.

9 **Pulau Ubin.** One of the few remaining slices of tropical Singapore.

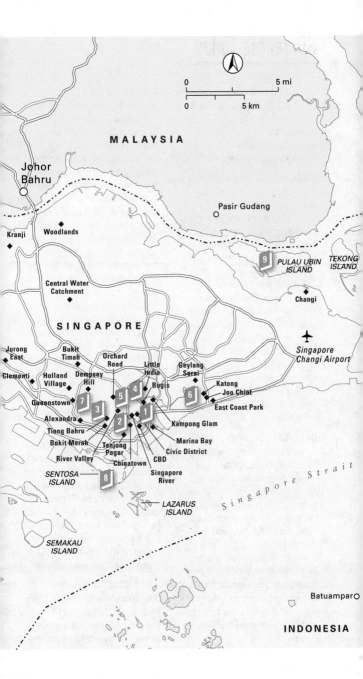

MALAYSIA

Johor
Bahru

Pasir Gudang

Kranji

Woodlands

9 PULAU UBIN
ISLAND

TEKONG
ISLAND

Central Water
Catchment

Changi

S I N G A P O R E

Jurong
East

Bukit
Timah

Orchard
Road

Little
India

Geylang
Serai

Singapore
Changi Airport

Clementi

Holland
Village

Dempsey
Hill

Bugis

Katong

5

4

6

Joo Chiat

Queenstown

7

3

1

East Coast Park

Alexandra

2

Kampong Glam

Tiong Bahru

Bukit Merah

Tanjong
Pagar

Marina Bay

River Valley

Chinatown

Civic District

CBD

SENTOSA
ISLAND

8

Singapore
River

LAZARUS
ISLAND

Singapore Strait

SEMAKAU
ISLAND

Batuampar

INDONESIA

0   5 mi

0   5 km

Singapore Today

Singapore's reputation as "Asia light" is a well-earned one. Everyone speaks English, transportation is clean and efficient, and there's plenty to see and experience.

CONSERVATIVE POLICIES

Singapore has a booming economy and is one of Asia's most stable nations, but state control is also strong. The Ministry of Home Affairs Internal Security Department still enforces the Internal Security Act (ISA), a draconian law that permits indefinite detention without recourse. The press and the LGBTQ community also face challenges in Singapore, and no antidiscrimination laws exist to protect them. Gay sex has been decriminalized, but same-sex relationships are not recognized under Singapore law.

DIVERSITY

Singapore is a remarkably peaceful multicultural society, where English acts as the common lingo. The city-state is composed by a majority of citizens of Chinese descent, followed by Malays and Indians. A big number of working Western expatriates, and an even bigger number of foreign immigrant workers, add to the mix, contributing to the creation of a dynamic workforce and cohesive multicultural society.

POPULAR CULTURE

Singapore certainly supports the arts, with performances and festivals throughout the year. From the 1960s pop music that imitated the rhythms of the Beatles and the Rolling Stones, to a vibrant local film industry, Singapore has always been at the forefront of popular culture in Asia. And, regardless of a few censorship incidents (most notably the cancellation of shows by Elton John and orders to "tone down" the stage act of artists like Avril Lavigne, Gwen Stefani, and the Pussycat Dolls), the Lion City is also the best place to catch international artists and bands on their Asian tours. Local and international literature is big, too: the yearly Singapore Writers Festival is one of the most acclaimed in the region.

THRIVING NIGHTLIFE

Singaporeans work hard and, maybe as a reflection of so many rules and fines, they also party very hard: clubs and discos stay open until the wee hours of the night, and in areas like Kampong Glam and the quays of the Singapore River, there's a bar on every corner.

CAFÉ CULTURE

Singapore's national obsession with kopi ("coffee" in Malay) means international cuppas are served everywhere, from the simple and ubiquitous hawker centers to all sorts of modern, stylish shops often housed in beautifully colored, century-old shophouses. Made with Robusta brew from nearby Indonesia, Singaporean coffee is usually long, frothy, and served with heavy doses of sugar or condensed milk.

THE ART SCENE

Singapore's many landmark art festivals (think of the Singapore Writers Festival or the Singapore Biennale) are also some of Southeast Asia's most important. The central areas of Bugis and Kampong Glam are the preferred haunts of local creative types, who fill the rows of hip hole-in-the-wall bars with art exhibits, spoken-word nights, and live music.

FOOD AND SHOPPING

For foodies, Singapore offers the best of both worlds: both traditional, casual street food at hawker centers and upscale establishments, Michelin-starred restaurants, and world cuisines. And, Singapore has some of the best malls in the world—air-conditioned paradises filled with designer brands and the latest technological gadgets.

A JEWEL OF AN AIRPORT

Few countries in the world have an airport hub as good as Singapore's—or one as beautiful and visit-worthy. Opened in 2019, Jewel Changi is a rain forest–themed entertainment complex on the landside of Changi International Airport, whose main centerpiece, the Rain Vortex, is the world's highest indoor waterfall.

LOOKING AHEAD

Singapore's tourism is in constant flux, and moving well beyond the city center. A new integrated development will transform the Jurong Lake District by 2026, in line with the government's aim of spreading hotel offerings across non-central areas of the island. Many hotels have just opened in Singapore: think of Mondrian Singapore Duxton, soaring above Chinatown's shophouses, or the oriental-chic Artyzen Singapore, which is the first Orchard Road property by this Hong Kong–based franchise. Pullman Singapore Hill Street, set to debut in October 2023, is one latest upscale business hotel in the thick of Singapore's Civic District.

What to Eat and Drink in Singapore

CHILLI CRAB

One of the country's signature dishes, chilli crab is on the must-try list for seafood-loving visitors. It's typically made using mud crabs, which are cooked in a mildly spicy, tomato-based gravy. Try it at Long Beach Seafood.

HAINAN CHICKEN RICE

Although it originated in the Hainan Province of China, Hainanese chicken rice is considered one of Singapore's national dishes. A plump chicken is poached, and the stock is used, along with garlic and ginger, to cook the rice. Both are then served with a ginger-and-garlic dipping sauce. The most famous Hainan chicken rice stall is Tian Tian at the Maxwell Food Court.

SINGAPORE SLING

The signature pink drink, made with gin, brandy, pineapple juice, and grenadine, was created at the iconic Raffles Hotel back in 1915. You can still drink it in the hotel's legendary Long Bar while munching on peanuts and throwing their shells on the floor— the only place in Singapore you can legally litter.

LAKSA

Not to be confused with Malaysian assam laksa, Singaporean katong laksa is a bowl of rice noodles and seafood in a curry-like broth of coconut milk, dried shrimp, and spices. One popular place to try it is 328 Katong Laksa (who beat Gordon Ramsay in a cooking showdown).

BAK KUT TEH

This pork rib soup in herbal broth is commonly eaten for breakfast and makes for a great hangover cure (the name translates to "meat bone tea," but there is no tea in the broth).

DURIAN

It's an acquired taste, but fans of this fruit, which smells dreadful but tastes good once you get past it, know that Singapore is one of the best cities to get durian.

SOY SAUCE CHICKEN

The Hong Kong–style soy sauce chicken can primarily be found in Chinatown, but the dish recently gained popularity worldwide when Liao Fan's hawker stall was awarded a Michelin star for its version.

Bak Kut Teh

SALTED EGG FISH SKIN CHIPS
This recent food trend is currently Singapore's number-one snack—and it's addictive. Crispy fish skin is coated with salted egg yolk and spices for an umami bomb. Pick up a bag of Irvin's at Changi International Airport.

HOKKIEN MEE
This popular hawker dish consists of stir-fried egg and rice noodles with eggs, prawn, and pork.

KAYA TOAST
White bread toast with a creamy spread made of coconut milk, caramelized sugar, and eggs is served for breakfast with soft-boiled eggs and soy sauce.

ES POTONG
Singapore's take on the ice cream sandwich, *es potong*, or "cut ice," is ice cream cut into blocks and wrapped in white bread.

Best Hotel Pools in Singapore

MARINA BAY SANDS

There can be no list of Singapore's hotel pools that does not include the iconic infinity pool on the 57th floor—650 feet above the ground—of the Marina Bay Sands Hotel. The view is nothing short of spectacular.

FAR EAST HOTELS OF SENTOSA

One amazing pool deck can be accessed from three Far East brand hotels: The Barracks Hotel Sentosa, Village Hotel Sentosa, and The Outpost Hotel Sentosa. Its highlight is a lazy river that flows through waterfalls.

CONRAD CENTENNIAL

It may not be brand new, but this 20-meter pool remains a sure-fire hotspot for a romantic date or a choreographic night swim with the twinkling lights of the Singapore Flyer and Marina Bay's skyline in the background.

SHANGRI-LA SINGAPORE

Sorry parents, this one's specifically designed for the kids. Developed around a boat equipped with water slides, this playground has six different water play areas, including lazy rivers, jet cannons, and shallow wading pools. It makes it easy to lounge with a cocktail on the surrounding poolside deck as you watch over your kids.

CAPELLA SINGAPORE

For a tranquil escape—one that recalls the rice terraces of Bali—wade in this multi-tiered, Sentosa Island hotel pool set amid lush greenery and colonial buildings next to Palawan Beach. The pool has ocean views and glimpses of the rain forest.

Parkroyal on Pickering

PARKROYAL ON PICKERING

This hotel's wellness floor features a spa, elevated garden, and this outdoor infinity pool, which offers city views. Greenery and partially enclosed cabanas shaped like birdcages give the pool a rather enchanted feel.

FULLERTON BAY HOTEL

Built over the water, the luxurious hotel offers sweeping views of Marina Bay, including from its rooftop infinity pool and whirlpool tubs. Framed by tropical plants, the pool sits next to the Lantern Rooftop Bar, so you can grab a cocktail between swims.

ANDAZ SINGAPORE

On the 25th floor of this sleek city hotel, the Andaz's infinity pool offers swimmers jaw-dropping views over the CBD and Marina Bay. Bugis and Haji Lane are just an elevator trip away, but the annexed sky bar Mr. Stork entices you to stay well after dusk.

SOFITEL SINGAPORE SENTOSA

Surrounded by colonial-style buildings and palm trees and adorned with aquamarine tiles, this Sentosa Island hotel pool is expansive enough for each guest to swim around with some privacy.

W SINGAPORE SENTOSA COVE

In addition to a swim-up bar, this sleek hotel pool has complimentary private cabanas (first come, first served) with their own iPads.

Best Cocktail Bars in Singapore

NATIVE
This small Chinatown bar connects cocktails to the local heritage by foraging for local ingredients and using Asian spirits such as jackfruit rum or arrak from Sri Lanka in its unique concoctions.

GIBSON BAR
Come to this cocktail and seafood bar with a casual vibe for the great oyster happy hour. The bar's namesake Gibson drink, created using house-made Ginjo sake vermouth, is a must-try. Seasonal offerings highlight Southeast Asian ingredients such as starfruit and pandan.

MANHATTAN BAR
Entering the Regent Hotel's bar is like stepping back into the golden age of New York City. The bar offers more than 150 whiskeys and crafts Negronis made with spirits that have been solera-aged in the hotel's own rickhouse.

NUTMEG & CLOVE
To taste true local flavors, order from the Flavour and Memories menu, using herbs, fruits, spices, and other ingredients commonly found in Singapore. There is a variation of Singapore Sling, of course, but also a cocktail made with crab.

28 HONG KONG STREET
Hidden behind an unmarked door, 28 Hong Kong Street was named the best bar in Asia at the very first Asia's 50 Best Bars Awards. Years later, the speakeasy remains at the forefront of Singapore's craft-cocktail movement, offering creative libations and an energetic vibe.

Atlas

ATLAS
A grand art deco–style temple of cocktails inspired by the Jazz Age, Atlas Bar is a sight to behold. Located in the lobby of the Parkview Square building, between Bugis and Kampong Glam, it has a three-story tower filled with more than 1,000 bottles of gin.

BITTERS & LOVE
Tell the bartenders at this 19th-century shophouse speakeasy your preferences and let them create a cocktail just for you. Prices are approachable,

but if you're feeling more extravagant, request a bespoke cocktail made using rare spirits they've collected.

JIGGER & PONY
This sultry bar and lounge specializes in traditional martinis and lesser-known Asian classics. The magazine-like menu offers lessons in cocktail history, and the renditions of the classics stand out.

TIPPLING CLUB
Not only is Tippling Club an award-winning restaurant, but it also pushes the mixology

boundaries. The chef and bartender collaborate closely to develop cocktails that are often inspired by culinary creations.

PAPA DOBLE
This outpost of Hong Kong's award-winning Hemingway-inspired bar has the same menu, but the bar is twice as big. Bartenders create drinks such as The Snows of Kilimanjaro, made with marshmallow gin and gruyere cheese, in a "mini-lab."

Outdoor Adventures in Singapore

MACRITCHIE NATURE TRAIL & RESERVOIR PARK

MacRitchie's highlight is its Treetop Walk, a suspension bridge that connects the park's two highest points and offers a bird's-eye view of the forest canopy.

PALAWAN BEACH

One of Sentosa Island's best free beaches for families, Palawan has white sands and facilities that include lockers, free showers, nearby restaurants, and kid-friendly attractions like the aviary and the animal show at the Palawan Amphitheatre.

CHESTNUT NATURE PARK

Singapore's largest nature park, at just over 200 acres, has two hiking trails: one on the north side that's just over 2 miles and a shorter route on the south-side that's 1.3 miles. There are also mountain biking trails.

BUKIT TIMAH NATURE RESERVE

Some know Bukit Timah as a posh residential district where wealthy expats and well-heeled Singaporeans live in expansive bungalows and high-rise condominiums, but it's also home to Singapore's tallest peak (at just 537 feet). Declared an ASEAN Heritage Park in 2011, the hill's eponymous, 163-acre nature reserve contains one of Singapore's last remaining primary rain forests, so-called because it is still in its untouched, original condition. You can hike, cycle the city-state's first mountain-biking trail, and take part to a monthly guided nature walk.

MARINA BAY WALK
You can take in several waterfront attractions along this easily accessible urban walk. Start at the Merlion statue in Merlion Park, and then stroll along the water to The Esplanade.

SUNGEI BULOH WETLAND RESERVE
The island nation's first ASEAN Heritage Park encompasses 500 acres of wetlands, including a mangrove forest. It's a haven for bird-watchers year-round, but especially from September to March.

MEGA ADVENTURE PARK
Thrill seekers love this park's attractions, which include the MegaZip, a 1,500-foot-long zip-line that starts off at 250 feet above the ground and traverses treetops before finishing just off Siloso Beach.

FORT SILOSO SKYWALK
This free skywalk on Sentosa Island was opened in 2015 as part of Singapore's Golden Jubilee celebration. The treetop trail is 11 stories high and 594 feet long, bringing explorers to historic Fort Siloso, a gun battery built in the late 1800s. The glass elevator up to the start of the skywalk runs from 9 am to 7 pm; in the off hours, you have to climb the stairs.

EASTERN COASTAL PARK CONNECTOR NETWORK CYCLING TRAIL
This 26-mile cycling loop runs through diverse scenery that include beach parks, mangroves, and areas forested with heritage trees. One easy starting point is Sun Plaza Park, near the Tampines MRT station.

What to Read and Watch

CRAZY RICH ASIANS

Kevin Kwan's laugh-out-loud story of a Singaporean man bringing his American girlfriend home to meet his obscenely wealthy family and friends was also a hit film.

THE SINGAPORE GRIP

J.G. Farrell's satirical look at a British family during Japan's entry into WWII and the occupation of Singapore.

12 STOREYS

A 1997 film looking into the sometimes tumultuous lives of several people living in one apartment in Singapore.

15

An expansion of director Royston Tan's 2002 short film of the same name, *15* (2003) is about teenage gangsters in Singapore's suburbs.

CHICKEN RICE WAR (JIYUAN QIAOHE)

Can love bring two people divided by secret family recipes together? Meet the Chans and the Wongs, two generations of street hawkers in this rom com from 2000.

LONG LONG TIME AGO

Zhao Di, the unwanted and pregnant second wife of an older man, is forced to return to her own family. The 2016 film is beautiful, fun, and touching.

THE ART OF CHARLIE CHAN HOCK CHYE

Sonny Liew's *New York Times* bestselling graphic novel tells the story of a fictional Singapore comic art genius and is a pungent metaphor of the autocratic development of Singapore's postwar politics.

GLASS CATHEDRAL

Winner of the 2014 Singapore Literature Prize Commendation Award, Andrew Koh's sensitive depiction of homosexuality in conservative Singapore is a landmark in local literature.

MINISTRY OF MORAL PANIC

Amanda Lee Koe's award-winning collection of short stories offers a frank yet improbable chance to understand Singapore and its denizens through a young, revelatory voice.

SAINT JACK

Adapted from a novel by Paul Theroux, Peter Bogdanovich's 1979 film tells the story of a good-hearted American pimp in pre-1980s Singapore.

17A KEONG SAIK ROAD

Charmaine Leung's insightful autobiography of growing up as the daughter of a brothel's madame in 1970s Chinatown.

TRAVEL SMART

Updated by
Marco Ferrarese

★ **CAPITAL:**
Singapore

♦ **POPULATION:**
5,982,361

💬 **LANGUAGE:**
English, Malay,
Mandarin Chinese,
and Tamil

$ **CURRENCY:**
Singapore Dollars

☎ **COUNTRY CODE:**
65

⚠ **EMERGENCIES:**
Fire and Ambulance:
995; Police: 999

🚗 **DRIVING:**
On the Left

⚡ **ELECTRICITY:**
220/240V/50 cycles;
electrical plugs have
three flat prongs
forming a triangle

🕘 **TIME:**
12 hours ahead of New
York

🌐 **WEB RESOURCES:**
www.visitsingapore.com

thehoneycombers.com/
singapore/

www.changiairport.com

✈ **AIRPORT:**
SIN

MALAYSIA

SINGAPORE

Singapore Strait

INDONESIA

Know Before You Go

Is Singapore as strict as everyone says? Can you drink the water? Is it safe to travel alone? You may have a few questions before you head to this thriving city-state in Southeast Asia. Here, we give you a few tips and tricks to make your trip a whole lot smoother so you can focus on other things—like which walking shoes will best carry you across the city.

IT'S GENERALLY SAFE

Singapore is one of the safest, easiest, and most efficient cities to navigate, which is why it's often named one of the best cities for solo travelers. Petty crime is rare in Singapore and violent crime even more uncommon. The streets are well-lit, and the public transportation system is safe and efficient, even after hours. But even though Singapore is a very safe place to travel, use general caution.

YES, THE LAWS ARE STRICT

Singapore charges hefty fines for what may be trivial acts in other countries. It's not a myth that chewing gum is banned, and jaywalking, the act of crossing the road outside the white stripes, could result in a fine of S$50 the first time, and up to S$1,000 and a jail term of 3 months for repeat offenders. You can be fined up to S$1,000 for smoking in prohibited areas and S$1,000 for littering. Other criminal offenses include vandalism, not flushing the toilet, and carrying or consuming drugs.

IT'S SUPER CLEAN AND GREEN

Lush greenery flourishes amid the urban sprawl, and the streets are so free of litter that you'd think thrice before dropping even the most miniscule of debris. And you won't have to—there's always a trash bin nearby whether you're indoors or out. The year-long tropical swelter is also real, which is where the verdant greenery comes in handy. When the unrelenting sun and humidity get to be too much, you'll be grateful for the benches beneath the tall, rainforest trees that line the streets.

WAYS TO SAVE

Singapore's astoundingly high prices are sometimes out of this world. Save by eating some (or even most meals) at the local hawker centres, which are still cheap, get an EZ-Link Card to take advantage of the city's excellent public transport, and look for cheaper hotels (the cheapest rooms sometimes have no windows!).

YOU'LL HEAR SINGLISH

Singapore's local patois is a mishmash of the island's four official languages—English, Mandarin, Malay, and Tamil—with regional dialects thrown in. Singlish is snappy, efficient, and casual, shortening words and sentences, and repeating things for emphasis ("ok ok" is a classic). Rather than say "yes, it can be done," Singaporeans will simply say "can." Rather than waste a full second on saying "excuse me," you might hear someone say, "scuse." And the most common word in the local parlance is "lah," which punctuates every sentence and can convey an exclamation, resignation, a question, or frustration. Singlish can be difficult to understand when spoken in its typical rapid-fire fashion. The good news is that Singaporeans are always happy to explain the nuances of Singlish to visitors—so use your questions as an ice breaker.

LOCALS CALL OTHERS "UNCLE" OR "AUNTY"

No, not everyone in Singapore is related—addressing someone (usually a stranger) who's older than you as "uncle" or "aunty" is a sign of respect. Most often, you'll hear Singaporeans addressing the likes of taxi drivers, hawkers, shopkeepers, and janitors in that manner. It's respectful to

address your friends' parents and older relatives as "aunty" or "uncle" too.

YOU CAN DRINK THE WATER

Singapore's tap water is perfectly safe to drink (though some say poor tasting from chlorination), so fill your water bottles before heading out into the tropical heat.

DON'T HAGGLE

Prices in Singapore are almost always fixed, and bargaining is not part of the consumer culture in Singapore as it is in other Southeast Asian countries. If a product is marked with a price tag, it's not up for negotiation.

USE PUBLIC TRANSPORTATION

The Mass Rapid Transit (MRT) system is the quickest, easiest, and most comfortable way to get around Singapore. The under- and over-ground network stretches throughout the entire city, with many attractions within walking distance of MRT stations. Singapore's bus system also covers an extensive

network of routes and is the most economical and scenic way to make your way across the city. Taxis and ride shares cover the rest.

FOLLOW LOCAL ETIQUETTE

There are a few cultural do's and don'ts. If you're invited for dinner by Chinese friends or acquaintances, leave some food on your plate to indicate that your host's generosity is so great, you can't eat another bite. There's no shame in asking for a knife and fork instead of chopsticks, which, by the way, should never be stuck straight up in your rice bowl, as this is considered bad luck (it recalls funerary offerings). Don't use your left hand for greeting, gesturing, giving something to, or eating with a Malay, Indonesian, or Indian person— it's the hand traditionally used for cleaning oneself with water after using the toilet. It's mandatory that you remove your shoes in places of worship.

Getting Here and Around

Sitting in the center of Southeast Asia, between Malaysia and the island of Sumatra in Indonesia, the small city-state of Singapore is one of the region's major transportation hubs.

✈ Air

Singapore is 14 hours and 30 minutes from San Francisco, 14 hours from Seattle and Vancouver, 20 hours from Chicago via Tokyo or Hong Kong, 18 hours from New York, and 8 hours from Sydney.

AIRPORT

International flights arrive and depart from Changi International Airport, which is on the island's eastern end and a 20-minute drive from downtown. It has four terminals, and all are connected by a free, two-minute ride on the Skytrain monorail.

Changi's facilities are second to none and contributed to making it the best airport in the world for nine years in a row between 2013 and 2021, and again in 2023. Each terminal is served by the Ambassador Transit Hotel, where you can shower or rent a room for six-hour periods. You take shorter naps at Terminal 2's Shower, Fitness and Lifestyle Centre. Terminal 2 also has a rooftop swimming pool and Jacuzzi, a movie theater, a supermarket, medical facilities, smoking rooms, and outdoor rest areas among other things. There are Free Internet Corners throughout the airport, as well as a children's playground, butterfly garden, and entertainment lounge. Just outside of the airport, the Jewel Changi Airport is Singapore's latest nature-themed entertainment and retail complex. Connected directly to three of the passenger terminals, it revolves around 130-foot-tall the Rain Vortex, the world's tallest indoor waterfall, surrounded by a stunning terraced forest setting. If you have at least 5.5 hours to kill between flights at Changi, register for one of three different 2.5-hour sightseeing tours of Singapore (Jewel, Heritage, or City Sights) at one of the clearly marked tour counters.

AIRPORT TRANSFERS

Buses 24, 27, 34, 36, 53, 110 and 858 stop at Terminal 1, 2 and 3 and, except for number 53 and 858, they all proceed to Terminal 4. Comfortable metro trains also run to the airport from 5:20 am to 11:50 pm. Catch the East West Line to Tanah Merah MRT Station, then transfer to the Changi International Airport MRT Station. Alternatively, use the Downtown Line to the Expo

MRT Station, then transfer to Changi Airport MRT Station. From Monday to Friday, there is also a free, first come, first-served shuttle bus leaving from Terminal 3, as well as a bus to the Tanah Merah Ferry Terminal, the gateway to the nearby Indonesian islands of Batam and Bintan, which leaves frequently from Terminal 1 between 6:30 am and 7:30 pm. Taxis and app-based ride-hailing services are also available.

🚲 Bicycle

It's easy to rent bikes via app-based services like SG Bike (⊕ www.sgbike.com.sg) and Anywheel (⊕ www.anywheel. sg), or from several bike rental shops such as the Bicycle Hut (⊕ bicyclehut.com.sg) and Biking Singapore (⊕ www. bikingsingapore.com). However-er, biking is a leisure activity here—especially outside the central part of the city—not a viable mode of transportation.

🚢 Boat

In Singapore, you can take a bumboat to Pulau Ubin. There is frequent scheduled ferry service between Singapore and Indonesia's Pulau Batam and Pulau Bintan; these ferries are

clean, fast, and air-conditioned, and they leave from the Tanah Merah Ferry terminal.

🚌 Bus

Air-conditioned private buses between Singapore and Malaysia are quite comfortable. The cheapest and best way to get to Singapore's nearest Malaysian city, Johor Bahru (aka JB), across the causeway, is to catch Singapore Bus Service (SBS) bus Number 170 to Larkin Terminal in JB. It's a one-hour ride that leaves from Queen Street bus station every 15 minutes and costs S$4.80 one-way. The bus will drop you at the Singapore checkpoint, but it will not wait, so bring all your belongings through immigration. After stamping, you can hop on the next bus that comes along and pay an additional S$2.60 cash or S$2 with a contactless credit card to continue across the cause-way to JB Sentral or onward to the Larkin bus terminal.

🚗 Car

Most travelers will not need a car in Singapore, but if you are traveling with kids or a large group and plan on visiting the far reaches of the island, you may consider renting one. You

Getting Here and Around

will need a valid driver's license in English or an International Driving Permit (IDP). Check the AAA website for more information and getting an IDP ($20).

CAR RENTALS

All major car rental companies such as Avis, Budget, and Europcar have offices at Singapore's Changi International Airport and downtown. Prices start from S$50 per day for a regular five-seater, and about S$150 per day for vans. Not all rental companies allow drivers to take their cars into Malaysia.

DRIVING

Cars drive on the left (British-style), and there are strict speed limits of 50 kph (30 mph) in the city, 70 kph (roughly 44 mph) on rural roads, and 90 kph (about 55 mph) on highways. It is compulsory to wear seatbelts, and there's a strict limit of 80mg of blood alcohol content.

GASOLINE

Gasoline in Singapore is quite expensive at S$2.72 per liter and S$10.28 per gallon. This, coupled with the high costs of car ownership permits and cars, is the main reason why very few Singaporeans can afford to have a vehicle.

PARKING

Parking in Singapore is not always easy and quickly gets expensive. Most hotels charge for parking, sometimes a great deal. On-street parking costs S$.60 per half-hour outside the Central Business District (CBD) and S$1.20 per half-hour within it. Dempsey Hill has 24-hour free parking, and you can also park at the Gardens by the Bay without any charge from 12 to 2 pm on weekdays. Parking in the many multistory car parks around the city is even more expensive. Check a local-approved list of 20 free car parks at ⊕ *thesmartlocal.com/read/free-carparks*

◉ Cable Car

Singapore Cable Car is a gondola lift connecting Mount Faber on Singapore's mainland across the Keppel Harbour to the resort island of Sentosa; a second line traverses Sentosa, but the two do not connect directly; both make several stops. When opened back in 1974, it was the first aerial ropeway system in the world to span a harbor. A round-trip ticket costs S$35 for adults and S$25 for children, and it takes 15 minutes to ride across the 1,650-meter-long (5,400-foot-long) line.

Public Transport

Singapore's local buses are frequent, air-conditioned, clean, and efficient. Together with an excellent subway system they cover routes across most of the island. The urban rail network in Singapore has 120 stations scattered over five metro lines and three light-rail lines. They are referred to as the Mass Rapid Transit (MRT) and the Light Rail Transit (LRT) respectively and operate from 5:30 am to 1:00 am daily.

URBAN TRAIN LINES

The North–South Line traverses the island connecting Jurong East to Marina Bay's South Pier, while the East–West line cuts the island side to side from Pasir Ris to the Tuas Link, with an extension to Changi International Airport jutting out from the Tanah Merah station. The North–East Line connects Harbour Front to Punggol Coast. The yellow Circle Line is very useful for visitors as it connects most of the central districts with the blue Downtown Line, with stops at important tourist attractions such as Little India, Chinatown, Bayfront, and Bugis. In addition, a system of three LRT loops extends from the MRT lines to service the areas of Bukit Panjang, Sengkang, and Punggol.

TICKETS

Trips on the MRT can be paid in cash or by tapping in and out with foreign contactless Mastercard and Visa bank cards, which is cheaper. The cost depends on the distance covered up to a maximum of S$2.80. Express and night services cost up to S$4.50. A standard ticket contactless smart card for a single trip costs between S$2 and S$4 (inclusive of a S$1 refundable card deposit). If staying in Singapore for a few days, however, the Singapore Tourist Pass (STP) is a better deal. It's a special stored-value card allowing unlimited travel on both buses and urban trains at a cost of S$22 for one day, S$29 for two days, and S$34 for three days, inclusive of a S$10 refundable rental deposit. The STP can be purchased at the Transit Link Ticket Offices at selected MRT stations, at the Concession Card Replacement Office at Somerset station, and at the Automated STP Kiosks at Changi Airport MRT Station, which can be accessed from Terminal 2 and 3.

Ride-Sharing

Ride-hailing services are very popular and efficient in Singapore and are a safe and cheaper alternative to

Getting Here and Around

taxis. Grab (⊕ *grab.com/sg*) acquired Uber's Southeast Asian divisions in March 2018 and is the dominant service. The most reliable are Gojek (⊕ *gojek.com/sg*), carpooling service RYDE (⊕ *rydesharing. com*), and TADA (⊕ *tada.global*), which emphasizes personalized rides and good customer service.

🚕 Taxi

Despite the numerous ride-hailing options available, taxis in Singapore are still plentiful. They can be hailed roadside or at the taxi stands found outside most shopping malls, MRT stations, hotels, and tourist attractions. Cabs in Singapore always use the meter, but there may be surcharges depending on the time of the day. To book a taxi, call 6–DIAL CAB (☎ *6342–5222*). ■ TIP→ **You don't typically tip taxi drivers in Singapore, but you may round up the fare if paying in cash.**

🚆 Train

From Singapore's Woodlands station there are 13 daily trains leaving roughly every 90 minutes from 8:30 am to 11:45 pm to Johor Bahru in Malaysia (in just 5 minutes). U.S. citizens don't need a visa for stays of up to 90 days, but proof of onward travel may be required

JB Sentral station is the starting point of a single railway line that travels north through Greater Johor (Kluang, Segamat) and ends at Gemas interchange in Malaysia. From there, the line splits: the main KTM railway line along Malaysia's western coast has Electric Train Service (ETS) trains going all the way to the Thai border at Padang Besar via Kuala Lumpur and Butterworth (for the island of Penang). The second line runs across Malaysia's interior to Kota Bharu, near Thailand's southeastern border. You can buy tickets online (⊕ *www. ktmb.com.my*).

Essentials

🍴 Dining

Eating like a Singaporean can be a casual and cheap affair at one of the many open-air *kopitiams* (coffee shops) and hawker centers that serve great street food all over the island. Those inside shopping malls cost a little more but are cleaner and fully air-conditioned.

Beyond the food courts, Singapore's dining scene gets very sophisticated but can be phenomenally expensive.

DISCOUNTS AND DEALS

Many upscale restaurants offer cheaper lunch deals with special menus designed to give customers a true taste of the place. Singapore also has some interesting smartphone apps that can give you discounts on food and drinks. Chope (⊕ *www.chope.co/singapore-restaurants*) offers real-time reservation booking. ChopeDeals has many buy-one, get-one-free offers and 50% discounts at more than 700 different dining spots. Eatigo (⊕ *eatigo.com/sg/singapore/en*) offers similar discounts.

PAYING

Most restaurants take credit cards, but some smaller places and hawker centers sometimes do not. Waiters expect a 20% tip at high-end restaurants.

RESERVATIONS AND DRESS

Although a few places don't accept reservations, they are generally needed for upscale establishments, which may book up weeks in advance. Singapore is fairly casual, so generally speaking, jeans and a button-down shirt will suffice. Some pricier restaurants, however, require jackets, and a few others also insist on ties. In reviews, we mention dress only where men are required to wear a jacket or a jacket and tie.

MEALS AND MEALTIMES

Many big-name restaurants shut down between lunch and dinner and close by 11 pm. Most restaurants are open seven days a week, but, for late-night dining, your best bets are food courts and kopitiams. Geylang Serai is a favorite late-night foodie hangout, as is Kampong Glam, where revelers head for quick, cheap bites after hitting the clubs.

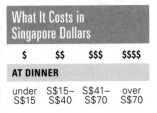

What It Costs in Singapore Dollars			
$	$$	$$$	$$$$
AT DINNER			
under S$15	S$15–S$40	S$41–S$70	over S$70

Essentials

SMOKING

Smoking is banned in all restaurants and bars, and like elsewhere in Singapore, it carries hefty fines of up to S$1,000.

⊕ Health

Singapore has first-rate doctors and well-equipped hospitals, all English-speaking.

IMMUNIZATIONS

Proof of vaccination against yellow fever is required if you've visited an infected area in the past six days. All Covid-19 vaccination requirements have been lifted.

FOOD AND DRINK

Tap water is safe to drink. Every eating establishment—from the most elegant hotel dining room to the smallest sidewalk stall—is regularly inspected by the strict health authorities. Look for "A" or "B" placards. MSG is still widely used.

PESTS AND OTHER HAZARDS

With the relentless heat in Singapore it's important to be aware of dehydration and sunstroke. Although there's virtually no malaria risk in Singapore, there are occasional flare-ups of dengue fever, so protect yourself at all times from mosquitoes. If you plan to visit Bintan and Batam islands, Indonesia, you may consider taking precautions against malaria, including bug spray.

🛜 Internet

The three major Internet service providers—Singtel, StarHub, and M1—all offer good-value tourist SIM cards with 100GB data that are valid for stays of up to two weeks. Singtel's S$15 100GB **Hi!Tourist EZ-Link SIM Card,** which also has a stored value of S$3 to use as an EZ-link card across the island's transport network, is the best value for most visitors.

🛏 Lodging

Singapore has an incredible array of accommodation options to fit all price categories. From trusted luxury brands to vacation rentals to hostels, you will have plenty to choose from.

FACILITIES

You can assume that all rooms have private baths, phones, TVs, and air-conditioning, unless otherwise indicated. Breakfast is noted when it is included in the rate. Most hotels have pools, some of which are on the top floor or terrace.

APARTMENTS AND HOUSE RENTALS

It is possible to rent apartments or townhouses for longer stays in Singapore. Some popular vacation rental websites to check out are Airbnb, Property Guru, and Edge Prop.

PARKING

With the bounty of affordable transportation connecting the island, few hotels have proper parking facilities. If you need to rent a car, try to return it after a day trip to avoid the hassle and the costs of finding suitable overnight parking near your hotel.

PRICES

Singapore is very expensive; even hostels aren't cheap (and prices have gone up at least 25% since the pandemic). Rooms are particularly expensive during peak tourist season (December to June). They climb even higher during the Christmas and Chinese New Year (usually January or February) holidays, and Indian festivals such as Thaipusam and Deepavali.

RESERVATIONS

It pays to reserve a room before national holidays like Chinese New Year when demand for rooms increase.

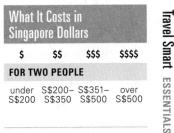

What It Costs in Singapore Dollars			
$	$$	$$$	$$$$
FOR TWO PEOPLE			
under S$200	S$200–S$350	S$351–S$500	over S$500

💲 Money

The Singapore dollar (S$, known on the street as the "sing-dollar") is the city-state's official unit of currency, with an exchange rate of roughly S$1 to USD0.74. Paper notes are denominated in S$2, S$5, S$10, and S$50 (and some larger denominations). There are 5-cent, 10-cent, 20-cent, 50-cent, and S$1 coins.

🌐 Passport

U.S. citizens need only a valid passport for stays of up to 90 days. Your passport must be valid for the next six months or more and in good condition. A confirmed round-trip airline ticket or other proof of onward travel is also required by most airlines upon boarding your flight to Singapore.

Where Should I Stay?

	NEIGHBORHOOD VIBE	PROS	CONS
Orchard Road	Where all the shopping and high-life is. A true experience of Singapore's heart.	Safe area; close to both Marina Bay and the heritage districts.	Busy with cars and people; some areas are known for prostitution, but generally safe.
Marina Bay	Located in the center of the city, Marina Bay overlaps with the CBD.	Super central; walking distance to the CBD and the Bay's main sights; good Metro access.	Expensive in general; can feel touristy.
Kampong Glam	Charming residential blocks of Chinese shophouses drawing artists and hipsters.	Great atmosphere; quiet yet vibrant; perfect MRT access.	Some streets are noisy at night; can become packed with tourists; not many high-end dining options around.
Chinatown	Iconic district packed with both great finds and tourist tat.	Slightly removed from the busiest part of town, and yet super-central; large selection of hotels, shops, and restaurants.	Crowded in the daytime; can feel like a tourist trap.
Little India	A stunning mix of temples and old lanes painted with stunning street art.	Safe; with historic charm; cheap and delicious Indian food.	Can get crowded; not many high-end dining options.
Dempsey Hill	Ritzy, lively area filled with bars and restaurants.	Plenty of modern hotels; good selection of bars and restaurants.	Few budget hotel options; not so well connected by MRT.
Sentosa	The island center of family entertainment, sun, and sea.	Theme parks, kid-friendly attractions, and family-oriented accommodations.	On the expensive side; very touristy.
Clarke Quay	Super-central and flashy with good restaurants and bars.	Safe; easy walk to the MRT and the Bay; more restaurants than you can try.	Can be noisy at night; filled with expats.

🕂 Safety

Singapore is very safe; you can walk around at night, and people often leave their bags unattended. But low crime doesn't mean no crime. Do not jaywalk; not only is it against the law, but Singapore drivers won't slow down or stop to let you cross.

👜 Shopping

Singapore is a real shopping paradise, and not only for high-end luxury goods. High-end boutiques and designer stores are in the malls on Orchard Road. Marina Bay has more malls that close late (11 pm during the week and 11:30 pm on Fridays and Saturdays). In Holland Village, you'll find made-in-Asia trinkets, carpets, antiques, and vintage furnishings. VIVOCity, on the western side of the Harbour Front, is the city's biggest mall.

Even Singapore's artsy districts have great shopping: Haji Lane in Kampong Glam is lined with cute vintage stores, and its Arab quarter offers an interesting mix of clothes, vintage cameras, and accessories. Little India is perfect for silks, jewelry, and Indian sarees. You'll get more bargains in Chinatown on spices, souvenirs, and low-cost clothing. Bugis

Street Market, between Little India and north Marina Bay, has 800-odd stalls loaded with the cheapest bargains, from clothes to electronics, housewares, and footwear.

💲 Taxes

VALUE-ADDED TAX

A 7% Goods and Services Tax (GST) is included in all prices. Visitors can get the tax refunded at Global Refund Singapore counters in the airport as you leave the country for purchases of at least S$100 made at a store displaying the Tax Free Shopping sticker (show your passport when you make purchases to get an eTRS transaction record). At the airport, you can process your refund request at a kiosk. You must apply for your GST refund *before* you check in your luggage since Singapore Customs may want to inspect your purchases. Visit ⊕ *www. changiairport.com*.

Everyone leaving Singapore by air pays a hefty departure tax, known as a Passenger Service Charge, of S$65.20. Transiting passengers only pay S$9 tax. This is almost always included in your airfare. Passengers who are in Singapore for less than 24 hours may leave the airport without paying this tax.

Essentials

💲 Tipping

Tipping isn't common in Singapore; however, if you feel that the service was exceptional you can leave a small tip. High-end hotels and restaurants automatically levy a 10% service charge.

🧭 Tours

Big Bus Tours
BUS TOURS | Singapore's Hop-on, Hop-off Tour circuit allows you to get on and off double-decker coaches as much as you wish from 9 am to 6 pm daily for either 24, 48, or 72 hours. Buses make over 33 stops on two different routes. The company also runs more traditional guided bus tours, night tours, as well as "duck" tours that go into the harbor from the SunTec Center. ✉ *SunTec Center, Singapore* ⊕ *www.ducktours.com.sg* 🎫 *Bus tours from S$37, Hop-on, Hop-off tours from S$57.*

Visa

U.S. passport holders do not require a visa to enter Singapore for up to 90 days. However, all travelers to Singapore must submit arrival details online to ICA for immigration clearance via the SG Arrival Card e-Services (⊕ *eservices. ica.gov.sg/sgarrivalcard/*) no later than three days before arrival. U.S. citizens can also now use automated entry gates.

📅 When to Go

High Season: It's hot and humid all year, but peak travel season is between December and June. The busiest time is from mid-December through Chinese New Year (falling in January or February depending on the lunar calendar).

Low Season: Rainy season is between November and January. Showers can last for hours or be heavy and finish within minutes, but full-out storms are rare. January is also the coolest month, but by only a few degrees.

Value Season: Because many office workers go on vacation themselves, hotel prices can be more reasonable during the summer months. Because locals schools are out, attractions are somewhat less crowded without school groups.

Contacts

Air

AIRPORT Changi International Airport. ✉ *Airport Blvd.* ☎ *6595–6868* ⊕ *www.changiairport.com.*

AIRLINES AirAsia. ☎ *80/4666–2222* ⊕ *www.airasia.com.* **Scoot.** ☎ *3138–4047* ⊕ *fly-scoot.com.* **Singapore Airlines.** ☎ *3027–7900* ⊕ *www.singaporeair.com.*

Embassy

CONTACTS U.S. Embassy in Singapore. ✉ *27 Napier Rd., Singapore* ☎ *6476–9100* ⊕ *sg.usembassy.gov.*

Lodging

CONTACTS Airbnb. ⊕ *www.airbnb.com/s/Singapore.* **Property Guru.** ☎ *6238–5971* ⊕ *www.propertyguru.com.sg.* **Edge Prop.** ⊕ *edgeprop.sg.*

Taxi

CONTACTS Gojek. ☎ *3135–3135* ⊕ *www.gojek.com/sg.* **RYDE.** ⊕ *www.rydesharing.com.* **TADA.** ⊕ *tada.global.*

Train

CONTACTS Singapore MRT. ⊕ *mrt.sg.* **Singapore Land Transport Authority.** ☎ *800/225–5582* ⊕ *www.lta.gov.sg.*

Visa

CONTACTS Immigration and Checkpoints Authority. ✉ *10 Kallang Rd.* ⊕ *www.ica.gov.sg.* **Ministry of Foreign Affairs.** ☎ *6379–8000* ⊕ *www.mfa.gov.sg.*

Visitor Information

CONTACTS Visit Singapore. ⊕ *www.visitsingapore.com.*

VISITOR CENTERS Orchardgateway Visitor Centre. ✉ *216 Orchard Rd., Orchard* Ⓜ *Somerset.* **Chinatown Visitor Centre.** ✉ *2 Banda St., Chinatown* Ⓜ *Chinatown.* **Kampong Glam Visitor Centre.** ✉ *55 Bussorah St., Kampong Glam* Ⓜ *Bugis.*

Great Itineraries

The Best of Singapore: City, Arts, and Nature in 7 Days

Singapore is compact and very well-connected by public transport, and you can definitely visit its main sights in just a couple of days. A week, however, is the perfect amount of time to experience the best of Singapore beyond the popular tourist areas.

DAY 1: BAYFRONT EXPLORATION

If you are flying in, visit **the Jewel** at Changi International Airport before catching an MRT or taxi to your hotel. You should start your Singapore exploration by the bay, visiting the iconic **Merlion Park**, the city-state's landmark. But first, grab breakfast at **Lau Pa Sat**, a popular food court in the Central Business District (CBD)— arrive before noon to avoid the crowds, or return in the evening for barbecue fish and casual outdoor dining. Then head to Marina Bay's **Gardens By the Bay**. You'll need about three hours to walk around these 250 acres of reclaimed land and three waterfront gardens. In the evening, the nearby **Marina Bay Sands Skypark**, perched 55-stories above ground like a surfboard on

top of three hotel towers, is a perfect spot to catch a sunset over the bay.

Logistics: Wear comfortable shoes as you'll have to walk a lot.

DAY 2: DOWNTOWN EXPLORATION

Start your day in the Civic District with a walking tour of the beautiful heritage buildings around the **Padang**, the immaculate lawn that marks the center of old Singapore. Before lunch, move to nearby **Chinatown**, where you can walk along historic streets to understand more about the lifestyles of Singapore's early immigrants. Be sure to visit some of Singapore's most important temples, like **Thian Hock Keng**, a Hokkien shrine dedicated to Sea Goddess Mazu, and the Hindu **Sri Mariamman**. You can have lunch at **Chinatown Food Street**, or keep that for dinner and hop to nearby **Tiong Bahru**, a hipster heaven, with plenty of cool cafés, indie boutiques, and iconic wall murals.

After lunch, head back to the Bugis and **Kampong Glam**, a former red-light district turned artsy neighborhood, for more shopping and café hopping. For a stark change of atmosphere, visit the **National Museum of Singapore**, the oldest in town, and the **Malay Heritage Centre**. From here, skirt the golden-domed **Sultan Mosque** to take in the heritage charm and abundant shops of hip **Haji Lane**.

Reserve your second evening for more window shopping at **Orchard Road**, Singapore's glitziest thoroughfare, stopping for a casual-chic dinner in one of **Emerald Hill's** alfresco restaurants, or catch a live band or poetry slam at the **Aliwal Arts Center** in Kampong Glam before visiting a local bar.

DAY 3: INTO THE WILD

Singapore Zoo, in Western Singapore, is one of the best in the world, and you should dedicate a solid day to see it. You can take the afternoon off at your hotel, or take a break at a café downtown, but you shouldn't miss a chance to experience the zoo's **Night Safari**, dining in a tepee tent before you start your night walk.

Logistics: Get an early start, or you won't see many active animals in the hottest hours of the day.

DAY 4: LITTLE INDIA AND THE GARDENS

After a break with nature, continue your exploration of Singapore's heart with breakfast in **Little India**. Browse the hawker stalls of **Tekka Market**, or try a *dosa* (crispy pancake) at the 70-year-old **Komala Villas** before you start traipsing down

streets lined with shops and temples. Peek at the elaborate pantheon of Gods etched on the *gopurams* (entrance towers) of the **Sri Veeramakaliamman** and **Sri Srinivasa Perumal** Hindu shrines. Continue your heritage hunt at the **Indian Heritage Centre**.

If you still have time before lunch, stroll through **Little India Arcade** to enjoy the 1920s architecture and the stacks of Indian textiles and flower garlands on offer. Have lunch at **Banana Leaf Apolo**, and then sweat off the calories by walking down glitzy **Orchard Road**. Stop as much as you need, but try to reach **Singapore Botanic Gardens**, a UNESCO World Heritage Site, by 3:30. Check out the rain forest, the Ethnobotany, and the extensive Orchid Gardens.

When you've had your fill of nature, catch a cab or the MRT to **Joo Chiat**, a delightful Peranakan enclave filled with colorful Chinese prewar architecture, for a coffee or dinner. If heritage shopping—think Kebaya traditional dresses and sarongs, beaded slippers, and Nonya ware—is not your thing, hop to nearby **Geylang Serai** and end the night in its thriving market.

Great Itineraries

DAY 5: EXPLORE PULAU UBIN

Tucked in the northeastern corner of Singapore right across from Malaysia, **Pulau Ubin** is an island stuck back in time. Shaped like a boomerang, this 2,500-acre land mass is home to Singapore's last village as well as the Chek Jawa Wetlands, one of the city-state's richest ecosystems. Cyclists will enjoy the 10-km (6.2-mile) **Ketam Mountain Bike Park** trail skirting around the Ketam Quarry. Otherwise, try to time your visit with one of the 2.5-km (1.5-mile) guided walking tours that showcase Pulau Ubin's kampung heritage and cultural, economic, and natural history.

Logistics: Board a bumboat at Changi Point Ferry Terminal and you'll reach Pulau Ubin's shores in about 15 minutes.

DAY 6: THEME PARK FUN AT SENTOSA

Singapore's entertainment island may not be everyone's cup of tea, but it's so packed with attractions that it's a must visit. **Universal Studios** here should top your list, with its 28 rides, as well as shows and attractions, across seven zones. If you still have time, check out the 1,000 species on display at **S.E.A. Aquarium**, or visit the **Butterfly Park and Insect Kingdom**. And if you are not exhausted, consider catching Universal Studios' nightly fireworks show before you depart.

Logistics: Sentosa can be reached on foot or by car, bus, monorail, and cable car. For those heading to Sentosa by train, take the MRT to Harbourfront Station, which is found on the North East Line.

DAY 7: SHOPPING AND DINING

Reserve your final day for last-minute shopping and relaxation. Start at **Orchard ION** for luxury branded items, and swing by **Lucky Plaza** for perfumes at bargain prices. In hip Bugis, **Bugis Junction** and **Bugis Plus** are two shopping arcades combined under one roof. You could also head farther west to **VivoCity** and experience the largest shopping mall in Singapore. For electronics, try **Sim Lim Square** in Rochor, the city-state's IT hub, but skip the pushy sellers on Levels 1 and 2. Make time for a relaxing evening at **Dempsey Hill**, filled with upscale stores and award-winning restaurants. Get one last nightcap in nearby **Holland Village**, where al fresco eateries, dessert bars, and old-fashioned cafés will make you feel sad to leave.

On the Calendar

January

Singapore Art Week. A nine-day annual island-wide celebration of the visual arts.

February

Chinese New Year. The Lunar New Year is celebrated with particular fervor in Singapore. It can take place in January or February.

Thaipusam. Celebrated on the full moon day of the Indian month of Thai, between the end of January and February in honor of Lord Murugan, the destroyer of evil, this religious festival attracts thousands of Hindu devotees who fulfill their vows (*kavadi*) with a 4-km walk from the Sri Srinivasa Perumal Temple to the Sri Thendayuthapani Temple.

March

Singapore Festival of Fun. Three festivals in one enliven Clarke Quay's scene for ten days of comedy, street performances, and more.

May

Singapore International Festival of Arts. Going strong for more than 40 years, this illustrious event has long been a jewel in Singapore's cultural calendar, presenting theatrical performances, music, and conferences by global luminaries and groundbreaking local artists alike.

Sundown Marathon Taking place between May and June every year, this is Asia's biggest night run.

June

Ultra Singapore. This outdoor electronic music festival at Marina Bay debuted in 2015 in Singapore as part of Ultra Music Festival's worldwide expansion, part of a dance empire spread across 20 countries.

July

Singapore Food Festival. Singapore food is celebrated in all its forms, including in workshops, chef collaborations, and food-themed tours of the tastiest neighborhoods in town.

On the Calendar

August

Baybeats. Baybeats is an annual 3-day alternative music festival organized by Esplanade. It showcases various Singaporean bands, who share an outdoor stage with Southeast Asian and international artists. The festival happens at Esplanade–Theatres on the Bay and is 100% free. ⊕ *www.esplanade.com*.

Singapore Night Festival. A lineup of arts, heritage, and cultural experiences transforms the Bras Basah and Bugis districts into an ethereal wonderland.

September

Singapore Grand Prix. Cars run a 3.14-mile F1 route at night during this event, which sees racers zipping around Marina Bay. ⊕ *www.singaporegp.sg*.

Hungry Ghost Festival. Just as Americans have Halloween, the Chinese have the Hungry Ghost Festival ("Zhong Yuan Jie"). According to local folklore, this is the time when the souls of the dead come back to earth and roam the streets looking for entertainment. Locals celebrate in the streets, knowing well that ignoring the ghosts can lead to mischief.

November

Deepavali. During the Indian festival of lights, Singapore's Little India fills with a thousand lamps and colors.

Singapore Biennale. This international contemporary visual arts exhibition, usually held once every two years for several months, promotes Singapore's art and culture to the world, while boosting the artistic and creative profile of the city state.

Singapore Writers Festival. One of Southeast Asia's most celebrated literary events returns every year to bring together an international array of writers and readers.

December

Marina Bay Countdown. End the year in a smorgasbord of fireworks and light shows at Singapore's enticing show by the bay.

Chapter 3

CIVIC DISTRICT AND MARINA BAY

Updated by
Marco Ferrarese

⊙ **Sights**   🍴 **Restaurants**   🏨 **Hotels**   🛍 **Shopping**   🍸 **Nightlife**

★★★★★   ★★★★★   ★★★★★   ★★★★☆   ★★★★☆

NEIGHBORHOOD SNAPSHOT

TOP EXPERIENCES

■ **Gardens by the Bay:** This man-made nature park (and architectural marvel) houses hundreds of thousands of plants in fantastical structures.

■ **Singapore Flyer:** Take a spin on Asia's biggest Ferris wheel and enjoy unparalleled views stretching as far as neighboring Indonesia.

■ **Sundown at Marina Bay Sands:** The hotel's stunning 150-meter infinity pool is the world's largest elevated outdoor body of water.

■ **World-Class museums:** The National Gallery, Peranakan Museum, and Asian Civilisations Museum are top-notch.

■ **Fort Canning Park:** This beautiful, historic park has nine gardens inspired by Singapore's heritage.

GETTING HERE

The Civic District is easily reachable via the Bras Basah MRT station on the Circle Line (yellow) and the City Hall MRT station on the North South Line (red). The Marina Bay area is accessible via the Bayfront MRT station on the Downtown and Circle lines or on a pleasant waterside walk from Raffles Place MRT station on the North South and East West (green) lines. The districts are compact and walkable.

PLANNING YOUR TIME

Allow at least one full day for exploring. Restaurants get busy during weekdays with the after-office crowd, so check out hawker stalls ahead of lunchtime. On weekends, the area is much quieter.

VIEW FINDER

■ **OCBC Skyway.** It's worth coming here at sunset to snap beautiful shots of the Supertrees as they light up against the darkening sky. ☒ *Bayfront.*

■ **Asian Civilisations Museum.** The translucent spheres parked in front of this colonial-looking museum make for an impressive mix of Singapore's future and past. ☒ *Raffles Place.*

■ **Marina Bay Sands Skypark Observation Deck.** Exceptional panoramic views above the Gardens by the Bay and the crowd of ships waiting to enter Singapore harbor—especially at night. ☒ *Bayfront South Station.*

Many of Singapore's top attractions are a short walk within or from this central part of the city.

Singapore's earliest example of urban planning is the Civic District, which runs alongside the Singapore River between the City Hall and Dhoby Ghaut MRT stations. The birthplace of the country's modern historical, architectural, and cultural heritage, it's dotted with imposing reminders of British rule.

Many of these colonial markers have been conserved and converted into government offices and museums (this is also the museum district), the stateliest of which is the National Gallery Singapore. It occupies two national monuments, the former Supreme Court building and City Hall. Other majestic landmarks include the storied Raffles Hotel—which completed an extensive renovation in 2019 and has accommodated many notable guests, from Charlie Chaplin to Elizabeth Taylor to Michael Jackson—and the Fullerton Hotel, which was once Singapore's first general post office.

Across from the Civic District and the Marina Bay waters, the futuristic buildings of the Marina Bay area sprout from 890 acres of reclaimed land. This is where some of Singapore's most famous skyline landmarks are located, from the iconic Marina Bay Sands and gleaming Marina Bay Financial Centre to Gardens by the Bay, a waterfront garden complex known for its larger-than-life Supertrees.

Civic District

Bras Basah Road and the surrounding streets were marked out by Sir Stamford Raffles as the European portion of the city in the 1800s. They're now home to many of the city's most important museums and national monuments. Although it's small, the area is highly concentrated, so allow a couple of days to explore thoroughly, especially if you love art and architecture.

◉ Sights

Armenian Church
CHURCH | Also known as the Church of St. Gregory the Illuminator and dating from 1835, this is one of the city's most elegant and oldest surviving churches. A dozen wealthy Armenian families

The Asian Civilisations Museum's fascinating galleries are dedicated to Asian heritage.

who had come to Singapore for a better life donated the funds for renowned colonial architect George Coleman to design this church. The main internal circular structure is imposed on a square plan with four projecting porticoes. In the churchyard is the weathered tombstone of Agnes Joaquim, who bred the pink-and-white orchid hybrid that has become Singapore's national flower. ✉ *60 Hill St., Civic District* ☎ *6334–0141* ⊕ *www.armeniansinasia. org* 🎫 *Free* Ⓜ *City Hall.*

★ The Arts House

ART GALLERY | George Coleman designed the Parliament House in 1827 as a mansion for wealthy merchant John Maxwell. Maxwell never occupied it, and instead leased it to the government, which eventually bought it in 1841 for S\$15,600. It is considered Singapore's oldest government building, housing the Supreme Court until 1939 followed by the Legislative Assembly in 1953 and then the Parliament in 1965. The building now contains The Arts House, a multidisciplinary venue offering film retrospectives, photo exhibitions, musicals, plays, and talks by experts. Note the bronze elephant statue on a plinth in front of the building; it was a gift from King Chulalongkorn of Siam during his state visit in 1871. ✉ *1 Old Parliament La., Civic District* ☎ *6332–6900* ⊕ *www. theartshouse.sg* 🎫 *Free* Ⓜ *City Hall.*

★ Asian Civilisations Museum

HISTORY MUSEUM | FAMILY | Constructed in the 1860s as a courthouse, the huge, white, Neoclassical Empress Place building is now home to the nation's first museum to look comprehensively at the all Asian regions, each of which has its own timeline and permanent displays. Spread over three levels, the 11 galleries have state-of-the-art interactive features, and there's also an educational center for kids. ⊠ *1 Empress Place, Civic District* ☎ *6332–7798* ⊕ *www.nhb.gov.sg/acm/* ⊠ *S$25* Ⓜ *Raffles Place.*

Cavenagh Bridge

BRIDGE | This gracious steel bridge, the oldest surviving bridge across the Singapore River, is named after Major General Orfeur Cavenagh, governor of the Straits Settlements from 1859 to 1867. Built in 1868 with girders imported from Glasgow, Scotland, it was the main route across the river until 1909. It's now a pedestrian bridge with a spectacular view of the Fullerton Hotel. On the riverbank, the whimsical sculptures of boys in half-dive over the water by local sculptor Chong Fah Cheong make for great pictures. ⊠ *Connaught Dr., Civic District* Ⓜ *City Hall.*

Chijmes

PLAZA/SQUARE | The oldest building in this walled complex is the Coleman-designed Caldwell House, a private mansion built in 1840. In 1852, it became the Convent of the Holy Infant Jesus, where nuns housed and schooled abandoned children. The church was added in 1903. After World War II, both the convent and the church fell into disrepair. In 1996, the complex was renovated and reopened as a shopping and entertainment complex. The lovingly restored church is also rented out for private functions (it stood in for the First Methodist Church in the film *Crazy Rich Asians*). ⊠ *30 Victoria St., Civic District* ☎ *6337–7810* ⊕ *www.chijmes.com.sg* Ⓜ *Bras Basah.*

Civil Defence Heritage Gallery

HISTORY MUSEUM | **FAMILY** | Housed in the stunning red-and-white brick building of the Central Fire Station built in 1908, this free museum is an exciting peek at Singapore's firefighting capabilities across the years. Besides a collection of dated firefighting artifacts and miniatures of Singapore's different fire stations from the 1980s, the museum's main attractions are two vintage fire engines—one horse-powered and one steam-powered—that were manually operated with pulley systems. A reenactment of the 1961 Bukit Ho Swee fire, with mock-up firefighters working hard to put out the flames, is a grim reminder of Singapore's biggest fire disaster. ⊠ *62 Hill St., Civic District* ☎ *6332–2996* ⊕ *www.scdf.gov.sg* ⊠ *Free* ☉ *Closed Mon.* Ⓜ *City Hall.*

Fort Canning Park

CITY PARK | **FAMILY** | Offering a green sanctuary from the bustling city below, Fort Canning is where modern Singapore's founder, Sir Stamford Raffles, built his first bungalow and experimented

Civic District

Sights

Armenian Church, **5**

The Arts House, **11**

Asian Civilisations Museum, **14**

Cavenagh Bridge, **15**

Chijmes, **7**

Civil Defence Heritage Gallery, **6**

Fort Canning Park, **1**

National Archives of Singapore, **4**

National Gallery Singapore, **10**

National Museum of Singapore, **2**

Peranakan Museum, **3**

Raffles City, **8**

Raffles Landing Site, **13**

St. Andrew's Cathedral, **9**

Victoria Theatre & Concert Hall, **12**

Restaurants

Artichoke, **1**

Flutes at the Fort, **2**

Lei Garden Restaurant, **3**

National Kitchen by Violet Oon, **9**

New Ubin Seafood CHIJMES, **4**

Odette, **10**

Shahi Maharani, **6**

Shinji by Kanesaka, **5**

SKAI, **8**

Szechuan Court & Kitchen, **7**

Quick Bites

ONALU Bagel Haus, **1**

Hotels

The Capitol Kempinski Hotel Singapore, **8**

Carlton Hotel, **3**

Lyf Funan Singapore, **9**

JW Marriott Hotel Singapore South Beach, **6**

Naumi Hotel Singapore, **4**

Raffles Hotel, **5**

Rendezvous Grand Hotel Singapore, **1**

Swissôtel The Stamford, **7**

YMCA @ One Orchard, **2**

KEY

1 *Sights*
1 *Restaurants*
1 *Quick Bites*
1 *Hotels*

with a botanical garden. Massive fig trees, luxuriant ferns, and abundant birdlife—including piping black-naped orioles and chattering collared kingfishers—flourish here. The hill's trails are well marked by signs, or you can explore the area with the help of augmented reality via the free BalikSG app offered by the National Heritage Board. In addition to the lush greenery, there are ancient artifacts for history buffs and occasional theater productions and music festivals for arts lovers. ⊠ *River Valley Rd., Civic District* ☏ *800/471–7300* ⊕ *www.nparks.gov.sg* Ⓜ *Fort Canning.*

National Archives of Singapore

ARCHIVE | Reopened in 2019 after a long revamp, which included expansion of the annexed Oldham Theater, this building is a treasure trove of archived materials of national and historical significance. The public can access over 200,000 audiovisual recordings, five million photographs, and almost 44,000 private records and copies of overseas records. English-language tours run by volunteers depart the lobby at 11 am and 3:30 pm on Saturday and Sunday, except for public holidays. A large part of the collection is also available to browse online. ⊠ *1 Canning Rise, Civic District* ⊕ *www.nas.gov.sg* 🖵 *Free* Ⓜ *City Hall.*

★ National Gallery Singapore

ART MUSEUM | **FAMILY** | A restoration and integration of Singapore's former City Hall and Supreme Court, this Southeast Asian visual arts museum is a work of art in itself. Immerse yourself in its extensive collection of modern art from the region—the world's largest public display—before grabbing a bite at one of the many globally acclaimed restaurants on site. ⊠ *1 St Andrew's Rd., Civic District* ☏ *6271–7000* ⊕ *www.nationalgallery.sg* 🖵 *S$20 (S$25 with special exhibitions)* Ⓜ *City Hall.*

National Museum of Singapore

HISTORY MUSEUM | **FAMILY** | Known as the Raffles Museum when it opened in 1887, this building with a silver dome has 20 dioramas depicting the republic's past. It's also home to the Revere Bell, donated to the original St. Andrew's Church in 1834 by the daughter of American patriot Paul Revere; the 380-piece Haw Par Jade Collection, one of the largest of its kind; the exquisite Farquhar Collection of regional flora and fauna paintings executed in the 19th century; occult paraphernalia from Chinese secret societies; and lots of historical documents. ⊠ *93 Stamford Rd., Civic District* ☏ *6332–3659* ⊕ *www.nationalmuseum.sg* ⏱ *S$15* Ⓜ *Bencoolen, Bras Basah, Dhoby Ghaut.*

Did You Know?

Fort Canning Park, once known as Forbidden Hill, is home to ancient artifacts., gardens, and a striking underground staircase.

★ Peranakan Museum

HISTORY MUSEUM | Formerly the Tao Nan School, built in 1910, this grand colonial building now houses the first museum in Southeast Asia devoted to the story of the Peranakans, the descendants of 17th-century Chinese and Indian immigrants who married local Malays. Its 10 galleries display artwork, jewelry, furniture, and clothing from members of the community. ⊠ *39 Armenian St., Civic District* ☎ *6332–3015* ⊕ *www.nhb.gov.sg/peranakanmuseum/* 🎟 *S$12* Ⓜ *Bras Basah.*

Raffles City

STORE/MALL | Designed by the famed Chinese-American architect I. M. Pei, the towering Raffles City complex contains an office tower; a variety of retail stores, including Robinsons Department Store; and two hotels, the Swissôtel The Stamford and the Fairmont Singapore. There's a stunning view of downtown and the harbor from the Swissôtel's 70th-floor restaurants, contemporary grill Skai and mod British fine diner Jaan by Kirk Westaway. ⊠ *252 North Bridge Rd., Civic District* ☎ *6338–7766* ⊕ *www.rafflescity.com.sg* Ⓜ *City Hall.*

Raffles Landing Site

MONUMENT | A statue of Sir Thomas Stamford Raffles keeps permanent watch over the spot where he first landed in Singapore on the morning of January 29, 1819. ⊠ *North Boat Quay, 1 Old Parliament Ln., Civic District* Ⓜ *Raffles Place.*

St. Andrew's Cathedral

CHURCH | Indian convicts were brought in to construct this cathedral in the English Gothic style. The structure, completed in 1861, has bells cast by the firm that made Big Ben's, and it resembles Netley Abbey, in Hampshire, England. So impressed were the British overlords that they granted freedom to the designer. The church was expanded in 1952 and again in 1983. Its lofty interior is white and simple, with stained-glass windows coloring the sunlight as it enters. On the walls are marble-and-brass memorial plaques, including one commemorating the British who died in a 1915 mutiny of native light infantry and another in memory of 41 Australian army nurses killed in the Japanese invasion. Services are held every Sunday. A few historical artifacts are in the south transept. ⊠ *11 St. Andrew's Rd., Civic District* ☎ *6337–6104* ⊕ *www.cathedral.org.sg* 🎟 *Free* 🕙 *Closed Mon.* Ⓜ *City Hall.*

Victoria Theatre & Concert Hall

ARTS CENTER | First established in 1862, the Victoria is one of the most recognizable historic buildings in the Civic District. The complex has two buildings and a tall clock tower joined by a common corridor. Completed in 1909, it was renovated entirely between

2010 and 2014. The concert hall is home to the Singapore Symphony Orchestra. ✉ *11 Empress Pl., 01–02, Civic District* ☎ *6338–8283 Victoria Theatre, 6338–6125 Concert Hall* ⊕ *artshouselimited.sg/vtvch* Ⓜ *Fullerton Jetty.*

 # Restaurants

★ Artichoke

$$ | MIDDLE EASTERN | This restaurant helmed by local celebrity chef Bjorn Shen serves up playful (and unabashedly inauthentic) Middle Eastern–inspired dishes like the cheekily titled Lambgasm, a 5.2-pound hunk of slow-roasted lamb; hummus with Iraqi spiced mushrooms; and raw tuna kebabs. The tranquil, tucked-away location in a cluster of historical buildings known as Sculpture Square only adds to the fun vibe. **Known for:** funky food with Middle Eastern flair; excellent playlist; chill vibes. ⑤ *Average main: S$25* ✉ *Sculpture Square, 161 Middle Rd., Civic District* ☎ *6336–6949* ⊕ *www.bjornshen.com/artichoke* ☺ *Closed Mon.* Ⓜ *Bugis.*

Bar & Billiard Room

$$$ | MEDITERRANEAN | Take your taste buds on a tantalizing tour of Italy with chef de cuisine Natalino Ambra. The classy eatery, located in the iconic Raffles Hotel, is complete with an open kitchen retrofitted with a wood-fired rotisserie and pizza oven and serves up bold food, including a flavorful octopus with white beans and pancetta ham; prime charcuterie; and pizzas spruced with 36-month aged Parmesan. **Known for:** celebrity chef; creative Italian food; energetic vibe. ⑤ *Average main: S$50* ✉ *Raffles Singapore, 1 Beach Rd., Civic District* ☎ *6412–1816* ⊕ *www.rafflessingapore.com* ☺ *Closed Tues. and Wed.* Ⓜ *City Hall.*

Flutes at the Fort

$$$ | MODERN EUROPEAN | Frangipani perfumes the air as you ascend the steps to this former colonial house among the well-manicured gardens of Fort Canning. The menu, which changes with the season, includes homemade breads and a hearty selection of international dishes, such as seared scallops, pan-fried foie gras, rack of lamb, and lobster. **Known for:** romantic setting; business lunch; wedding venue. ⑤ *Average main: S$50* ✉ *National Museum of Singapore, 93 Stamford Rd., #01–02, Civic District* ☎ *6338–8770* ⊕ *www.flutes.com.sg* ☺ *No dinner Sun.* Ⓜ *City Hall.*

Lei Garden Restaurant

$$$ | CANTONESE | FAMILY | Located within the Civic District's historic Chijmes building, Singapore's branch of Hong Kong's Lei Garden is known for having one of the best dim sum spreads in the city (prixe-fixe and à la carte menus are also available). It's packed with lunching office workers on weekdays and with families on weekends, but the jostle is worth it to savor such standout dishes as Peking duck, grilled rib-eye beef, and scallops with bean curd in black bean sauce. **Known for:** dim sum; big-group dining; sophisticated setting. $ *Average main: S$50* ✉ *Chijmes, 30 Victoria St., #01–24, Civic District* ☎ *6339–3822* ⊕ *leigarden.hk/branch/chijimes/* Ⓜ *City Hall.*

★ National Kitchen by Violet Oon

$$ | ASIAN FUSION | Get a taste of Singapore's culinary heritage at this luxurious, colonial-style dining destination helmed by veteran local chef Violet Oon. It's known for serving elevated local and Peranakan classics like fish head curry and *mee siam* (thin rice vermicelli noodles), as well as modern reinventions like pasta tossed with spicy *buah keluak* (a bitter and earthy nut labelled the "truffle of the east") sauce. **Known for:** refined Singaporean fare for lunch, dinner, and high tea; lovely ambience; local approval. $ *Average main: S$30* ✉ *National Gallery Singapore, 1 St. Andrew's Rd., #02–01, Civic District* ☎ *9834–9935* ⊕ *violetoon.com* Ⓜ *City Hall.*

★ New Ubin Seafood CHIJMES

$$$ | ASIAN FUSION | With creations like Heart Attack Fried Rice (rice stir-fried in beef drippings and served with U.S. Angus beef cubes on the side) and foie-gras satay, this Michelin Bib Gourmand listee specializing in creative Singaporean food is decidedly not for those on a diet. **Known for:** local foodie favorite; innovative use of flavors; Heart Attack Fried Rice. $ *Average main: S$50* ✉ *Chijmes, 30 Victoria St., #02–01B/01C, Civic District* ☎ *9740–6870* ⊕ *newubinseafood.com* ⊘ *No lunch Mon.* Ⓜ *City Hall, Bras Basah, Esplanade.*

Odette

$$$$ | EUROPEAN | Any self-proclaimed gourmand needs to add this classy restaurant, often considered one of Asia's best (and certainly one of Singapore's top tables), to their culinary bucket list. The dishes in its four- to six-course (called "acts") lunches and seven-course dinners vary seasonally but maintain the same respect for great artisanal produce, brought to life by French culinary arts and a touch of Japanese flair. **Known for:** mod-French fine dining; numerous accolades; cozy and minimalist space. $ *Average main: S$358* ✉ *National Gallery Singapore, 1 St. Andrew's Rd., #01–04, Civic District* ☎ *6385–0498* ⊕ *www.odetterestaurant.com* ⊘ *Closed Sun. No lunch Mon.* Ⓜ *City Hall.*

Shahi Maharani

$$ | INDIAN | Teak tables, gold-plated chairs, Indian artifacts, and live Nepalese music combine for a regal experience at this lavish North Indian restaurant, where each dish is categorized as mild, spicy, or very spicy (though the chef can turn the heat up or down based on your preference). You can't go wrong with any of the biryani (rice casserole) or tandoori meals, and the well-chosen wine list, which includes labels from many of the world's top wine-producing regions, runs surprisingly deep. **Known for:** North Indian fine dining; value-for-money lunch buffet; refined biryani dishes. $ *Average main: S$30* ⊠ *Raffles City, 252 North Bridge Rd., #03–21B, Civic District* ☎ *6235–8840* ⊕ *www.shahimaharani. com* Ⓜ *City Hall.*

Shinji by Kanesaka

$$$$ | **SUSHI** | For some of the best sushi outside of Japan, make your way to this spartan Edo-style restaurant by lauded chef Shinji Kanesaka inside the Carlton Hotel, where you'll be served sublime nigiri sushi across a counter carved from a single, 220-year-old, Japanese cypress tree. Here, simplicity takes precedence so that the cultural and culinary traditions can shine. **Known for:** true-to-tradition sushi; elegant Japanese setting; acclaimed chef. $ *Average main: S$280* ⊠ *Carlton Hotel Singapore, 76 Bras Basah Rd., L1, Civic District* ☎ *6338–6131* ⊕ *www.shinjibykanesaka.com/raffles-place* ⊗ *Closed Sun.* Ⓜ *City Hall.*

SKAI

$$$$ | **MODERN EUROPEAN** | This contemporary restaurant and Rosé bar on the 70th floor of the Swissôtel The Stamford hotel doesn't just serve up beautifully plated sharing dishes, it also doles out fabulous views of Singapore (and, on a clear day, Malaysia and Indonesia). The staff's quiet, attentive service contributes to the elegance, as does the warm, modern decor. **Known for:** panoramic views; Instagrammable interiors; refined sharing plates. $ *Average main: S$60* ⊠ *Swissôtel The Stamford, 2 Stamford Rd., Level 70, Civic District* ☎ *6431–6156* ⊕ *www.skai.sg* Ⓜ *City Hall.*

Szechuan Court & Kitchen

$$ | **CHINESE** | **FAMILY** | The extensive menu at this contemporary Szechuan and Cantonese restaurant includes dishes designed to be *xian* (salty), *tian* (sweet), *suan* (sour), *la* (hot), *xin* (pungent), and *ku* (bitter). Specialties include thinly sliced beef rolls with garlic sauce, spare ribs in honey sauce, and spicy rice noodles with diced chicken; dim sum and six- to eight-course prix-fixe menus are also available. **Known for:** dim sum; refined Szechuan and Cantonese cooking; hairy crabs (when in season). $ *Average main: S$40* ⊠ *Fairmont Singapore, 80 Bras Basah Rd., Level 3, Civic District* ☎ *6339–7777* ⊕ *www.fairmont.com* Ⓜ *City Hall.*

☕ Coffee and Quick Bites

Onalu Bagel Haus

$ | **BAKERY** | Ideally located between the National Museum and Fort Canning Park, Onalu is a popular and pit stop for freshly rolled, boiled, and baked bagels and cups of tea and coffee. The classic bacon, egg, and cheese (stuffed full of creamy scrambled eggs and bacon strips) and smoked salmon bagels (with thinly sliced smoked salmon and cream cheese) are highly recommended. **Known for:** generous servings; reasonable prices; relaxed vibes. $ *Average main: S$12* ✉ *60 Stamford Rd., #01–11, Civic District* ☎ *8268–5900* ⊕ *onalu.co* ⊗ *No dinner* Ⓜ *Esplanade.*

🛏 Hotels

⭐ The Capitol Kempinski Hotel Singapore

$$$ | **HOTEL** | No two rooms are the same at this luxury hotel in the neoclassical, 1930 Capitol Building and the Venetian Renaissance–style, 1904 Stamford House, where it took Pritzker Prize–winning architect Richard Meier years to renovate in a way that seamlessly marries European elegance with local heritage. **Pros:** steps from City Hall MRT station and Raffles City shopping mall; walking distance to top sights; beautifully restored heritage site. **Cons:** lowest-tier room option feels small and closed-in; small pool; poorer-than-average breakfast selection. $ *Rooms from: S$486* ✉ *15 Stamford Rd., Civic District* ☎ *6368–8888* ⊕ *www.kempinski.com* 🛏 *157 rooms* ⦿ *No Meals* Ⓜ *City Hall.*

Carlton Hotel

$$ | **HOTEL** | Raffles City, Chijmes, the arts and cultural district, the convention and business areas, and major public transportation are all near this understated, contemporary hotel, where the marble lobby is dotted with modern artwork, and the lounges are perfect spots for sipping afternoon tea. **Pros:** center of town; spacious rooms; poolside drinks. **Cons:** some wings have rooms that are better than others; not a showstopper like some other hotels in the area. $ *Rooms from: S$288* ✉ *76 Bras Basah Rd., Civic District* ☎ *6338–8333* ⊕ *www.carlton.com.sg* 🛏 *940 rooms* ⦿ *No Meals* Ⓜ *Bras Basah.*

Lyf Funan Singapore

$$ | **APARTMENT** | Designed for mobile workers and longer stays, this modern apartment-style hotel by Ascott is located inside the Funan Mall and is a stone's throw away from most of the Civic District sights and City Hall metro station. **Pros:** cleanliness; fast Wi-Fi; modern design. **Cons:** housekeeping is only once-weekly; some rooms have no TVs; can be noisy as it faces a busy road. $ *Rooms*

from: S$230 ⊠ 67 Hill St., #04–01, Civic District ☎ 6970–2288 ⊕ www.discoverasr.com ⇄ 412 rooms ⦿ *No Meals* Ⓜ *City Hall.*

JW Marriott Hotel Singapore South Beach

$$$ | HOTEL | Sophistication meets eccentricity at this towering, artsy JW Marriott outpost with contemporary rooms designed by Philippe Starck and five eclectic bars—from a jazz joint to a Champagne bar with mermaids. **Pros:** sky gardens, a spa, and two infinity pools; plenty of dining in the hotel and connected buildings; underground passage links hotel to subway stations. **Cons:** poor views from low-level rooms; some rooms are small; not many attractions in the immediate vicinity. ⑤ *Rooms from: S$360* ⊠ *30 Beach Rd., Civic District* ☎ *6818–1888* ⊕ *www.marriott.com* ⇄ *634 rooms* ⦿ *No Meals* Ⓜ *City Hall.*

★ Naumi Hotel Singapore

$$ | HOTEL | In an effort to pay tribute to the Peranakan-style townhouses used to form this boutique hotel, its designers left details like the original timber flooring and French-style windows intact. **Pros:** free snacks and minibar; Nespresso machines; rooftop infinity pool. **Cons:** TV reception could be better; noise from traffic; rooms could do with a refresh. ⑤ *Rooms from: S$350* ⊠ *41 Seah St., Civic District* ☎ *6403–6000* ⊕ *www.naumihotels. com/singapore* ⇄ *79 rooms* ⦿ *No Meals* Ⓜ *City Hall, Bras Basah, Esplanade.*

★ Raffles Hotel

$$$$ | HOTEL | An extensive 2019 makeover added elegant new suites, restaurants, and bars to this 1887 Grande Dame, which was once the home of a British sea captain and is still Singapore's history-steeped showpiece—not only has its guest list included the likes of Rudyard Kipling, Somerset Maugham, Elizabeth Taylor, and Michael Jackson, but its chic plantation-themed Long Bar is the original purveyor of the Singapore Sling cocktail and the only place where you can litter legally (help yourself to peanuts from the gunny sack, then throw their shells onto the floor). **Pros:** a Singapore landmark; legendary service; Long Bar, the original purveyor of the Singapore Sling cocktail. **Cons:** very expensive; lots of curious non-guests milling around; still somewhat old-fashioned after the renovation. ⑤ *Rooms from: S$1200* ⊠ *1 Beach Rd., Civic District* ☎ *6337–1886* ⊕ *www.raffles.com/singapore* ⇄ *115 suites* ⦿ *No Meals* Ⓜ *City Hall.*

Rendezvous Grand Hotel Singapore

$$ | HOTEL | With its mix of colonial and modern architecture, this hotel retains its 1930s-era charm; the rooms are styled with warm, bright colors, and the retro bathroom tiles reflect shades of days gone by. **Pros:** Balinese-inspired swimming pool; Straits Café

The Singapore Sling

Like the legendary shooting of Singapore's last wild tiger under the billiard table at Raffles Hotel (that's for another time), the Singapore Sling is part of Singaporean folklore. The consensus is that Ngiam Tong Boon, a Raffles Hotel bartender, created the pink-colored drink with ladies in mind. That's where the agreement ends: some claim the first Sling was concocted in 1915, others contend that it was given life in 1913, and the hotel insists that it was created prior to 1910. Many purists insist that the original recipe was lost in the 1930s. They contend that the drink, in its current incarnation, is based on the memories of retired bartenders. The hotel's museum shop has what it claims is the safe where Mr. Ngiam locked away his recipe books, and the original Sling

recipe. Leave the debate to the die-hards. Order a tall glass at the peanut shell–covered Long Bar at Raffles Hotel or make your own version with these ingredients:

- 1½ ounces gin
- ½ ounce Cherry Herring brandy
- ¼ ounce Cointreau
- ¼ ounce Benedictine
- 4 ounces pineapple juice
- ½ ounce lime juice
- ⅓ ounce grenadine
- a dash of bitters

Shake the mix with ice, pour it into a chilled glass, and garnish the drink with cherries or pineapple. Sip with care: the juices often mask the gin, brandy, Cointreau, and Benedictine.

restaurant on-site; central location. **Cons:** rooms could use updating; busy road; limited dining options within the hotel. $ *Rooms from: S$270* ⊠ *9 Bras Basah Rd., Civic District* ☎ *6336–0220* ⊕ *www.rendezvoushotels.com.sg/en* ⇥ *298 rooms* ⧉ *No Meals* Ⓜ *Dhoby Ghaut.*

Swissôtel The Stamford

$$$ | HOTEL | Catering to business executives, this 70-story hotel, among the tallest in the world, is connected to the busy Raffles City office and retail tower, with dozens of restaurants, more than 100 shops, and convention facilities. **Pros:** all rooms have balconies; central location; five-star business hotel. **Cons:** busy lobby; might be too crowded for some people; getting public transport can be challenging, especially during peak hours. $ *Rooms from: S$460* ⊠ *2 Stamford Rd., Civic District* ☎ *6338–8585* ⊕ *www. swissotel.com/hotels/singapore-stamford/* ⇥ *1,261 rooms* ⧉ *No Meals* Ⓜ *City Hall.*

YMCA @ One Orchard

$ | **HOTEL** | **FAMILY** | This well-run YMCA at the bottom of Orchard Road has a range of room types and suites (including family rooms), plus an impressive gym and a rooftop pool. **Pros:** low rates; central location; rooftop pool. **Cons:** basic accommodation; crowded on weekdays; poor breakfast selection. ⑤ *Rooms from: S$140* ✉ *1 Orchard Rd., Civic District* ☎ *6336–6000* ⊕ *www. ymcaih.com.sg* ⇨ *110 rooms* ⦿ *No Meals* Ⓜ *Dhoby Ghaut.*

Nightlife

The Auld Alliance

BARS | Sporting leather sofas and bar stools in timeless British colonial style, the intimate boutique shop of this famous independent whisky company welcomes patrons with a mix of glitzy modern and historical chic. Lined on the bar and stocked along the walls, close to 70 different choices of top-notch single-cask whisky, rum, cognac, calvados, and Armagnac wait for the pick of drinking connoisseurs. ✉ *Rendezvous Hotel Gallery, 9 Bras Basah Rd., #02–02A, Civic District* ☎ *6337–2201* ⊕ *theauldalliance.mys-hopify.com* Ⓜ *Bras Basah.*

Cool Cats

LIVE MUSIC | A part of the NCO club, the new concept in Singapore's haute bar scene blends sophisticated mixology with premium live music. From 8 pm, an international cast of musicians steps on stage to fire up the bar with performances ranging from jazz to flamenco, rumba, and other Cuban and Latin rhythms; soulful singers round out the mix. ✉ *The NCO Club, 32 Beach Rd., Civic District* ⊕ *www.coolcats.sg* Ⓜ *City Hall.*

Long Bar

BARS | The home of the Singapore Sling cocktail reopened in 2019 after a major makeover and now sports stylized, earthy decor inspired by the Malayan plantations of the 1920s. But some things haven't changed: you can still knock back the original-recipe Singapore Sling and chuck peanut shells on the floor, technically the only place you're allowed to litter legally in Singapore. As you might expect of a bar inside Singapore's best-known and most historic hotel, it's touristy and pricey. ✉ *Raffles Arcade, 328 North Bridge Rd., Civic District* ⊕ *www.rafflessingapore.com/dining/ long-bar* Ⓜ *City Hall.*

Nutmeg & Clove

COCKTAIL LOUNGES | A low-key, homey gastronomic cocktail bar, a stalwart in the local bar scene, specializes in award-winning artisanal cocktails with creative names inspired by Singapore's history and modern personalities. It's all explained in their creative menu, "Vol. 6: The Cocktail Diaries," but think about getting the Ramos at Home, which celebrates local singer Kit Chan with its fruity pineapple-and-egg-white-spiked Singaporean take on Gin Fizz. Don't miss the happy hour deals with a free flow of crispy chicken sandwiches from 5 to 7 pm. ⊠ *8 Purvist St., Civic District* ☏ *9389–9301* ⊕ *www.nutmegclove.com* Ⓜ *Esplanade.*

★ Smoke and Mirrors

BARS | Cocktail aficionados need to make a pit stop at this rooftop bar, where mixologists favor adventurous ingredients such as gentian root and "pencil aroma" and create experimental concoctions such as a whisky sour with Asian flavors like black sesame and rice. Bonus: There are unblocked views of the Marina Bay skyline. ⊠ *National Gallery Singapore, 1 St. Andrew's Rd., #06–01, Civic District* ☏ *9380–6313* ⊕ *www.smokeandmirrors.com.sg* Ⓜ *City Hall.*

🎭 Performing Arts

Singapore Symphony Orchestra

CONCERTS | The nearly 100 members of the Singapore Symphony Orchestra, Singapore's flagship orchestra, regularly deliver a mix of Western classical music and new Asian compositions. Performances are usually held at the Esplanade Concert Hall or Victoria Theatre & Concert Hall. ⊠ *Victoria Concert Hall, 11 Empress Place, #01–02, Civic District* ☏ *6602–4200* ⊕ *www.sso.org.sg* Ⓜ *City Hall.*

🛍 Shopping

CAMERAS

The Camera Workshop

ELECTRONICS | This shop in Peninsula Shopping Centre carries not just the latest cameras and accessories from Nikon, Canon, Pentax, and Mamiya, but also analogue models and serious shutterbug equipment like dry cabinets. You can even get camera issues diagnosed by the staff, have your cam cleaned, or sell a pre-loved gadget. ⊠ *Peninsula Shopping Centre, 3 Coleman St., #01–06, Civic District* ☏ *6336–1956* ⊕ *www.thecameraworkshop. sg* Ⓜ *City Hall.*

HOUSEWARES

★ Supermama

CERAMICS | Perhaps the best way to bring home a piece of Singapore is to buy from this local brand helmed by husband and wife Edwin and Mei Ling. They design and produce meaningful omiyage (contemporary gift ware) using Singapore's rich culture as inspiration. Plates, cups, and bowls are emblazoned with uniquely, local icons like the Merlion, the Singapore Flyer, and Jewel Changi's Vortex (that jaw-dropping airport waterfall you've been hearing about). Their Supermama Porcelain line is made in collaboration with Kihara, a well-known Japanese porcelain label and their stockist now includes glassware, tea towels, and commemorative bone china. ✉ *National Museum of Singapore, 93 Stamford Rd., Civic District* ☎ *6291–1946* ⊕ *www.supermama. sg* Ⓜ *Dhoby Ghaut.*

SHOPPING CENTERS AND MALLS

Capitol Piazza

MALL | Within its four sleek floors, this swanky mall that's part of the historic Capitol Singapore complex houses many cult labels from around the globe, including the flagship stores for local designers like SABRINA GOH and Max Tan. There are also three art galleries for you to visit amid all your shopping. ✉ *13 Stamford Rd., Civic District* ☎ *6499–5168* ⊕ *capitolsingapore.com* Ⓜ *City Hall.*

The Cathay

MALL | This complex, inside what was Singapore's first skyscraper when it was built in 1939, has eight floors of quirky stores and entertainment outlets, including an eight-screen cineplex and the funky Brunswick Pool & Billiards. Check out Leftfoot (#01–19/20) for an excellent selection of hard-to-find sneakers and VOL.TA Marque (#02–09) for sharp men's fashion. The complex is across the street from the Dhoby Ghaut MRT station; look for the building's original art deco facade. ✉ *2 Handy Rd., Civic District* ☎ *6732–7332* ⊕ *www.thecathay.com.sg* Ⓜ *Dhoby Ghaut.*

★ Funan

MALL | Following a renovation that was completed in 2019, this electronics and tech-lifestyle center now has funky retail, dining, and entertainment offerings like a food court where you can pay with cryptocurrency, a theater, a rock-climbing wall, and more. One of the most interesting things is the 5,000 square-foot rooftop urban farm that's part of the city's commitment against food insecurity, and whose produce is directly sourced by Noka, a modern-Japanese restaurant on Funan's 7th floor. ✉ *107 North Bridge Rd., Civic District* ☎ *6970–1665* ⊕ *www.capitaland.com/sg/ malls/funan/en* Ⓜ *City Hall.*

Raffles City

MALL | Get everything you need at this mega mall, which has more than 200 tenants within its walls, including Robinsons Department Store and Ode to Art, a contemporary art gallery. Both traveling to and spending time in the mall is a breeze—it is easily accessed from the City Hall and Esplanade train stations. It also offers services like the loan of portable chargers and umbrellas. ✉ *252 North Bridge Rd., Civic District* ☎ *6318–0238* ⊕ *www. capitaland.com/sg/malls/rafflescity* Ⓜ *Esplanade.*

🏃 Activities

WALKING TOURS

Jane's Tours

WALKING TOURS | The buildings in the Civic District, Singapore's earliest example of urban planning, are clustered in the downtown area, so they're easy to cover on foot. You can do the walk yourself using Google Maps (just search for "Singapore Civic District DIY Walk Itinerary"), or go with a tour agency like Jane's Tours, a small-group operator offering out-of-the-ordinary and bespoke tours that focus on culture and history. Either way, sunscreen, comfortable shoes, and a bottle of water are essential take-alongs. ✉ *Civic District* ⊕ *janestours.sg* 🎫 *From S$60* Ⓜ *City Hall, Bras Basah, Esplanade, Promenade.*

Marina Bay

Along the water from the Civic District is Marina Bay, an extension of the business district that was created through land reclamation in the 1970s. It's now one of the most architecturally significant parts of town, with Marina Bay Sands hotel-casino and the futuristic Gardens by the Bay.

👁 Sights

ArtScience Museum

SCIENCE MUSEUM | FAMILY | Part of Marina Bay Sands, this Moshe Safdie–designed structure is often compared to an open hand or a lotus flower. Inside, the exhibitions combine—you guessed it—art and science. Since its opening in 2011, major international exhibitions have been set up within the 21 gallery spaces, totaling 50,000 square feet. Guided tours leave at 4 and 5 pm from the Exhibition Entrance on basement level 2. Upstairs, the Sweet Spot has excellent coffee, cakes, and snacks. ✉ *Marina Bay Sands, 6 Bayfront Ave., Marina Bay* ☎ *6688–8868* ⊕ *www.marinabaysands. com/museum.html* 🎫 *From S$19* Ⓜ *Bayfront.*

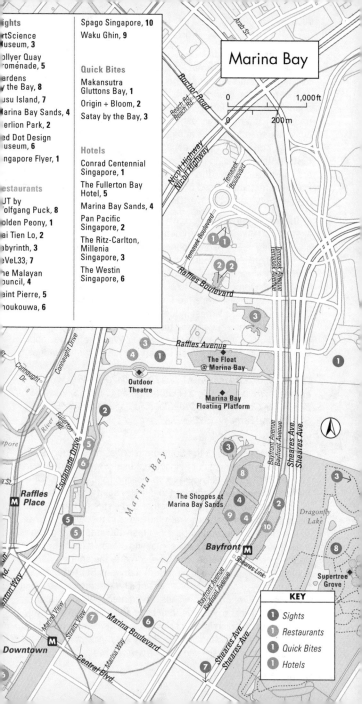

Collyer Quay Promenade

PROMENADE | Land reclamation projects throughout the 19th century pushed the seafront several blocks away from Collyer Quay. At that time, the view from here would have been a virtual wall of anchored ships. Today, you look out onto Marina Bay. European traders once arrived by steamship and Chinese immigrants arrived by wind-dependent junks at **Clifford Pier,** a covered jetty with high, vaulted ceilings that ceased operations in 2006. Nearby, the **Customs House** building once facilitated the arrival of leisure seekers and traders. Now, the historical buildings host some of the trendiest restaurants and bars in town, with **The Fullerton Bay Hotel** nestled between. ⊠ *Collyer Quay, Marina Bay* Ⓜ *Raffles Place.*

★ Gardens by the Bay

GARDEN | FAMILY | The government-funded, large-scale gardens next to Marina Bay Sands opened with much well-deserved pomp in 2012. Highlights include a futuristic grove of "Supertrees"— giant vertical gardens—and two armadillo-shaped conservatories. The Flower Dome is home to plants from the Mediterranean and subtropical regions, while the Cloud Forest is veiled in mist and houses the world's largest indoor waterfall. The OCBC Skyway is a 420-foot (128-meter) walkway that connects several of the Supertrees and offers a great view from above. While hefty fees apply for the Skyway, the SuperTree Observatory, and conservatories, visitors can wander around the Gardens until 2 am free of charge. ⊠ *18 Marina Gardens Dr., Marina Bay* ☎ *6420–6848* ⊕ *www. gardensbythebay.com.sg* ⊠ *Outdoor gardens free; Skyway S$14; SuperTree Observatory S$14; Cloud Forest and Flower Dome S$53; Floral Fantasy S$20* Ⓜ *Bayfront.*

Kusu Island

ISLAND | FAMILY | One of the Southern Islands and situated less than 4 miles southwest of Singapore, Kusu, whose name means "turtle" in Chinese, is known for its beaches and temples. One of these is **Kramat Kusu,** dedicated to a Malay saint named Haji Syed Abdul Rahman, who, with his mother and sister, is said to have disappeared supernaturally from the island in the 19th century. To reach the shrine, you climb more than 100 steps that go up through a forest. Plastic bags containing stones have been hung on the trees by devotees who have come to the shrine—particularly during the ninth lunar month (between September and November)—to pray for forgiveness of sins and the correction of wayward children. If their wishes are granted, believers return the following year to remove their bags and give thanks. Staying overnight or camping is not permitted, and it's best to pack food and drink. ⊠ *Kusu Island, Marina Bay* ⊕ *www.islandcruise.com.sg/ places-of-interest/kusu-island/* ⊠ *Ferry from S$15.*

The Flower Dome at Gardens by the Bay is the largest glass greenhouse in the world.

★ Marina Bay Sands

NOTABLE BUILDING | One of the most iconic structures on the Singapore skyline, Marina Bay Sands includes the biggest hotel in Singapore; **The Shoppes at Marina Bay Sands,** a glitzy mall filled with top fashion brands and its own casino; celebrity-chef restaurants; and the cavernous Marquee nightclub. Don't miss out on the atelier Louis Vuitton, set on an island accessible via a tunnel, and the state-of-the-art Apple Store Marina Bay Sands, an all-glass dome sphere floating on water and offering 360-degree views of the city's skyline. There's also the SkyPark, an observation deck that's 660 feet (200 meters) high and home to the hotel's much-Instagrammed, 150 meter-long infinity pool—the world's largest outdoor elevated body of water. ⊠ *1 Bayfront Ave., Marina Bay* ☎ *6688–8868* ⊕ *www.marinabaysands.com* Ⓜ *Bayfront.*

Merlion Park

PUBLIC ART | This waterfront space is where you will find two statues of the Merlion, a mythical beast and Singapore icon that symbolizes courage, strength, and excellence. Half lion, half fish, it's based on the national symbol, the lion (from which the name Singapore was derived), while its fish tail represents the country's past as a fishing town. The larger, 28-foot statue gushes water into the Singapore River through its mouth and looks even more dramatic after dark when it's floodlit and its eyes glow. The other statue, sometimes known as the "cub" for its smaller size, faces landward and is an equally unique photo opportunity. ⊠ *1 Fullerton*

Rd., Marina Bay ⊕ *Opposite the Fullerton Hotel* ☎ *6736–6622*
⊕ *www.visitsingapore.com* Ⓜ *Raffles Place.*

Red Dot Design Museum

ART MUSEUM | A second physical location of the Red Dot Design Award (one of the world's largest displays of contemporary design, first held in Germany) occupies a quiet corner of Marina Bay. The striking full-glass and geometrical facade of its pavilion packs over 300 design works on exhibition. The annexed design shop is a good place to buy peculiar mementoes, and the museum café serves good desserts and coffee. ⊠ *11 Marina Blvd., Marina Bay* ☎ *6514–0111* ⊕ *museum.red-dot.sg* 🖭 *S$10* Ⓜ *Bayfront, Downtown, Marina Bay.*

Singapore Flyer

AMUSEMENT RIDE | **FAMILY** | One of the largest observation wheels in the world, and the biggest in Asia, the Singapore Flyer offers one of the most exciting ways to soar over Marina Bay and capture its best views. The 30-minute journey provides unparalleled day and night views that, with good weather, stretch up to 45 km away to Changi, Sentosa, and parts of Indonesia and Malaysia. Packages that include dinner are available. ⊠ *30 Raffles Ave., Marina Bay* ☎ *6333–3311* ⊕ *www.singaporeflyer.com* 🖭 *S$40* Ⓜ *Promenade.*

🍽 Restaurants

CUT by Wolfgang Puck

$$$$ | **STEAKHOUSE** | Dine with Adele, Denzel Washington, and Katy Perry—or their portraits by award-winning photographer Martin Schoeller, at least—at this storied steakhouse by Wolfgang Puck. The Austrian-American celebrity chef's first foray into Asia offers up an amazing selection of USDA Prime, Australian Angus, American, and Japanese wagyu cuts and an impressive list of artisanal cocktails with not-suitable-for-work names, including Bound & Gagged (vodka, elderflower liquer, yuzu, and shiso) and The Full Frontal (gin, pineapple, and orgeat). **Known for:** perhaps the best steak in Singapore; celebrity status; sharp service. Ⓢ *Average main: S$90* ⊠ *The Shoppes at Marina Bay Sands, 2 Bayfront Ave., #B1–71, Marina Bay* ☎ *6688–8517* ⊕ *wolfgangpuck.com/dining/cut-singapore* ⊗ *No lunch* Ⓜ *Bayfront.*

Golden Peony

$$ | **CANTONESE** | Join the power-lunchers at this swanky, Michelin-starred hotel dining room for what has been described as "maverick Hong Kong cuisine." Alongside an impressive selection of conventional dim sum delicacies you'll also find more adventurous Cantonese dishes, like crispy prawns with walnuts or golden crispy chicken stuffed with glutinous rice. Both prix-fixe and à la carte menus are available for lunch and dinner. **Known for:** business lunches; Chinese fine dining; classic cooking with a contemporary twist. $ *Average main: S$25* ⊠ *Conrad Centennial Singapore, 2 Temasek Blvd., Marina Bay* ☎ *6432–7482* ⊕ *conrad-hotels3.hilton.com* ⊗ *No dinner Mon. and Tues.* Ⓜ *City Hall.*

Hai Tien Lo

$$ | CANTONESE | You'll enjoy sweeping views of Singapore from most tables at this contemporary Cantonese restaurant, curated by Hong Kong Chef Ricky Leung, high up in the Pan Pacific hotel. Dim lighting, carved wooden screens, and waitresses in cheongsams (Chinese-style dresses with Mandarin collars and side slits) all contribute to the restaurant's distinct sense of place. **Known for:** dim sum; great views; business lunches. $ *Average main: S$34* ⊠ *Level 3, Pan Pacific Singapore, 7 Raffles Blvd., Marina Bay* ☎ *6826–8240* ⊕ *www.panpacific.com* Ⓜ *City Hall.*

★ Labyrinth

$$$$ | ASIAN FUSION | The inventive dishes at this seafood-centric, Michelin-starred restaurant reinvent Singaporean classics with local produce. Within its five-course lunch and nine-course dinner menus, chicken rice is packaged into dainty dumplings, chilli crab is transformed into ice cream, and kaya toast is elevated with caviar—but the flavors stay distinctively Singaporean. **Known for:** modern Singaporean cuisine; inventive flavor pairings; chilli crab ice cream. $ *Average main: S$200* ⊠ *Esplanade Mall, 8 Raffles Ave., #02–23, Marina Bay* ☎ *6223–4098* ⊕ *www.restaurantlabyrinth. com* ⊗ *Closed Mon. and Tues. No lunch weekdays* Ⓜ *Esplanade.*

LeVeL33

$$ | INTERNATIONAL | At what's billed as "the world's highest urban craft brewery," the pricey platters of meat and seafood served in the slick indoor dining area are beside the point. Instead, get here no later than 6 pm on a clear day, hunker down in one of the too-few outdoor deck tables, and bask in the stunning panoramas over the marina, with the spaceship-like pool deck of the Marina Bay Sands hotel to your right and the impressive CBD skyscrapers to your left. **Known for:** panoramic views; craft beers; sharing plates. $ *Average main: S$36* ⊠ *Marina Bay Financial Centre Tower 1, 8 Marina Blvd., #33–01, Marina Bay* ☎ *6834–3133* ⊕ *www. level33.com.sg* Ⓜ *Bayfront.*

The Malayan Council

$$ | ASIAN FUSION | Decked in a charming mix of modern-meets-colonial—think vintage brown leather padded chairs, wooden tiles, hanging metallic wire lamps, and a minimalist bar that resembles a British Malayan colonial pub—the Esplanade branch of this classy yet casual franchise has breathtaking views over the bay and a menu that fuses English and Malaysian staples. Wagyu beef flank Wellington, cone trios rillette, and fish & chips pair with local chicken *percik* and an assorted selection of satay to help bring the "talk, makan, and chill" tagline to life. **Known for:** bay views; value for money; relaxed family ambience. $ *Average main: S$30* ⊠ *8 Raffles Ave., #02–14, Marina Bay* ☎ *9009–7345* ⊕ *themalayan-council.sg* Ⓜ *City Hall.*

★ Saint Pierre

$$$$ | FRENCH FUSION | At this intimate 24-seater run by celebrated chef Emmanuel Stroobant, you'll be served delicate, Asian-inflected French cuisine alongside a panoramic view of the Marina Bay waterfront. The chic, Michelin-starred establishment is a favorite among many not just for its fine food but also its inclusive offerings such as special menus for vegetarians. **Known for:** impeccable food and service; vegetarian-friendly fine dining; picturesque waterfront views. $ *Average main: S$398* ⊠ *One Fullerton, 1 Fullerton Rd., #02–02B, Marina Bay* ☎ *6438–0887* ⊕ *www.saintpierre.com.sg* ☾ *Closed Mon.–Wed.* Ⓜ *Raffles Place.*

Shoukouwa

$$$$ | SUSHI | The two-Michelin-starred Shoukouwa offers perhaps the most intimate dining experience in all of Singapore, with just eight counter seats and a private room for six. Reservations are a must, but for your trouble, you get elegant omakase meals created with obsessive attention to detail—even the sushi rice is dressed in a meticulously crafted mix of artisanal vinegars. **Known for:** fastidiously fashioned sushi; attention to detail; intimate dining experience. $ *Average main: S$520* ⊠ *One Fullerton, 1 Fullerton Rd., #02–02A, Marina Bay* ☎ *6423–9939* ⊕ *www.shoukouwa.com.sg* ☾ *Closed Sun. and Mon.* Ⓜ *Raffles Place.*

★ Spago Singapore

$$$$ | MODERN AMERICAN | The second Singaporean venture by Wolfgang Puck serves Californian food with an Asian twist, including a locally-inspired "kaya toast" with foie gras. Perched on the 57th floor of Sands SkyPark in the Marina Bay Sands, the restaurant offers unparalleled views of the hotel's famed infinity pool and the city skyline from its alfresco bar and lounge and its indoor dining room. **Known for:** sky-high views; celebrity chef; casual-chic ambience. $ *Average main: S$80* ⊠ *Sands SkyPark, 10 Bayfront Ave., Level 57, Marina Bay* ☎ *6688–9955* ⊕ *wolfgangpuck.com/dining/spago-singapore* Ⓜ *Bayfront.*

Waku Ghin

$$$$ | **MODERN AUSTRALIAN** | Celebrated chef Tetsuya Wakuda expertly melds Australian, Japanese, and classic French cuisine to craft the innovative menus at this two-Michelin-starred spot. The dinner experience begins with a 10-course degustation meal in one of the three private cocoon rooms, which is followed by dessert in the drawing room with a view of Marina Bay and then a Japanese-style cocktail or sake at The Bar at Waku Ghin. **Known for:** memorable experience; fusion that isn't confusion; intimate, personal service. $ *Average main: S$450* ⊠ *The Shoppes at Marina Bay Sands, 2 Bayfront Ave., #02–01, Marina Bay* ☎ *6688–8507* ⊕ *www.tetsuyas.com/waku-ghin* ☉ *No lunch Sat.–Thurs.* Ⓜ *Bayfront.*

☕ Coffee and Quick Bites

Makansutra Gluttons Bay

$ | **ASIAN** | Located just off the boardwalk by the Esplanade–Theatres on the Bay, this outdoor, hawker-style cluster of food stands offers a delicious (albeit slightly expensive) variety of local and regional specialties. Here you'll find chili crab, grilled prawns, chicken rice, fried carrot cake, meat satay, and much more served into the wee hours of the morning. **Known for:** authentic hawker fare; wide variety of food in one spot; local vibes. $ *Average main: S$14* ⊠ *8 Raffles Ave., #01–15, Marina Bay* ☎ *6438–4038* ⊕ *www.makansutra.com* 🚫 *No credit cards* ☉ *No lunch* Ⓜ *City Hall.*

Origin + Bloom

$$ | **DESSERTS** | Take a break in the lush garden setting of this lavish Marina Bay Sands bistro, where Instagram-worthy gourmet cakes, sandwiches, and salads pair well with signature brews and cold-drip coffee. **Known for:** garden setting; confections and cakes; gourmet sandwiches. $ *Average main: S$20* ⊠ *Marina Bay Sands, 10 Bayfront Ave., Tower 3 Lobby, Marina Bay* ☎ *6688–8588* ⊕ *www.marinabaysands.com/restaurants/origin-and-bloom.html* ☉ *No dinner* Ⓜ *Bayfront.*

Satay by the Bay

$$ | **SINGAPOREAN** | In a quiet and green corner of Gardens by the Bay, this alfresco food court is a popular, reasonably priced choice in an otherwise expensive area. As the name suggests, the focus here is on all-meat variants of the satay, including pork, chicken, beef, and mutton. **Known for:** reasonable prices; picturesque waterfront location; local hawker food. $ *Average main: S$15* ⊠ *Gardens by the Bay, 18 Marina Gardens Dr., #01–19, Marina Bay* ☎ *6538–9956* ⊕ *sataybythebay.com.sg* Ⓜ *Bayfront.*

🛏 Hotels

Conrad Centennial Singapore

$$$ | HOTEL | Spaces throughout this swank business hotel—situated near Suntec City, three national museums, and the CBD—are brightened by original Asian-influenced artwork, and guest rooms have pillow menus, Conrad teddy bears, bath salts, and other little extras. **Pros:** 24-hour restaurant; convenience; great service. **Cons:** swimming pool is showing its age; limited spa treatments; rooms can be noisy. *$ Rooms from: S$400 ⊠ 2 Temasek Blvd., Marina Bay ☎ 6334–8888 ⊕ conradhotels3.hilton.com ➴ 512 rooms ⏐⊙⏐ Free Breakfast Ⓜ City Hall.*

★ The Fullerton Bay Hotel

$$$$ | HOTEL | Sitting on a historic pier, the Fullerton Bay Hotel is built completely over water, with a glass facade that sets it apart from the historic buildings nearby. **Pros:** great views; large pool; contemporary art. **Cons:** small lobby; breakfast buffet can get cramped; more expensive than other similarly-sized rooms. *$ Rooms from: S$850 ⊠ 80 Collyer Quay, Marina Bay ☎ 6333–8388 ⊕ www.fullertonhotels.com ➴ 99 rooms ⏐⊙⏐ Free Breakfast Ⓜ Raffles Place.*

Marina Bay Sands

$$$$ | HOTEL | It's all about the view at this world-famous hotel, with its three towers offering plenty of vantage points from which to enjoy Singapore's cityscape. **Pros:** iconic rooftop infinity pool; lots of excellent restaurants; award-winning Banyan Tree Spa. **Cons:** very expensive; large crowds milling about; service can feel impersonal. *$ Rooms from: S$530 ⊠ 10 Bayfront Ave., Marina Bay ☎ 6688–8868 ⊕ www.marinabaysands.com ➴ 2,561 rooms ⏐⊙⏐ No Meals Ⓜ Bayfront.*

Pan Pacific Singapore

$$$ | HOTEL | FAMILY | The vast, 35-story atrium of this luxury hotel is filled with greenery and has an exterior elevator with impressive city views. **Pros:** central location; award-winning spa; great views. **Cons:** not overly baby-friendly; bathroom taps aren't in a user-friendly position; turndown service is by request only. *$ Rooms from: S$380 ⊠ 7 Raffles Blvd., Marina Bay ☎ 6336–8111 ⊕ www.panpacific.com ➴ 821 rooms ⏐⊙⏐ No Meals Ⓜ City Hall.*

★ The Ritz-Carlton, Millenia Singapore

$$$$ | HOTEL | One of the most dramatic of the luxury hotels in Marina Bay has 32 floors of unobstructed harbor and city views; sculptures by Frank Stella; prints by David Hockney and Henry Moore; and large rooms with sofas as well as bathrooms where tubs have pillows and large octagonal windows. **Pros:** top floors have great views; top-notch service; central. **Cons:** some corner rooms overlook the highway; all this luxury is costly; doesn't participate in Marriott's Bonvoy loyalty rewards program. ⑤ *Rooms from: S$780* ✉ *7 Raffles Ave., Marina Bay* ☎ *6337–8888* ⊕ *www. ritzcarlton.com* ⮑ *608 rooms* ⦿ *No Meals* Ⓜ *City Hall.*

The Westin Singapore

$$$ | HOTEL | This large, family-friendly hotel—part of the Marriott group—is located on levels 32 to 46 of Asia Square Tower, conveniently positioned near Marina Bay, offering communal spaces, including the lobby and outdoor infinity pool, that are larger than commonly found in Singapore. **Pros:** complimentary fitness amenities; very spacious; excellent buffet breakfast. **Cons:** some views blocked by nearby buildings; limited choice for in-room dining; neighborhood is empty on weekends. ⑤ *Rooms from: S$390* ✉ *Asia Square Tower 2, 12 Marina View, Marina Bay* ☎ *6922–6888* ⊕ *www.marriott.com* ⮑ *305 rooms* ⦿ *No Meals* Ⓜ *Shenton Way.*

🍸 Nightlife

AVENUE Singapore

DANCE CLUBS | Within the same complex as Marquee Singapore, this bespoke club appeals to a completely different crowd. The plush custom banquettes and fun features—like a karaoke room, mini bowling alley, and arcade game–cum–pool table room—are inspired by vintage spots in New York and Los Angeles. The regular DJs and craft cocktails alternate with a program of hip-hop, deep house, and open-format music experience. It opens late (at 10 pm) and only allows guests who are 21 and up. ✉ *The Shoppes at Marina Bay Sands, 2 Bayfront Ave., Basement 3, Marina Bay* ☎ *6688–8680* ⊕ *avenuesingapore.com* Ⓜ *Bayfront.*

Cé La Vi Singapore

BARS | At this stunning restaurant-bar 57 stories above ground, you can take in Singapore's late-night vistas while vibing to resident and celeb DJs. To make a full night of it, you can start with a mod-Asian dinner at Cé La Vi Restaurant, before enjoying a tipple at the Skybar and then hitting the dance floor at the Club Lounge. ✉ *Marina Bay Sands SkyPark, 1 Bayfront Ave., Level 57, Marina Bay* ☎ *6508–2188* ⊕ *www.celavi.com* Ⓜ *Bayfront.*

Lantern

BARS | The Lantern, which is named for Clifford Pier (i.e., Red Lantern Pier), is a great place to chill out with a cocktail or sparkling wine on the rooftop of The Fullerton Bay Hotel. There's a menu of gourmet snacks if you're hungry, and a DJ usually plays relaxing tunes from Wednesday to Sunday. To get seats with the best views, book well ahead. ⊠ *Fullerton Bay Hotel, 80 Collyer Quay, Level 8, Marina Bay* ☎ *3129–8229* ⊕ *www.fullertonhotels.com* Ⓜ *Raffles Place.*

★ Marquee Singapore

DANCE CLUBS | For a night you will (or possibly won't) remember, party at this glittering club kid hotspot with Vegas vibes. Also Singapore's largest nightclub, it goes big with eight private dance pods suspended 20 meters in the air as well as a massive Ferris wheel you can board for a spin. ⊠ *The Shoppes at Marina Bay Sands, 2 Bayfront Ave., #B1–67, Marina Bay* ☎ *6688–8660* ⊕ *marqueesingapore.com* Ⓜ *Bayfront.*

Synthesis

BARS | Part restaurant, part speakeasy, and part music club, this classy venue is decked out as a vintage Chinese medicine hall. Neon lights, dark corridors strewn with hanging paper lanterns, and a well-choreographed menu of modern Singaporean food (think *char siew* but with Iberico pork) make for an exclusive ambience—but entering through the Suntec Mall spoils part of the fun. Happy Hour is from 4 to 6 pm daily. Reservations are recommended, but tables are also available for walk-ins. ⊠ *Suntec Mall, 3 Temasek Blvd., #01–643, Marina Bay* ☎ *9727–4649* ⊕ *www.synthesis.sg* Ⓜ *Esplanade.*

🎭 Performing Arts

The Esplanade–Theatres on the Bay

ARTS CENTERS | FAMILY | The Esplanade hosts many of Singapore's top ticketed performances, but it also offers free concerts, shows, and talks every week. Most take place at the Esplanade Concourse or the Outdoor Theater in the evenings when the weather is cooler—all you have to do is drop by and take a seat. There's a performance schedule on the Esplanade website, but it's much more fun to visit and be surprised by what's on, which could be anything from a classical guitar performance from Latin America to a Chinese puppet show. ⊠ *1 Esplanade Dr., Marina Bay* ☎ *6828–8377* ⊕ *www.esplanade.com* Ⓜ *Esplanade.*

🛍 Shopping

MUSIC

★ Analog Vault

MUSIC | Founded in 2015, the Analog Vault established as the go-to place for electronic, jazz and fine music lovers in Singapore. The curated selection of thousands of vinyl records ranges from jazz to funk and soul, Singaporean retro music to hip-hop, and Japanese music. The shop is also home to TAV Records, founded in 2019 to showcase emerging Asian artists of the genres Analog selects with clinical zeal. ✉ *Esplanade Theatres on the Bay, 8 Raffles Avenue, #02–10, Marina Bay* ☎ *9026–5215* ⊕ *theanalogvault.com* Ⓜ *Esplanade.*

SHOPPING CENTERS AND MALLS

Marina Square

MALL | FAMILY | Home to more than 250 shops and restaurants, Marina Square was once the largest shopping mall in Singapore, an honor that now belongs to VivoCity. Banks, convenience stores, a movie theater, a bowling alley, a large food court, coffee shops, and spas and salons are all here. Some nearby hotels and attractions, including Esplanade–Theatres on the Bay, Pan Pacific Singapore, and Suntec City, can be accessed directly from here via underground walkways. ✉ *6 Raffles Blvd., Marina Bay* ☎ *6339–8787* ⊕ *www.marinasquare.com.sg* Ⓜ *City Hall.*

The Shoppes at Marina Bay Sands

MALL | You can while away a whole day at this mega mall that has over 170 stores and restaurants. Look out for the contemporary cuts of local fashion label In Good Company (#B1–65) and the unique handiwork of custom sneaker design artist SBTG at Limited Edt Chamber (#B2–112). While you're at it, make time for the mall's casino, theater, and boat rides along its indoor river. ✉ *2 Bayfront Ave., Marina Bay* ☎ *6688–8868* ⊕ *www.marinabaysands.com/shopping* Ⓜ *Bayfront.*

Suntec City Mall

MALL | This sprawling complex has over 600 stores, including local designer boutiques and the funky Pasarbella food court featuring stalls by some of Singapore's most creative culinary entrepreneurs. In the middle is the photo-worthy Fountain of Wealth, which was listed in the 1998 Guinness Book of Records as the world's largest fountain. There are nightly laser shows, and walking around the fountain supposedly brings good luck. ✉ *3 Temasek Blvd., Marina Bay* ☎ *6825–2669* ⊕ *www.sunteccity.com.sg* Ⓜ *Suntec City.*

Activities

BIKING

City Scoot Bicycle Rental and Tours

BIKING | FAMILY | You can rent regular or folding bicycles, scooters, tandem bikes, or kick scooters at this handy outlet located outside The Esplanade Mall on the bay. Bicycles can be rented by the hour, but the full-day package is more convenient and cost-effective. The outlet serves walk-ins, but reservations are best to avoid disappointment. If you don't feel like pedaling by yourself, their 2.5-hour long day or night Marina Bay and city tours with a licensed tour guide cover 15 km of terrain and a load of local insight. ⊠ *The Esplanade Mall, 8 Raffles Ave., #01–18, Marina Bay* ☏ *9355–5881* ⊕ *www.cityscoot.com.sg/esplanade* ⊠ *Bicycle rentals from S$15 per hour, from S$40 per day; guided tours from S$50 (per person, based on 2-person min.)* Ⓜ *Esplanade.*

GOLF

Marina Bay Golf Course

GOLF | Singapore's only public 18-hole green is an award-winning links-style course—and it's one of the best in Asia. Course A has an outer and inner loop of two nines and Course B (a new configuration) has holes crossing over to the inner loop after hole 5. It's also one of the few golf courses in Singapore to have night golfing. ⊠ *80 Rhu Cross, Marina Bay* ☏ *6345–7788* ⊕ *www.mbgc. com.sg* ⵌ *18 holes, 7100 yds., par 72* Ⓜ *Bayfront.*

SPAS

Banyan Tree Spa

SPAS | There's a more relaxing way to take in the views than from the perpetually packed Marina Bay Sands rooftop: from a spa bed. The award-winning Banyan Tree Spa sits just two stories below the hotel's famous infinity pool, so you can enjoy the same stunning views through floor-to-ceiling windows as your knots get kneaded. There are more than 30 treatments available, from facials, massages, and body scrubs to hand, foot, and hair treatments. Post session, further unwind in the tea lounge, or visit the in-house boutique to stock up on products so you can re-create the experience at home. ⊠ *Marina Bay Sands Tower 1, 10 Bayfront Ave., Level 55, Marina Bay* ☏ *6688–8825* ⊕ *www.banyantree.com/ spa/banyan-tree-spa-marina-bay-sands-hotel* Ⓜ *Bayfront.*

Chapter 4

CHINATOWN, THE CBD, AND TANJONG PAGAR

Updated by
Olivia Lee

⊙ Sights 🍴 Restaurants 🛏 Hotels 🛍 Shopping 🍸 Nightlife
★★★★☆   ★★★★★   ★★★★☆   ★★★★☆   ★★★★☆

NEIGHBORHOOD SNAPSHOT

TOP EXPERIENCES

■ **Bargain hunt:** Browse Chinatown's colorful market stalls in search of silk fabrics, trinkets, and charms.

■ **Snack in Chinatown Complex:** Vendors on the second floor serve everything from crispy duck to dim sum.

■ **Enjoy a tipple:** Chinatown and Tanjong Pagar are home to some of the city's top cocktail bars.

■ **Explore Keong Saik Road:** Stroll along this colorful up-and-coming street full of artisan coffee shops, and trendy bars.

■ **Join the line:** On Tanjong Pagar Road, especially on the weekend, you'll find lines at every good Korean and Japanese spot.

GETTING HERE

The Chinatown stop is on the North East Line (purple), though you can also reach area sights from the Outram Park and Tanjong Pagar stations on the East West Line (green)—the latter of which also serves Tanjong Pagar, naturally. For the CBD, there's Shenton Way on the Thomson-East Coast Line (brown) and Downtown, on the Downtown Line (blue).

PLANNING YOUR TIME

Chinatown is particularly pretty at night, when the neon lights flick on, but it's also a good place for shopping at the market stalls by day. Tanjong Pagar is a foodie haven, so plan to spend at least one evening eating here, and ideally an afternoon strolling past the temples and markets.

VIEWFINDER

■ The 280m-high **CapitaSpring** building (⊠ 88 Market St.) in the CBD is one of the tallest in Singapore. Though primarily a commercial block, it has a leafy sky garden on the roof, with amazing views of Marina Bay—and it's free to visit. Opening hours are fairly limited though, so plan carefully: weekdays only from 8:30 am to 10:30 am, and 2:30 pm to 6:00 pm.

PAUSE HERE

■ Although Singapore is a very green city, green spaces in the center are a little harder to come by. In Telok Ayer, though, you'll find a small oasis called **Ann Siang Hill Park.** Rising up steeply behind the shophouses, this little park has a spiral staircase lookout and quiet benches so you can pause beneath the palm trees.

Chinatown and Tanjong Pagar lie side by side but have distinctly different feelings. The former is a place for traditional Chinese food and bargain shopping, where you can explore the twisting streets packed with vibrant market stalls. The latter is often referred to as "Koreatown," where queues of locals spill out of the many Korean restaurants filling the shophouses.

Chinatowns are typically found in cities where the Chinese are a minority. In Singapore, though, where ethnic Chinese substantially outnumber all other groups, a Chinatown may seem out of place. This Chinatown dates to the colonial period, when Sir Stamford Raffles was attempting to organize immigrants by their race. The Chinese received the largest portion of land, southwest of the Singapore River. Over the years, the neighborhood has had its ups and downs, but recently it's gotten a lot more touristy. Smith, Temple, and Pagoda streets are filled with shops selling souvenir Buddhas and tea sets, "I Love SG" key chains, and T-shirts poking fun at Singapore's love for strict fines. It's a fun place to explore at night, with traditional lanterns lighting the streets and the smell of deep-fried food filling the air.

Tanjong Pagar, by contrast, feels a lot more upscale. There are glossy office blocks and shiny hotels alongside traditional shophouses that have ben converted into cool bars and restaurants. This gives the area an interesting mix of old and new charm—both home to one of the oldest Historic Districts with its beautifully conserved shophouses and local hawker centers—as well as Singapore's tallest building, the modern mirror-like Guoco Tower. With its Koreatown reputation, you know the Korean food is going to be good, but the area also has a substantial number of great Japanese restaurants and cool cafés, too.

Adjacent to both neighborhoods is a district with a different vibe altogether: the Central Business District (CBD), where locals march to work in the shiny highrises and pile back out to the bars come sundown. During the week you'll find yourself swamped by locals, while on the weekend it's eerily quiet.

Keong Saik Road buzzes at night with Singapore's top restaurants and bars.

Chinatown

Chinatown is a dynamic and colorful part of the city, where you feel Singapore's heritage along every street. There are plenty of individual sights to explore, but the greatest experience is taking in the neighborhood as a whole. Red lanterns, masterful street art, and ornate architecture lie around each corner, and chaotic market stalls and street vendors offer up all kinds of goods.

◉ Sights

Al-Abrar Mosque

MOSQUE | Standing on a busy road in Chinatown, this ornate mosque was once just a thatched hut, built in 1827 as one of Singapore's first mosques for Indian Muslims. Also known as Kuchu Palli (Tamil for "mosque hut"), the existing structure dates from 1855. Though much of the mosque's original ornamentation has been replaced, its original timber panels and fanlight windows have remained. You can visit during the week except on a Friday lunchtime, when devotees flock in for the midday prayers. ✉ *192 Telok Ayer St., Chinatown* ☎ *6220–6306* ⊕ *www.muis.gov.sg* 🖃 *Free* ⊙ *Closed Sat. and Sun.* Ⓜ *Telok Ayer.*

Baba House

HISTORIC HOME | Take the hour-long heritage tour to explore the ancestral home of a Chinese Peranakan family who lived in this three-story townhouse in 1895. The building and furnishings are stunning, with gold-gilded beds, mother-of-pearl inlay chairs, and striking works of calligraphy art. Heritage tours take place Tuesday to Friday at 10 am. You can also opt for a self-guided tour on Saturday. ■TIP→ **Appointments are required.** ⊠ *157 Neil Rd., Chinatown* ☎ *6227–5731* ⊕ *babahouse.nus.edu.sg* ⊠ *S$10* ⊙ *Closed Sun. and Mon.* Ⓜ *Outram Park.*

Blair Road
STREET | The heritage houses that line Blair Road are a sight to be seen with their beautiful Peranakan floor tiles, mint green facades, and French-style shutters. They were built in the 1900s in response to the increasing demand from well-to-do Chinese merchants who wanted new homes for their families. Nowadays, they look too pretty to live in, but some people are lucky enough to call them home—which means you can't go inside and should be conscientious with your photography. Still, just strolling the street outside is enough to give you a taste of what it might be like to live here. ⊠ *3–57 Blair Rd., Chinatown* Ⓜ *Outram Park.*

★ Buddha Tooth Relic Temple
TEMPLE | Beautiful by day but especially lovely by night, Chinatown's most iconic landmark is tiered in ornate red and gold, the design inspired by the Buddhist mandala, a symbol of Buddhist culture that represents the universe. The temple takes its name from what's thought to be the left canine tooth of the Buddha, recovered from his funeral pyre in India and displayed inside the temple grounds. ⊠ *228 South Bridge Rd., Chinatown* ☎ *6220– 0220* ⊕ *www.buddhatoothrelictemple.org.sg* ⊠ *Free* Ⓜ *Maxwell.*

Chinatown Complex
MARKET | Typically, this market is swamped. On the first floor, hawker stalls sell local eats that are great for a quick, cheap meal, but it's the basement floor that fascinates. Here, you'll find a wet market—so called because water is continually sloshed over the floors to clean them—where meat, fowl, and fish are bought and sold. There's also an open-air produce market where you can find bargain local fruit—including the infamous durian—for an after-lunch snack. ⊠ *335 Smith St., Chinatown* Ⓜ *Chinatown.*

Jamae Mosque
MOSQUE | Popularly called Masjid Chulia, this simple, almost austere mosque was built in 1826 by Chulia Muslims from India's Coromandel Coast, on its southeast shore. So long as it's not prayer time and the doors are open, you're welcome to step inside for a look. Note that you must be dressed conservatively and take your shoes off before entering. ⊠ *218 South Bridge Rd.,*

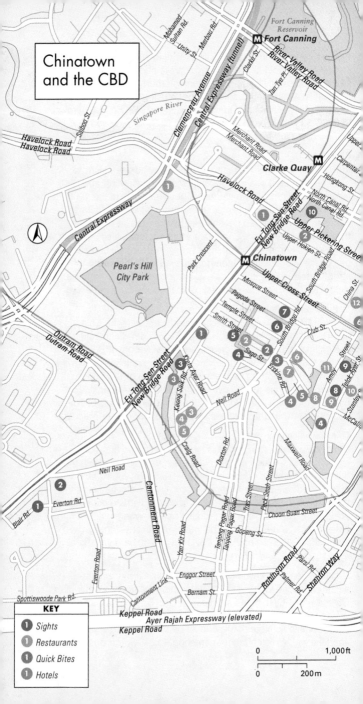

Chinatown
and the CBD

Fort Canning
Reservoir

M **Fort Canning**

Mohamed Sultan Rd.
Merbau Rd.
Clarke St.
River Valley Road
River Valley Road
Tan Tye Pl.

Saiboo St.

Singapore River

Havelock Road
Havelock Road

Merchant Road
Merchant Road

Clarke Quay **M**

Upper Carpenter
Hongkong St.

Havelock Road

1

North Canal Rd.
North Canal Rd.

Eu Tong Sen Street
New Bridge Road

1

10

Upper Pickering Street

2

Central Expressway

Upper Hokien St.

South Bridge Road

M **Chinatown**

*Pearl's Hill
City Park*

Park Crescent

Upper Cross Street

China St.
12

Outram Road
Outram Road

Mosque Street

Pagoda Street **7**

6

Temple Street **5**

Smith Street **2**
1
Sago St. **2**
4

South Bridge Rd.
Club St.
6

3
Erskine Rd. **7**

Amoy Street
11 **9**

Keong Saik Rd.
3
3

3 **6**

Eu Tong Sen Street
New Bridge Road

Kreta Ayer Road

Neil Road

4 **5** **8**
8

Telok Ayer St.
10

4 **3**
4 **5**
4 **9**

Stanley
McCall

Craig Road

Duxton Rd.

Maxwell Road

Peck Seah Street

Choon Guan Street

Neil Road

2

Cantonment Road

1 Everton Rd.

Yan Kit Road

Tanjong Pagar Road
Tanjong Pagar Road

Tras Street

Gopeng St.

Robinson Road
Parsi Rd.
Palmer Rd.

Shenton Way

Blair Rd.

Everton Road

Enggor Street

Bernam St.

Cantonment Link

Spottiswoode Park Rd.

Keppel Road
Ayer Rajah Expressway (elevated)
Keppel Road

KEY	
1	*Sights*
1	*Restaurants*
1	*Quick Bites*
1	*Hotels*

0   1,000ft
0   200m

Map Labels

Stamford Rd.

City Hall M

War Memorial Park

North Bridge Road

Coleman St.

Hill Street

Hill Street

High Street

Supreme Ct. Ln.

Saint Andrew's Road

Nicoll Highway

Nicoll Highway

Raffles Boulevard

Temasek Boulevard

Temasek Avenue

Connaught Dr.

Empress Pl.

Connaught Drive

Fullerton Rd.

Esplanade Drive

Esplanade Drive

Raffles Avenue

Singapore River

Circular Road

Chulia St.

Market St.

Raffles Place M

Marina Bay

Telok Ayer

Boon Tat St.

Cecil St.

Robinson Road

Boon Tat Link

Shenton Way

Marina Boulevard

Marina View

Bayfront M

Shears Link

Shears Ave.

Bayfront Avenue

Bayfront Avenue

Straits Boulevard

Numbered markers: 8, 7, 11, 6, 7, 13, 5, 12, 14, 15

Sights

Al-Abrar Mosque, **8**

Baba House, **2**

Blair Road, **1**

Buddha Tooth Relic Temple, **4**

Chinatown Complex, **5**

Jamae Mosque, **7**

Lau Pa Sat, **12**

Speakers' Corner, **10**

Sri Layan Sithi Vinayagar Temple, **3**

Sri Mariamman Temple, **6**

Thian Hock Keng Temple, **9**

Yueh Hai Ching Temple, **11**

Restaurants

ALTRO Zafferano, **15**

Chilli Pan Mee (Batu Rd), **12**

Chinatown Food Street, **2**

Cloudstreet, **11**

L'Angelus, **6**

Lime House, **3**

Lolla, **7**

Meta Restaurant, **5**

My Awesome Café, **9**

NAE:UM, **10**

Nouri, **8**

Pagi Sore, **13**

Red Star Restaurant, **1**

Thevar, **4**

Thunder Tea Rice, **14**

Quick Bites

Coffee Break at Amoy Street, **4**

Grain Traders, **5**

Hellu Coffee, **6**

Maxi Coffee Bar, **3**

Nanyang Old Coffee, **2**

Surrey Hills Deli, **7**

Tiong Shian Porridge, **1**

Hotels

Amoy Hotel, **7**

Ann Siang House, The Unlimited Collection by Oakwood, **5**

The Clan Hotel Singapore, **6**

The Fullerton Hotel, **8**

Furama City Centre, **1**

KēSa House, The Unlimited Collection by Oakwood, **3**

PARKROYAL on Pickering, **2**

The Scarlet Singapore, **4**

Chinatown ☎ 6221–4165 ⊕ www.masjidjamaechulia.sg ⧉ Free
Ⓜ Chinatown.

Speakers' Corner

PLAZA/SQUARE | Also known as Hong Lim Park, this spot was
declared a "free speech zone" by the government in 2001. It looks
like nothing more than a small patch of grass, but from 7 am to
7 pm on some days, you may be able to catch carefully craft-
ed words and speeches from people with an opinion to share.
Those who wish to speak need to register with the police at the
park station or online. This was intended as a place for people to
express their opinions freely, but it hasn't been very successful:
you can't address religious or racial issues, and having to register
means that your presence has been noted. ⊠ Hong Lim Park,
New Bridge Rd., Chinatown ☎ 800/471–7300 ⊕ www.nparks.gov.
sg Ⓜ Clarke Quay.

Sri Layan Sithi Vinayagar Temple

TEMPLE | This small but incredibly ornate temple is covered with
tiny pale blue and baby pink statues in typical Hindu style. It was
first built in 1925 in honor of Lord Vinayagar—also known as Lord
Ganesha, the most widely worshipped Hindu god. He has three
deity statues dedicated to him in the main sanctum, one of which
was brought from India. It's worth visiting just to admire from the
outside as you breathe in the heavy scents of incense, but you
can go inside as long as there isn't a worship session taking place.
⊠ 73 Keong Saik Rd., Chinatown ☎ 6221–4853 ⊕ www.sttemple.
com Ⓜ Outram Park.

★ Sri Mariamman Temple

TEMPLE | Singapore's oldest Hindu temple has a pagoda-like
entrance topped by one of the most ornate gopurams (pyramidal
gateway towers) you're likely to ever see outside of South India.
Hundreds of brightly colored statues of deities and mythical
animals line the tiers of this towering porch; glazed concrete cows
sit, seemingly in great contentment, atop the surrounding walls.
The story of this temple begins with Naraina Pillay, Singapore's
first recorded Indian immigrant, who arrived on the same ship as
Sir Stamford Raffles in 1819 and set up his own construction business, often using convicts sent to Singapore from India, quickly
making a fortune. The first temple, built in 1827 of wood and attap
(wattle and daub), was replaced in 1843 by the current brick structure. The gopuram was added in 1936. Inside are some spectacular paintings that have been restored by Tamil craftsmen brought
over from South India. This is where Hindu weddings, as well as
the firewalking festival Thimithi, take place. ⊠ 244 South Bridge
Rd., Chinatown ☎ 6223–4064 ⊕ www.smt.org.sg Ⓜ Chinatown.

Singapore's Hawker Centers 👁

Singapore's hawker centers are a way of life. These vibrant food markets, dotted across the island in large numbers, play an integral role in the country's heritage and identity. They act as a kind of community dining center, where people from all walks of life can gather to eat, drink, and bond over the cheap, local food.

The hawker centers started out in the 1800s as street food stalls and grew rapidly until the colonial British government tried (and failed) to stop them in the early 1900s. The government eventually issued licenses, and in the 1970s, moved them to new centers in residential areas—many have survived.

These days, a trip to Singapore wouldn't be complete without eating at a hawker center: Chinatown has **Maxwell Food Centre**, **Amoy Street Food Centre**, and **Chinatown Complex Food Centre** and Tanjong Pagar has **Tanjong Pagar Plaza Market & Food Centre**, though you can find centers in just about every central neighborhood.

There are no real rules to observe. Many like to find a seat first, a practice called "choping" in Singlish, in which you leave a personal item (like a packet of tissues) on a table while you line up for their meal. Usually you wait while the food is cooked, then pay when you collect it a few minutes later. When you're done, leave the tray on the table. No napkins are provided, but there are sinks for washing your hands.

★ **Thian Hock Keng Temple** (*Temple of Heavenly Happiness*)
TEMPLE | This structure was completed in 1842 to replace a simple shrine built 20 years earlier. It's one of Singapore's oldest Chinese temples, built on the spot where, prior to land reclamation, immigrants stepped ashore after a hazardous journey across the China Sea. In gratitude for their safe passage, the Hokkien people dedicated the temple to Ma Chu P'oh, the goddess of the sea. It's richly decorated with gilded carvings, sculptures, tile roofs topped with dragons, and fine carved-stone pillars. On either side of the entrance are two stone lions. The one on the left is female and holds a cup symbolizing fertility; the other, a male, holds a ball, a symbol of wealth. If the temple is open, note that as you enter, you must step over a high threshold board. ✉ *158 Telok Ayer St., Chinatown* ☎ *6423–4616* ⊕ *www.thianhockkeng.com.sg* 🎫 *Free* Ⓜ *Telok Ayer.*

🍴 Restaurants

★ Chinatown Food Street

$ | **CHINESE** | A stretch of Smith Street that is closed to traffic, this outdoor eating area packed with stalls is the only place you'll find real "street food" in Singapore. Though it isn't totally open-air (there is a high-ceiling glass canopy in case of rain), it makes a welcome change from the often hot and sweaty hawker centers. **Known for:** street food in a novel setting; open rain or shine; cold beer and chicken satay. $ *Average main: S$7* ✉ *41 Smith St., Chinatown* ⊕ *chinatownfoodstreet.sg* Ⓜ *Chinatown.*

Cloudstreet

$$$$ | **ASIAN FUSION** | Chef Rishi Naleendra's Cloudstreet is rooted in both his Sri Lankan heritage and his training in Australia. The menu promises to "champion ingredient-driven cuisine," and there's always a heavy focus on seasonality in the creative tasting menus. **Known for:** creative fine dining; chef's counter experience; separate dining space for dessert courses. $ *Average main: S$388* ✉ *84 Amoy St., Chinatown* ☎ *6513–7688* ⊕ *cloudstreet. com.sg* ☾ *Closed Sun. and Mon.* Ⓜ *Telok Ayer.*

L'Angelus

$$$$ | **FRENCH** | Potted plants line the entrance of this chic, Parisian-style restaurant, and, in its casual dining area, French film posters cover the walls from floor to ceiling. Daily specials are scrawled on chalkboards, but the set menu includes meat, seafood, and such French specialities as snails, foie gras, and crème brûlée, and there's an exhaustive selection of French wines, as well as a large range of whiskies, vodkas, gins, liqueurs, rums, and Armagnacs. **Known for:** poster-covered walls; perfectly cooked steaks; French wines. $ *Average main: S$72* ✉ *85 Club St., Chinatown* ☎ *6225–6897* ⊕ *www.langelus.sg* ☾ *Closed Sun.* Ⓜ *Maxwell.*

Lime House

$$ | **CARIBBEAN** | Spend time "liming"—the Caribbean slang for "hanging with friends"—at this vibrant eatery inside a four-story heritage shophouse decorated with leafy plants, natural woods, and colorful prints. Wash down such classic Caribbean dishes as jerk chicken and curry goat with a rum cocktail from the restaurant's tiki-style bar, Bago. **Known for:** Caribbean classics; tiki bar; light and airy atmosphere. $ *Average main: S$35* ✉ *2 Jiak Chuan Rd., Chinatown* ☎ *6222–3130* ⊕ *limehouse.asia* ☾ *Closed Mon.* Ⓜ *Outram.*

★ Lolla

$$$ | **MEDITERRANEAN** | Inspired by the food of the Mediterranean, Lolla's small plates menu combines flawless technique with seasonal, high-quality ingredients. Perched on Ann Siang Hill, the restaurant belies its status with a lively atmosphere that makes you feel instantly welcome. **Known for:** weekend tasting menus; open kitchen countertop; refined Mediterranean small plates. ⑤ *Average main: S$45* ✉ *22 Ann Siang Rd., Chinatown* ☎ *6423–1228* ⊕ *lolla.com.sg* ⊘ *Closed Sun.* Ⓜ *Maxwell.*

★ Meta Restaurant

$$$$ | **KOREAN FUSION** | If you're celebrating a special occasion or looking to experience some Michelin-starred fine dining, you won't be disappointed by Meta's multi-course fixed menu inspired by Chef Sun Kim's Korean heritage. With a minimalist design and open kitchen, the restaurant gives you the opportunity to watch the chefs at work as you enjoy a languid afternoon or evening of tasting (the restaurant advises customers plan 2.5 hours for their meal). **Known for:** Korean food prepared using both Japanese and Western techniques; high-quality fine dining; warm yet polished service. ⑤ *Average main: S$298* ✉ *1 Keong Saik Rd., Chinatown* ☎ *6513–0898* ⊕ *www.metarestaurant.sg* ⊘ *Closed Sun. and Mon. No lunch Tues.–Thur.* Ⓜ *Outram Park.*

My Awesome Café

$$ | **CONTEMPORARY** | Inside a historic shophouse tucked away on a quiet street, this café-by-day, bar-by-night has all the makings of a hipster hangout. Seated at a table with legs made out of old piping—amid fairy lights and exposed brickwork—you can order fresh salads, sandwiches, or platters, as well as excellent coffees and even better wine. **Known for:** hearty sandwiches by day; great beers by night; lively evening atmosphere. ⑤ *Average main: S$25* ✉ *202 Telok Ayer St., Chinatown* ☎ *8798–1783* ⊕ *www.myawesomecafe.com* Ⓜ *Telok Ayer.*

NAE:UM

$$$$ | **KOREAN FUSION** | NAE:UM— meaning a fragrance that evokes memories—is a contemporary take on traditional Seoul cuisine, blending Western cooking techniques wth Korean flavors. Founder and chef Louis Han regularly changes the seasonal tasting menu to reflect the stories and memories of home, with menu titles like "Han River Sunset" and "Front Yard Barbecue." The dining room is a calming space just back from the busy Telok Ayer Street, with impeccable service from Han's team. **Known for:** seasonal Korean menus; calming birch dining space; somewhat affordable fine dining. $ *Average main: S$198* ✉ *161 Telok Ayer St., Chinatown* ☎ *8830–5016* ⊕ *naeum.sg* ⊗ *Closed Sun. and Mon. No lunch Tues.–Fri.* Ⓜ *Telok Ayer.*

Nouri

$$$$ | FUSION | Chef Ivan Brehm's mixed background—Italian, Spanish, German, and Brazilian—provides the inspiration for what he calls "crossroads cooking." Nouri's dedicates himself to combining ingredients, techniques, and flavors from across the globe in intriguing tasting menus. The light, airy dining room and marble chef's counter create a serene atmosphere, with service and wine pairings that are both top-notch. **Known for:** dishes inspired by different geographies and cultures; communal marble table; appealing wine pairings. $ *Average main: S$328* ✉ *72 Amoy St., Chinatown* ☎ *9230–2477* ⊕ *nouri.com.sg* ⊗ *Closed Mon. and Tues. No lunch Sat.* Ⓜ *Telok Ayer.*

Red Star Restaurant

$$ | CANTONESE | Shuffling waiters push dim sum trolleys from table to table at this wonderfully outdated Cantonese restaurant. Although the old-school decor (red carpets, cream table cloths, strip lights) makes it feel like a giant community center, the crispy spring rolls, siew mai dumplings, fried wantons, and egg tarts are classic and delicious. **Known for:** suckling pig; roast duck; delicious dumplings (served at lunchtime only). $ *Average main: S$20* ✉ *#07–23, 54 Chin Swee Rd., Chinatown* ☎ *6532–5266* Ⓜ *Chinatown.*

Thevar

$$$$ | MODERN INDIAN | Situated at the heart of foodie Keong Saik Road, chef Mano Thevar's eponymous modern Indian restaurant provides a refreshing take on cuisine not often considered fine dining. Recognizable dishes like Chettinad chicken roti are given a unique twist with European techniques and flavors from the Malay peninsula. **Known for:** far-ranging Chef's tasting menu the only option; fun, lively atmosphere; unique vegetarian options. $ *Average main: S$288* ✉ *9 Keong Saik Rd., Chinatown* ☎ *9750–8275* ⊕ *thevar.sg* ⊗ *Closed Sun. and Mon. No lunch* Ⓜ *Outram Park.*

☕ Coffee and Quick Bites

★ Coffee Break at Amoy Street

$ | **CAFÉ** | Head to level 2 of the Amoy Street food center for a cup of traditionally-brewed local *kopi* with a twist; the menu includes a dizzying array of latte flavors, including black sesame, hazelnut, and butter pecan. For a quick bite, pair it with their equally-eclectic toast flavors, like earl grey creme or matcha coconut. **Known for:** unique kopi and toast breakfast; traditional sock-brewed coffee; popular with the Telok Ayer work crowd. $ *Average main: S$4* ✉ *7 Maxwell Rd., Chinatown* ⊕ *coffeebreaksg.com* ▭ *No credit cards* ☉ *Closed Sat. and Sun.* Ⓜ *Telok Ayer.*

Maxi Coffee Bar

$ | **CAFÉ** | This small, blue-decked café on the side of Ann Siang Hill serves some of the best coffee on the island. Grab an iced latte and perch on one of the outside tables for a quick break from the Chinatown sightseeing and shopping. **Known for:** seasonal coffee selections; friendly staff; outdoor seating. $ *Average main: S$7* ✉ *6 Ann Siang Hill, Chinatown* ☎ *9776–7400* ⊕ *maxicoffeebar.com* ☉ *Closed Mon.* Ⓜ *Maxwell.*

Nanyang Old Coffee

$ | **CAFÉ** | "Bringing back the good old taste of Singapore traditional coffee" is the motto here, and you definitely won't be disappointed in the way that's done. Try the strong, sweet ubiquitous in Singapore's history, in an old-fashioned, bright red coffee house. **Known for:** supports historic Singaporean coffee culture; strong coffee and milk tea; kaya toast sets. $ *Average main: S$4* ✉ *268 South Bridge Rd., Chinatown* ☎ *6221–6973* ⊕ *nanyangoldcoffee. com* Ⓜ *Maxwell.*

Tiong Shian Porridge

$ | **CHINESE** | This humble store on the edge of Chinatown, with its metal chairs and bright strip lights, doesn't look very inviting— until you see the hoards of people waiting to get inside. *Congee,* or savory porridge, is a popular local dish, and nowhere does it better than Tiong Shian, where thick, hot white rice is served with everything from meatballs to frogs legs. **Known for:** cheap prices; delicious congee; quick service. $ *Average main: S$7* ✉ *265 New Bridge Rd., Chinatown* ☎ *6222–3911* Ⓜ *Chinatown.*

🛏 Hotels

Ann Siang House, The Unlimited Collection by Oakwood

$$$ | **HOTEL** | In a restored heritage building, this boutique property is much-loved for its architecture and style. **Pros:** excellent location; complimentary laundrette; near to popular hawker centers. **Cons:** no swimming pool; no breakfast; some rooms have small windows. $ *Rooms from: S$380* ✉ *28 Ann Siang Rd., Chinatown* ☎ *8608–8190* ⊕ *www.discoverasr.com* 🛏 *20 rooms* ⦿ *No Meals* Ⓜ *Maxwell.*

Furama City Centre

$$ | HOTEL | This modern curvilinear building stands out amid the surrounding shophouses on the edge of Chinatown. **Pros:** great views from high floors; easy access to Chinatown; 24-hour room service. **Cons:** amenities are outdated; some rooms have interior-facing windows; check-in and check-out can take a while. *⑤ Rooms from: S$225 ✉ 60 Eu Tong Sen St., Chinatown ☎ 6533–3888 ⊕ www.furama.com/citycentre ⇌ 445 rooms* ⦿ *No Meals* Ⓜ *Chinatown.*

KēSa House, The Unlimited Collection by Oakwood

$$ | HOTEL | Designed in bold turquoise and green hues, this colorful boutique hotel is in a heritage townhouse from the 1920s, right in the heart of Chinatown. **Pros:** complimentary all-day refreshments; central Chinatown location; outdoor terrace area. **Cons:** some rooms are small; street-facing rooms can be noisy; limited facilities. *⑤ Rooms from: S$260 ✉ 55 Keong Saik Rd., Chinatown ☎ 6958–1588 ⊕ discoverasr.com ⇌ 60 rooms* ⦿ *No Meals* Ⓜ *Outram.*

★ PARKROYAL on Pickering

$$$ | HOTEL | The stunning architecture at this hotel integrates environmental principles both inside and out, including lush sky gardens almost 1,000 feet above street level, floor-to-ceiling glass windows throughout to decrease the need for artificial lighting, use of recycled stone and glass in guest room baths, and rainwater used to water greenery in the lobby. **Pros:** great spa facilities; eco-conscious initiatives; city views from infinity pool. **Cons:** limited in-house restaurants; some rooms are considered small for price; outdoor walkways not so great in the rain. *⑤ Rooms from: S$400 ✉ 3 Upper Pickering St., Chinatown ☎ 6809–8888 ⊕ www.panpacific.com ⇌ 367 rooms* ⦿ *No Meals* Ⓜ *Chinatown.*

The Scarlet Singapore

$$ | HOTEL | Singapore's first luxury boutique hotel opened in 2004 in one of the oldest conservation buildings on the island, a row of restored shophouses dating back to 1868, offering both historical charm and modern-day luxury, with a highly eclectic design. **Pros:** late (2 pm) checkout with direct bookings; panoramic views from rooftop; custom pillow menu. **Cons:** small pool; cheapest rooms don't have windows; street-facing rooms can be a little noisy. *⑤ Rooms from: S$250 ✉ 33 Erskine Rd., Chinatown ☎ 6511–3333 ⊕ thescarletsingapore.com ⇌ 80 rooms* ⦿ *No Meals* Ⓜ *Maxwell.*

Nightlife

Bitters and Love

COCKTAIL LOUNGES | A 19th-century shophouse in Chinatown is the perfect location for this speakeasy-like cocktail bar, where you'll have a one-of-a-kind experience. Tell the bartenders what you like, and they'll create a cocktail especially for you. There are also signature cocktails and bar bites available. Be sure to call for reservations in advance. ✉ *118 Telok Ayer St., Chinatown* ☎ *6438–1836* ⊕ *www.bittersandlove.com* Ⓜ *Telok Ayer.*

Chinese Theatre Circle

THEMED ENTERTAINMENT | The Chinese Theatre Circle (CTC) is a nonprofit organization that's been cultivating an appreciation of Cantonese opera since 1981. Check out one of their dinner performances every Friday and Saturday night from 7 to 9 pm and gain some insight into this particular art form (translations are provided). For S$40, you can dine on a set Chinese dinner with special-brewed tea while you watch, or for S$25 you can simply sit back and enjoy the show. There are daily karaoke singing concerts held in the afternoons, as well. The Theatre Circle is set up along a stretch of Smith Street that transforms into a pedestrian zone nightly and brings to mind the hustle and bustle of the street hawkers from the 1970s. ✉ *5 Smith St., Chinatown* ☎ *6323–4862* ⊕ *www.ctcopera.com.sg* Ⓜ *Chinatown.*

★ Employees Only

COCKTAIL LOUNGES | Conceived in downtown New York City back in 2004, Employees Only has become one of the most iconic cocktail bars in Singapore since it opened here in 2016. Describing itself as a "neo-speakeasy restaurant and bar," this slice of the Big Apple has been ranked among Asia's best bars in the annual "Best Bars" awards every year since its inception. Enjoy classic small plates like steak tartare and shrimp cocktail as you drink the innovative NYC creations. ✉ *112 Amoy St., Chinatown* ☎ *6221–7357* ⊕ *employeesonlysg.com* Ⓜ *Chinatown.*

Gibson Bar

BARS | This casual cocktail and seafood bar comes from the team behind Jigger & Pony (another renowned Singapore bar), so you already know it's good. Their seasonal cocktail menu does a good job of highlighting southeast Asian ingredients such as passionfruit and pandan. Try the oysters along with their namesake cocktail, the Gibson, which incorporates a homemade Ginjo sake vermouth. ✉ *20 Bukit Pasoh Rd., Level 2, Chinatown* ☎ *9114–8385* ⊕ *www.gibsonbar.sg* Ⓜ *Outram.*

Kult Yard

BARS | Part beer garden, part taqueria, part art café, this cool hangout is set in a former police barrack in leafy Pearl's Terrace—a stone's throw from the bustling streets of Chinatown. The courtyard is a great place to chill with a beer or (Kult Yard cocktail creation) while listening to some live music or checking out the local artwork on display. ⊠ *195 Pearl's Hill Terr., 01–53/54/55, Chinatown* ☎ *8361–1848* ⊕ *www.facebook.com/kultyard* Ⓜ *Chinatown.*

★ Native

BARS | At this sophisticated cocktail lounge and restaurant, the drinks are designed around stories and cultures from around southeast Asia. Many drinks are made using ingredients foraged from nearby areas and include local alcohols such as jackfruit rum; there's a strong focus on in-house, seasonal fermentation. Enjoy bespoke cocktails with a full restaurant menu on level one, or head upstairs for a more intimate drinking experience. ⊠ *52A Amoy St., Chinatown* ☎ *8869–6520* ⊕ *tribenative.com* Ⓜ *Chinatown.*

No Sleep Club

BARS | Since moving to a new home on buzzy Keong Saik Road, this neighborhood bar-cum-restaurant has gone from strength to strength. Drinks are inventive, the atmosphere cool and welcoming, and the food always hits the spot, with the Sunday roast a highlight among locals. ⊠ *20 Keong Saik Rd., Chinatown* ☎ *8838–0188* ⊕ *www.nosleepclub.sg* Ⓜ *Outram Park.*

Nutmeg and Clove

COCKTAIL LOUNGES | This avant-garde cocktail bar, a regular in Asia's 50 Best Bars, delivers a proudly Singaporean-influenced experience. Drawing inspiration from Singapore's progression from colony to independent metropolis, the extensive cocktail menu uses herbs, fruits, spices, and flora in concoctions that reflect Singapore's history in every sip. Accompanying nibbles are as experimental (and delicious). ⊠ *8 Purvis St., Chinatown* ☎ *9389–9301* ⊕ *www.nutmegclove.com* Ⓜ *Esplanade.*

★ Papa Doble

BARS | Opened in 2019, this Hemingway-inspired bar was formerly an outpost of Hong Kong's Old Man bar (the Singapore outpost also used to share its name), which was deemed "Best Bar in Asia" by the World's 50 Best Bars. The cocktails live up to the hype, with high-quality takes on classics like old fashioned and sazerac, alongside inventive, delicious signatures. ⊠ *55 Keong Saik Rd., Chinatown* ☎ *9022–7908* ⊕ *papadoblesg.com* Ⓜ *Outram.*

Potato Head

BARS | Hailing from the sandy shores of Bali, this bar with a cult following brings a beach-chic aesthetic to the art deco heritage building it occupies. Although it has an Asian burger restaurant and quirky speakeasy-style bar, head for the rooftop bar—a place of fairy lights, bright murals, lush greenery, lovely night views over the city, and tropical cocktails that will have you believing you're really in Bali. ☒ 36 Keong Saik Rd., Chinatown ☎ 6327–1939 ⊕ singapore.potatohead.co Ⓜ Outram Park.

Sago House

BARS | This raw, pared-back cocktail bar was built almost entirely with upscaled materials, lending a vibe to the place more akin to a friend's house rather than a smooth-operating business. There's a weekly rotating menu of exciting cocktails that use local produce, and an accompanying menu of tasty bar bites. Climb three stories and look for the iron hand on the shophouse door. ☒ 40B Sago St., Chinatown ☎ 8874–9936 ⊕ sagohouse.sg Ⓜ Maxwell.

★ Smith Street Taps

PUBS | Occupying a space on Level 2 of the Chinatown Complex Food Centre, this tiny bar is a hidden gem. It would be easy to mistake it as just one of the hundreds of food vendors that occupy the center if it weren't for the number of people drinking the excellent craft drafts at the tables that surround it. The friendly, knowledgeable staff will happily talk you through the tasting notes of each beer, many of which are brewed in Singapore. Grab some food from one of the many excellent hawker stalls around the bar and spend an evening watching the crowds throng through Chinatown below. ☒ Chinatown Complex, 335 Smith St., #02–062, Chinatown ☎ 8853–8535 ⊕ www.facebook.com/smithstreettaps Ⓜ Chinatown.

★ Underdog Inn

BARS | Moodily lit and uniquely designed, this lively bar is a great choice for an evening drink. Choose from one of the whiskeys or agaves of the month, or from the regular cocktail menu, which offers a twist on the classics. There's also a rotating menu of draft beers, and a specials board centered around nose-to-tail dining. ☒ 115 Amoy St., Chinatown ☎ 8751–0354 ⊕ underdoginn.com Ⓜ Telok Ayer.

🛍 Shopping

Chinatown is one of the best places in Singapore to buy cheap souvenirs, from keyrings and T-shirts to paintings and silk scarves. The market also sells interesting antiques and vintage Chinaware, while the surrounding malls are known for having some of the cheapest toiletries on the island.

ANTIQUES

Wing Antiques & Collectibles

ANTIQUES & COLLECTIBLES | It's a shame that no photography is allowed at this dusty old antiques shop. Its remarkable groupings of vintage goods, arranged in what you might call haphazard symmetry, make for one of the more photogenic mishmashes of random items in Singapore. Then again, photos might sully the surprises an hour of treasure hunting might yield. It's a great shop if you like thrifting. ⊠ *Havelock 2, 02 Havelock Rd., #03–27/28, Chinatown* Ⓜ *Chinatown.*

★ East Inspirations

ANTIQUES & COLLECTIBLES | At this family-run Chinese antiques shop, the treasure trove of ceramics, vases, furniture, and textiles could keep you entertained for hours. Each item has been curated by the shop's owner, Mr. Cheong, who fell in love with antiques more than 40 years ago and has been selling them ever since. He stocks all manner of elaborate items, from huge ornate wardrobes to tiny, intricately designed vases, while orange silks embroidered in dragons and flowers hang from the walls. ⊠ *256 South Bridge Rd., Chinatown* ☎ *6323–5365* ⊕ *www.east-inspirations.com* Ⓜ *Chinatown.*

CERAMICS

★ Peranankan Tiles Gallery

CERAMICS | This Chinatown gallery houses a collection of over 30,000 Peranakan tiles—colorful ceramics based on designs created by descendants of Chinese traders who settled in Singapore as early as the 15th century. A blend of Malaysian, Indonesian, and Singaporean influences, the intricate tiles can be seen adorning shophouses and residential properties across the island. Peranakan tiles make a distinctive (if fragile) souvenir of your time in Singapore, so Victor Lim's gallery is well worth a visit if you still have room in the suitcase. ⊠ *37 Pagoda St., Chinatown* ☎ *6684–8600* ⊕ *asterbykyra.sg* Ⓜ *Chinatown.*

DEPARTMENT STORES

Yue Hwa

DEPARTMENT STORE | Inside this aging, five-level, Chinese department store you'll find plenty of unique (and often pricey) products, including medicinal herbs, tea, silks, fashion, and home furnishings. Many of the items are from mainland China. ⊠ *70 Eu Tong Sen St., Chinatown* ☎ *6538–9233* ⊕ *www.yuehwa.com.sg* Ⓜ *Chinatown.*

Chinatown's outdoor shops are a good spot to pick up souvenirs.

MARKETS
★ Chinatown Street Market
SOUVENIRS | This is one of the most popular spots in the city to souvenir shop. The stalls sprawl across Pagoda Street, Trenggga-nu Street, Sago Lane, Smith Street, and Temple Street, so you just need to pick a starting point and get walking. You can buy everything from lacquerware and handmade fans to paintings and T-shirts. Prices are usually fixed. ✉ *Pagoda St., Chinatown* Ⓜ *Chinatown.*

SHOPPING CENTERS AND MALLS
Chinatown Point
MALL | One of the more modern shopping malls in the Chinatown area, this mall is a great place to grab a cool drink in the crisp air-conditioning—a welcome break from the busy market streets nearby. You'll also find a range of chain restaurants if you are looking for a quick lunch, as well as such expected amenities as drugstores in the basement. There are regular promotions and events held in the main area on the first floor, near the Cross Street entrance. ✉ *133 New Bridge Rd., Chinatown* ☎ *6702–0114* ⊕ *chinatownpoint.com.sg* Ⓜ *Chinatown.*

People's Park Centre
MALL | People's Park Centre—not to be confused with the distinctive yellow People's Park Complex—is an older mall often frequented by local Chinese residents. The mall is mixed-use, so you'll find everything from cheap grocery stores and massage

and beauty services, to traditional Chinese medicine practitioners. The mall is a good place to pick up a bargain or peruse interesting Chinese collectibles, and is very handily connected to Chinatown MRT. ✉ *101 Upper Cross St., Chinatown* Ⓜ *Chinatown.*

🏃 Activities

COOKING CLASSES

Cultural Cooking Class

FOOD AND DRINK TOURS | Appreciate Singapore's national pastime—eating—with a three-hour hands-on cooking class. Learn more about Singapore's colorful, multicultural history while you cook three quintessential Singaporean dishes, guided by friendly local instructors. Menus differ each day, but you can expect to be eating your way through classics like *nasi lemak, Nonya laksa,* and *char kway teow* by the end of class. Each session begins with an introduction to Singaporean food markets, hawkers, and local ingredients. ✉ *24A Sago St., Chinatown* ☎ *9452–3669* ⊕ *www. foodplayground.com.sg* ✑ *From S$119* Ⓜ *Maxwell.*

WALKING TOURS

Indie Singapore Tours

WALKING TOURS | This free, 3-hour walking tour of Chinatown runs every Tuesday and Friday morning. The guide points out local highlights and main attractions in addition to illustrating how this diverse part of Singapore is made up of a unique blend of cultures and religions. Bookings are essential (on the Indie Singapore site or via email) and can be made up to four weeks in advance. Tips at the end are appreciated. ✉ *151 New Bridge Rd., Chinatown* ⊕ *indiesingapore.com* ✑ *Free* Ⓜ *Chinatown Exit A.*

★ Monster Day Tours

WALKING TOURS | The free walking tour takes you on a 2.5-hour trip around the area, starting at Telok Ayer MRT (exit B). It's a great way to get your bearings and learn the history of the area as you tour the food streets, markets, and temples with a knowledgeable guide. At the end, tips (S$10–S$20, or even S$30) are appreciated but not compulsory if you think your guide was professional. Tours are available Tuesday, Thursday, and Saturday at 4 pm, and pre-registration is required. ✉ *7 Cross Street, Chinatown* ☎ *8749–7346* ⊕ *www.monsterdaytours.com* Ⓜ *Telok Ayer Exit B.*

The CBD

On weekdays, the Central Business District is packed with professionals traveling to and from work. High-rise office buildings and hotels fill the area next to Chinatown and many of its surrounding streets, but this is also the area where you'll find many heritage buildings and other reminders of Singapore's history.

Plan on spending at least a half-day here. The two-mile walk from Raffles Place to Gardens by the Bay will give you a good feel for this bustling, business-heavy part of town. Several of the city's biggest attractions will take up more of your time along the way.

There are MRT stations in the area covering most MRT lines, including the North–South and East–West lines at Raffles Place, Downtown line at Telok Ayer, and Thompson–East Coast line at Shenton Way. Several buse lines also serve the area, and taxi stands are fairly numerous.

◉ Sights

★ Lau Pa Sat

MARKET | This market is the largest Victorian cast-iron structure left in Southeast Asia. Already a thriving fish market in 1822, it was redesigned as an octagon by George Coleman in 1834 and again redesigned, as seen today, in 1894. It now serves as a food court, with hawker stalls that are busy during the day with office workers. After 7 pm, Boon Tat Street is closed to traffic, and the mood turns festive: hawkers wheel out their satay carts, and buskers often perform. ⊠ *18 Raffles Quay, CBD* ☏ *6220–2138* ⊕ *laupasat. sg* Ⓜ *Raffles Place*.

Yueh Hai Ching Temple

TEMPLE | Built in 1826 by Teochew Chinese from Guangdong Province and dedicated to the goddess of the sea, this is one of Singapore's oldest Taoist temples. It's also known as Wak Hai Cheng Bio Temple, which means Temple of the Calm Sea. Traders and travelers returning from China visited the temple on disembarking—believe it or not, Philip Street was then very close to the water—to offer their thanks for a safe journey. It has been maintained by the Ngee Ann Clan Association since 1845 and was rebuilt in 1895. Inside, there's an imperial signboard presented by Qing Dynasty Emperor Guang Xu in 1907. Each of the structure's twin wings can be accessed by its own entrance, each of which has different ornamental features. Besides dragons and pagodas, human figurines and scenes from Chinese operas are depicted on the temple's roof. ⊠ *30B Phillip St., CBD* ☎ *6536–6851* 🎫 *Free* Ⓜ *Raffles Place.*

🍴 Restaurants

ALTRO Zafferano

$$$ | MODERN ITALIAN | This corporate executive favorite encased by floor-to-ceiling windows serves up mod Italian food with a side of sweeping Marina Bay views. Wine aficionados can pair their meals with a selection from more than 200 premium Italian wines and collection of vintages. **Known for:** contemporary Italian cuisine; stunning views; personable service. ⑤ *Average main: S$70* ⊠ *Ocean Financial Centre, 10 Collyer Quay, Level 43, CBD* ☎ *6509–1488* ⊕ *altrozafferano.sg* ⊘ *Closed Sun.* Ⓜ *Raffles Place.*

Chilli Pan Mee (Batu Rd)

$ | MALAYSIAN | The lines outside this small noodle shop on a weekday at lunchtime speak for themselves. Owned by a Malaysian restaurant group, Restoran Super Kitchen, with locations also found in Kuala Lumpur, the simply-fitted, compact restaurant is often crowded, but turnover is quick. **Known for:** spicy Malaysian noodles; well-known brand from Kuala Lumpur; long lines at lunchtime. ⑤ *Average main: S$11* ⊠ *Far East Square, 22 China St., CBD* ☎ *6787–7889* ⊕ *www.chillipanmee.com* Ⓜ *Telok Ayer.*

★ Pagi Sore

$$ | INDONESIAN | FAMILY | This restaurant has been serving Indonesian classics in the CBD for decades. Its focus on authentic recipes and Indonesian spice blends results in vibrant dishes loved by families and workers alike. **Known for:** ikan ota kukus (fish in a rich sauce) or tahu telor (crispy tofu omelet); well-established CBD restuarant; family-style dining. ⑤ *Average main: S$16* ⊠ *Far East Square, 88 Telok Ayer St., CBD* ☎ *6225–6002* ⊕ *pagi-sore. com* ⊘ *No dinner Mon.* Ⓜ *Telok Ayer.*

Thunder Tea Rice

$ | CHINESE | Among the heaving mass of eateries in Lau Pa Sat food center, this locally-renowned stall serves an exemplary version of thunder tea rice, a rice dish topped with peanuts, chilli, and anchovies and served alongside herby, green tea soup. The dish is a specialty of the Hakka people—one of Singapore's largest Chinese dialect groups—and is apparently named after the sound the ingredients make when being pounded to make the soup. **Known for:** limited menu; healthy food center option; busy at lunchtime with work crowds. ⑤ *Average main: S$7* ⊠ *Lau Pa Sat, 18 Raffles Quay, Stall 25, CBD* ☎ *6342–0223* ⊕ *www.thunder-tearicesg.com* Ⓜ *Raffles Place.*

🍵 Coffee and Quick Bites

Grain Traders

$$ | **INTERNATIONAL** | Reminiscent of the hip Melbourne café scene, this CBD lunch spot is a great place to grab a healthy snack. The veggies are always fresh, the meat high-quality, and there's a great range of tasty bowls like chicken breast, quinoa, mushrooms, and cucumber pickle. **Known for:** build-your-own bowls; healthy salad options; busy at lunchtime with work crowd. $ *Average main: S$18* ✉ *CapitaGreen, 138 Market St., CBD* ☎ *9776–8379* ⊕ *www.graintraders.com* ☉ *Closed weekends* Ⓜ *Raffles Place.*

★ Hellu Coffee

$ | **CAFÉ** | Grab a quick coffee at this hole-in-the-wall joint, one of the few independent coffee shops in the CBD. The space is definitely small—so you'll want to take your perfectly-roasted flat white to go—but don't forget to check out the pastry and waffle options. **Known for:** cute hole-in-the-wall spot; iced lattes as well as hot coffee; tasty pastries and waffles. $ *Average main: S$7* ✉ *Far East Square, 137 Amoy St., #01–05, CBD* ☉ *Closed Sun.* Ⓜ *Telok Ayer.*

Surrey Hills Deli

$$ | **SANDWICHES** | Run by the team behind well-stocked Australian market Surrey Hills Grocer, this deli serves great coffee and hearty sandwiches in a light, rustic setting. For extra snacking on the go, don't miss the gourmet yogurts and fresh fruit bowls at the mini grocer. **Known for:** thick, hearty sandwiches; good Aussie coffee; snack options for on-the-go. $ *Average main: S$18* ✉ *6 Battery Rd., CBD* ☎ *8036–7818* ⊕ *www.surreyhillsgrocer.sg* ☉ *Closed Sun.* Ⓜ *Raffles Place.*

🛏 Hotels

The CBD might feel like it would be better suited to business travelers, but its prime location between Chinatown and Marina Bay makes it a good choice for exploring—though keep in mind it's quieter on the weekend.

★ Amoy Hotel

$$$ | **HOTEL** | Named after the Zhangzhou people, who came from China to settle in Singapore, this boutique hotel is a tribute to the area's trading past and full of character. **Pros:** excellent location; digital check-in; unique historical design. **Cons:** lighting is a little dim in some rooms; no pool; late-night noise from local bars in some rooms. $ *Rooms from: S$400* ✉ *Far East Square, 76 Telok*

Ayer St., CBD ☎ *6580–2888* ⊕ *www.fareasthospitality.com* ⮑ *37 rooms* ⦿ *Free Breakfast* Ⓜ *Telok Ayer.*

The Clan Hotel Singapore

$$$ | HOTEL | Moody lighting and traditional Chinese design define this modern 30-story hotel, which is located perfectly at the edge of the CBD, overlooking the intricate red-tiled shophouses of Telok Ayer. **Pros:** great benefits for Master Series rooms; shower suites for early/late arrivals; amazing views. **Cons:** deluxe rooms are quite compact; breakfast area is crowded; fairly small pool area. Ⓢ *Rooms from: S$450* ✉ *10 Cross St., CBD* ☎ *6228–6388* ⊕ *www.theclanhotel.com.sg* ⮑ *324 rooms* ⦿ *No Meals* Ⓜ *Telok Ayer.*

The Fullerton Hotel

$$$$ | HOTEL | FAMILY | Singapore's former General Post Office-turned-hotel has many historic details paying tribute to its past, making this an atmospheric setting to base yourself; plus, its central location means that you'll be within walking distance of many of the top sights. **Pros:** iconic building; award-winning restaurants; great city views. **Cons:** small pool that can get crowded; small TVs; starting to show its age. Ⓢ *Rooms from: S$530* ✉ *1 Fullerton Sq., CBD* ☎ *6733–8388* ⊕ *www.fullertonhotels.com* ⮑ *400 rooms* ⦿ *Free Breakfast* Ⓜ *Raffles Place.*

🍸 Nightlife

The Good Beer Company

BARS | Craft beers and thin-crust pizzas are the main draws for thirsty workers at this bar in China Square. You'll find a large selection of ales, IPAs, and lagers on tap, many brewed in Singapore, plus a well-stocked fridge for perusing. Pizza and pint deals are available on most days, and happy hour runs until 8 pm. ✉ *3 Pickering St., Nankin Row #01–30, CBD* ☎ *8120–5060* ⊕ *www. facebook.com/goodbeerchinasquare* Ⓜ *Telok Ayer.*

The Secret Mermaid

COCKTAIL LOUNGES | This speakeasy-style bar serves exceptional cocktails, developed from both their large collection of boutique spirits from American distilleries, and from their homemade infusions and concoctions. There's also a short selection of beers and wines, and a snack menu led by the renowned oyster happy hour. ✉ *Ocean Financial Centre, 10 Collyer Quay, #B1–09, CBD* ☎ *6634–8593* ⊕ *www.thesecretmermaid.com* Ⓜ *Raffles Place.*

★ Taylor Adam

COCKTAIL LOUNGES | Walk through the bespoke tailor shop in front, built in collaboration with Meiko Tailor, to get to this hidden, charming speakeasy. As you may expect, cocktails can be "tailored" to taste and preference, alongside a regularly changing menu of signature creations. ⊠ *1 Raffles Place, #01–03, CBD* ☏ *8878–3395* ⊕ *tayloradam.bio.link* Ⓜ *Raffles Place.*

Performing Arts

★ Singapore Chinese Orchestra

CONCERTS | Singapore's only professional Chinese orchestra is comprised of more than 80 musicians. It stages annual blockbusters, both locally and internationally, that push the boundaries of traditional Chinese music, and it holds free performances to promote appreciation of the genre. ⊠ *Singapore Conference Hall, 7 Shenton Way, CBD* ☏ *6557–4034* ⊕ *www.sco.com.sg* Ⓜ *Shenton Way.*

Shopping

CLOTHING

Le Petit Society

CHILDREN'S CLOTHING | **FAMILY** | One of Singapore's most well-loved family lifestyle brands has an "in real life" concept store at Downtown Gallery. If you are looking for high-quality kids clothing or gifts, this should be your first stop. ⊠ *DownTown Gallery, 6A Shenton Way, #01–06, CBD* ☏ *6224–6288* ⊕ *www.lepetitsociety. com* Ⓜ *Shenton Way.*

JEWELRY AND WATCHES

★ Bold & Craft

JEWELRY & WATCHES | A team of craftsmen and designers makes the unique handmade products, including jewelry, accessories, leather goods, and woodwork that are sold in this boutique. You're bound to find something unique here. ⊠ *OUE Downtown 2, 6A Shenton Way, #01–42, CBD* ☏ *8611–8233* ⊕ *www.boldandcraft. com* Ⓜ *Shenton Way.*

SHOPPING CENTERS AND MALLS

The Arcade

MALL | If you're traveling around SEA, the second floor of the Arcade mall is by far the best place in Singapore to buy currency, with over 20 vendors competing for the best rates. If you are at lunch hour, though, expect long lines. ⊠ *11 Collyer Quay, CBD* Ⓜ *Raffles Place.*

Downtown Gallery

MALL | One of the CBD's few dedicated retail spaces, Downtown Gallery houses unique shops, including Bold&Craft and

The Fashion Pulpit, as well as a range of barbers and healthcare studios. The mall is also home to fitness and gym spaces, with a concentration of sports, cycling equipment, and apparel shops. There's also a nice selection of cafés and restaurants here for a quick refuel. ⊠ *6A Shenton Way, CBD* ☎ *6513–7727* ⊕ *downtown-gallery.com.sg* Ⓜ *Shenton Way.*

VINTAGE
★ The Fashion Pulpit

SECOND-HAND | A unique concept in Singapore allows you to trade in your unwanted clothing and "swap" for pieces you do fancy. The store, with a goal to "make fashion a force for good," has saved over 200,000 fashion items since inception, reducing the energy and resources needed to create new items. It's great fun to search through the racks for a new look, especially with a clear conscience. ⊠ *OUE Downtown 2, 6A Shenton Way, #02–08, CBD* ☎ *8399–5343* ⊕ *www.thefashionpulpit.com* Ⓜ *Shenton Way.*

🏃 Activities

GOLF
Clubhouse SG

GOLF | Billed as Singapore's premier indoor golf pub and café, this is a great place to have a round of (virtual) golf in the middle of the CBD. The GC Hawk simulators allow play on courses from around the world for seasoned pros. For those new to golf, there are fun carnival games to play. Grab a well-earned beer or a bite to eat as you play. ⊠ *Capital Tower, 168 Robinson Rd., #01–07, CBD* ☎ *6327–8045* ⊕ *clubhousesg.com* 🎟 *From S$75 per hour* Ⓜ *Shenton Way.*

ROCK CLIMBING
Origin Boulder

ROCK CLIMBING | **FAMILY** | You won't find mountains to climb amidst the CBD's skyscrapers, but you can still reach great heights at this bouldering gym in Cross Street Exchange. The gym caters to beginners and intermediate climbers, and there's also an introductory class option to get you into the swing of the sport. It's a fun way to burn a few of those hawker-induced calories. ⊠ *Cross Street Exchange, 18 Cross St., B1–117 and B1–118, CBD* ☎ *8818–6879* ⊕ *originboulder.sg* 🎟 *From S$26 (including climbing shoes)* Ⓜ *Telok Ayer.*

Tanjong Pagar

In the 1830s, Tanjong Pagar was a simple fishing village, although no sign of that sleepy image remains today. Now famed for its range of dining options, cocktail bars, and coffee shops, it's a fun and fast-paced neighborhood to spend your time.

◉ Sights

Pinnacle@Duxton

VIEWPOINT | If you visit Tanjong Pagar, you can't miss the Pinnacle, which towers imposingly over the area with its geometric black-and-white design. Though the building is actually a local government housing block, the 50th-story skybridge is open to all visitors, offering dramatic views across the city. You need an EZ Link card to enter, which you can buy from any 7-11 or MRT Ticket Office. ⊠ *1G Cantonment Rd., Tanjong Pagar* ⊕ *Go to the MA office at Level 1 Block G* ☎ *8683–7760* ⊕ *www.pinnacleduxton. com.sg* 🖾 *S$6 per person* Ⓜ *Tanjong Pagar.*

Singapore Chinese Cultural Centre

HISTORY MUSEUM | Discover what it means to be a Chinese Singaporean at the center's permanent interactive Singapo▨ Exhibition. This new identity is complex and ever-changing, where Chinese culture has been shaped over many years by Singapore's other diverse ethnicities. From historic influences to modern-day food, language, and culture, it tells a fascinating story of this uniquely Singaporean identity. ⊠ *1 Straits Blvd., Tanjong Pagar* ☎ *6812– 7222* ⊕ *www.singaporeccc.org.sg* 🖾 *Free* Ⓜ *Shenton Way.*

Singapore City Gallery

OTHER MUSEUM | Explore the rapid rise of Singapore's city skyline, from trading port to metropolis in just five decades, in this interactive exhibition from Singapore's Urban Redevelopment Authority. The exhibition details the country's unique planning challenges, conservation efforts, and future urban planning, with a large city model and 270-degree panoramic show being two of the key attractions. ⊠ *The URA Centre, 45 Maxwell Centre, Tanjong Pagar* ☎ *6221–6666* ⊕ *www.ura.gov.sg* 🖾 *Free* ☾ *Closed Sun.* Ⓜ *Maxwell.*

★ Singapore Art Museum at Tanjong Pagar Distripark

ART MUSEUM | Housed in an old industrial port building, this large, airy art museum showcases contemporary southeast Asian art, with a regularly changing lineup of exhibitions and residencies.

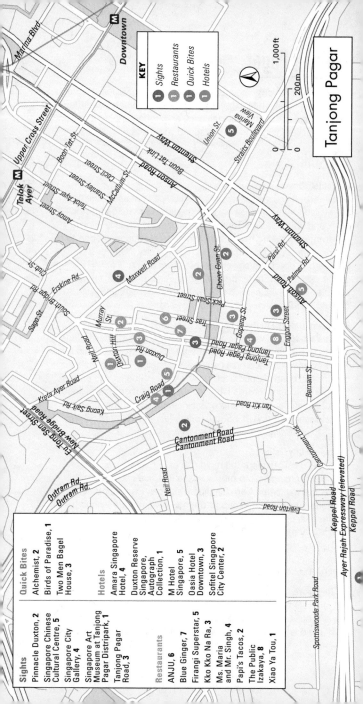

Tanjong Pagar

KEY

- **1** Sights
- **1** Restaurants
- **1** Quick Bites
- **1** Hotels

Sights

Pinnacle Duxton, **2**

Singapore Chinese Cultural Centre, **5**

Singapore City Gallery, **4**

Singapore Art Museum at Tanjong Pagar Distripark, **1**

Tanjong Pagar Road, **3**

Restaurants

ANJU, **6**

Blue Ginger, **7**

Firangi Superstar, **5**

Kko Kko Na Ra, **3**

Ms. Maria and Mr. Singh, **4**

Papi's Tacos, **2**

The Public Izakaya, **8**

Xiao Ya Tou, **1**

Quick Bites

Alchemist, **2**

Birds of Paradise, **1**

Two Men Bagel House, **3**

Hotels

Amara Singapore Hotel, **4**

Duxton Reserve Singapore, Autograph Collection, **1**

M Hotel Singapore, **5**

Oasia Hotel Downtown, **3**

Sofitel Singapore City Center, **2**

Permanent exhibit "The Everyday Museum" commissions art that interacts with local communities, giving a unique perspective into some of the areas you may have already visited. The museum also hosts an ongoing selection of weekly programs, including family art classes, live music, and art wellness courses—check the website for more information. ⊠ *39 Keppel Rd, Tanjong Pagar* ☎ *6697–9730* ⊕ *www.singaporeartmuseum.sg* 🖃 *S$10* Ⓜ *Tanjong Pagar.*

Tanjong Pagar Road

STREET | You'll struggle not to pull out your camera as you walk along this road. The 220 shophouses that line the street have been restored to an idealized version of their 19th-century appearance—a collection of brightly-colored facades standing in symmetrical unity. The buildings contain tea houses, calligraphers, mahjong tile makers, shops, bars, and restaurants, and although there is no one house that is especially worth visiting, the road itself makes for a pleasant stroll as you admire the striking architecture. ⊠ *Chinatown* Ⓜ *Tanjong Pagar.*

🍴 Restaurants

ANJU

$$$ | KOREAN FUSION | Amongst the many BBQ-grilling, beer-swilling Korean joints on Tanjong Pagar, ANJU stands out as a more refined way to experience Korean food and drink. Named after the term for small plates served with alcohol, ANJU's goal is to redefine Korea's dining and drinking experience, moving away from the perceptions of "green bottle" soju (a cheap rice-based spirit, often flavored with fruit). **Known for:** impeccable Korean small plates; excellent Korean spirits; calm, sophisticated dining space. ⑤ *Average main: S$45* ⊠ *62 Tras St., Tanjong Pagar* ☎ *6612–1172* ⊕ *anju. com.sg* 🕙 *Closed Sun. and Mon. No lunch* Ⓜ *Tanjong Pagar.*

★ Blue Ginger

$$ | SINGAPOREAN | Established in 1995 by a group of friends, this is one of Singapore's first spots to serve Peranakan cuisine. In a beautifully restored shophouse, the restaurant offers a range of well-prepared Malaysian/Chinese fare, including signature *ayam panggang* (smoky chicken with spiced coconut milk) and rich beef rendang. **Known for:** historical setting; authentic Peranakan food; specialty dessert made with durian. ⑤ *Average main: S$30* ⊠ *97 Tanjong Pagar Rd., Chinatown* ☎ *6222–3928* ⊕ *www.theblueginger.com* Ⓜ *Tanjong Pagar.*

Firangi Superstar

$$$ | **MODERN INDIAN** | Billed as a love letter to India, this restaurant focuses on modern Indian cuisine. The food tries to tell a story, with the signature "This Is Also Not Aloo Gobi" offering a fun play on the traditional cauliflower potato dish, while cocktails use South Asian ingredients like ghee and masala to elevate classics. **Known for:** all options can be made vegetarian-friendly; extravagant colonial-style setting; weekend Champagne brunch. $ *Average main: S$45 ⊠ 20 Craig Road, #01–03, Tanjong Pagar ☎ 3129–7552 ⊕ www.firangisuperstar.com ⊗ Closed Sun. Ⓜ Tanjong Pagar.*

Kko Kko Na Ra

$$ | **KOREAN** | In an area with seemingly countless Korean places to choose from, there is one obvious destination if you want traditional Korean fried chicken. Supposedly the first restaurant in Singapore to introduce Chi-Maek (Korean-style fried chicken and beer), its menu also features soups, savory pancakes, and rice dishes too. **Known for:** addictive fried chicken; Korean staples like bibimbap and kimchi jjigae; lively atmosphere. $ *Average main: S$30 ⊠ 68 Tg Pagar Rd., Tanjong Pagar ☎ 6225–9282 ⊕ www. kkokkonara.com Ⓜ Tanjong Pagar.*

Ms. Maria and Mr. Singh

$$ | **MEXICAN FUSION** | Helmed by renowned chef Gaggan Anand, this unique fusion restaurant blends homestyle Indian and Mexican cooking to make what is billed as "a marriage of salsa and curries." The tasting menu showcases the best of the affair, with snacks that include *papdi chaat* (crackers with chutney and yogurt), larger dishes of tacos, biriyani, and tamales, all the way through to meal-ending churros. If you are more particular, there's a full à la carte menu to enjoy in the low-lit, vibe-heavy dining room, with plenty of vegetarian options. **Known for:** Indian/Mexican fusion; elaborate tasting menu; multiple vegetarian options. $ *Average main: S$25 ⊠ 43 Craig Rd., Tanjong Pagar ☎ 9654–4351 ⊕ www.mariaandsingh.sg ⊗ Closed Mon. No lunch Tues.–Thurs. Ⓜ Tanjong Pagar.*

Papi's Tacos

$$ | **MEXICAN** | With its neon signs, loud music, and Mexican street art plastered across the walls, this taqueria stands out from the rows of Korean BBQ restaurants along Tangjong Pagar Road. The food here is fresh, colorful, and authentic, with popular tacos such as the cult favorite al pastor (marinated pork shoulder) and pescado (fried dory). **Known for:** authentic Mexican classics; neon, music, Mexican decorations; ice-cold margaritas. $ *Average main: S$30 ⊠ 33 Tanjong Pagar Rd., Tanjong Pagar ☎ 9127–4922 ⊕ www.papis-tacos.com Ⓜ Maxwell.*

★ The Public Izakaya

$$ | JAPANESE | Tables and diners noisily spill out onto the street at one of the best Japanese *izakaya* experiences you can get outside of Japan. The casual menu and quintessential design pay homage to Japanese pub food, with excellent *yakitori* (meat/vegetable skewers) and light bites best shared by the table. **Known for:** lively outside dining; charcoal-grilled meat and vegetable skewers; ice-cold Japanese beers. $ *Average main: S$40* ⊠ *100 Tras St., #01–09, Tanjong Pagar* ☎ *6604–9622* ⊕ *www.hachi-group.com* ◷ *No lunch weekends* Ⓜ *Tanjong Pagar.*

Xiao Ya Tou

$$ | ASIAN FUSION | Retro posters adorning the walls and old-school lanterns hanging from the ceilings decorate this lively space that's almost always packed with diners. The modern Asian menu focuses on local classics with fun, playful twists, like truffle-roasted duck and angus beef satay, as well as a large menu for vegetarians. **Known for:** Singaporean classics with a twist; lively weekend atmosphere; fun cocktail menu. $ *Average main: S$35* ⊠ *6 Duxton Hill, #01–01, Tanjong Pagar* ☎ *6226–1965* ⊕ *www.xyt. sg* Ⓜ *Tanjong Pagar.*

☕ Coffee and Quick Bites

Alchemist

$ | CAFÉ | For a quick coffee on the go, Alchemist at International Plaza is a small, hole-in-the-wall joint that nevertheless deserves all the attention it gets. Aside from espresso, latte, and iced options, the rotating filter coffee is a great value, and the hot chocolate is rich and addictive. **Known for:** specialty coffee roasts; seasonal filter coffee; rich hot chocolate. $ *Average main: S$6* ⊠ *International Plaza, 10 Anson Rd., #01–34, Tanjong Pagar* ⊕ *www.alchemist.com.sg* ◷ *Closed weekends* Ⓜ *Tanjong Pagar.*

★ Birds of Paradise

$ | ICE CREAM | Cool down with some gelato at at this shop where the flavors are unique and the portions enormous. The makers incorporate culinary influences of southeast Asia when creating their gelato, using natural and botanical local ingredients like basil and blue ginger. **Known for:** exotic, botanical flavors; popular with locals; long weekend lines. $ *Average main: S$7* ⊠ *53 Craig Rd., Tanjong Pagar* ☎ *9823–4091* ⊕ *birdsofparadise.sg* Ⓜ *Tanjong Pagar.*

★ Two Men Bagel House

$$ | SANDWICHES | Grab a hefty bagel from this cult favorite. The menu is comprehensive, so you can design your bagel by type (plain, sesame, etc.) and schmear (cream cheese, vegemite etc.); and add a whole world of extras. **Known for:** freshly baked bagels; cold-brew coffee; create-your-own bagelwiches. $ *Average main: S$16* ⊠ *Icon Village, 16 Enggor St., #01–12, Tanjong Pagar* ☎ *6509–4125* ⊕ *www.twomenbagels.com* ⊗ *Closed Wed.* Ⓜ *Tanjong Pagar.*

🛏 Hotels

★ Amara Singapore Hotel
$$ | HOTEL | This 18-story hotel—part of a vibrant entertainment and shopping complex in the business district's south end and convenient to the MRT station—is soothing, thanks to a minimalist lobby, a Balinese-style pool, and guest rooms decorated in earth tones and timber. **Pros:** central location; huge range of dining options; spacious bedrooms. **Cons:** hotel could do with refreshing; some rooms are a little tired; TVs on the small side. $ *Rooms from: S$250* ⊠ *165 Tanjong Pagar Rd., Chinatown* ☎ *6879–2555* ⊕ *singapore.amarahotels.com* 🛏 *384 rooms* ⦿ *Free Breakfast* Ⓜ *Tanjong Pagar.*

Duxton Reserve Singapore, Autograph Collection
$$$ | HOTEL | This ornate hotel, with interiors by former Bond girl Anouska Hempel, aims to reflect 19th-century Singapore with large golden fans, calligraphy wallpaper, and a palette of black and gold that exudes both luxury and theater. **Pros:** nightly turndown service; organic cotton-linen towels and robes in all rooms; unique boutique design. **Cons:** interiors are dimly lit; no swimming pool; some rooms are small. $ *Rooms from: S$420* ⊠ *83 Duxton Rd., Tanjong Pagar* ☎ *6914–1428* ⊕ *duxtonreserve.com* 🛏 *49 rooms* ⦿ *No Meals* Ⓜ *Maxwell.*

M Hotel Singapore
$$ | HOTEL | The dull exterior makes the modern and stylish interior of this business hotel a bit of a surprise, and, though it's near the business district, it's removed from all the hurly-burly. **Pros:** central location; great service; plenty of dining options in the area. **Cons:** can seem dull on weekends; small pool; impersonal lobby. $ *Rooms from: S$270* ⊠ *81 Anson Rd., CBD* ☎ *6224–1133* ⊕ *www.millenniumhotels.com* 🛏 *413 rooms* ⦿ *Free Breakfast* Ⓜ *Tanjong Pagar.*

Oasia Hotel Downtown
$$ | HOTEL | The Oasia Hotel is best described as a tropical skyscraper, a 27-story metallic tower draped in greenery (21 different kinds of vines), with two rooftop pools open to all guests, and

a breezy sky terrace with a lawn for the hotel's yoga sessions. **Pros:** great perks for Club-room guests; 24-hour gym; cool craft gin bar. **Cons:** breakfast options are limited; views are sometimes compromised by nearby buildings; slow elevators. ⑤ *Rooms from: S$350* ⊠ *100 Peck Seah St., Tanjong Pagar* ☎ *6812–6900* ⊕ *www. oasiahotels.com* ➥ *314 rooms* ❍❙ *No Meals* Ⓜ *Tanjong Pagar.*

Sofitel Singapore City Center

$$$ | HOTEL | Sofitel's city hotel is characterized by bold artwork and botanical motifs, and rooms that offer views of the sleek buildings and colorful shophouses nearby. **Pros:** right next to MRT; grand lobby; Bose sound systems in all rooms. **Cons:** pool area is a little small; hotel restaurants are expensive; limited breakfast options. ⑤ *Rooms from: S$380* ⊠ *Guoco Tower, 9 Wallich St., Tanjong Pagar* ☎ *6428–5000* ⊕ *all.accor.com* ➥ *223 rooms* ❍❙ *No Meals* Ⓜ *078885.*

Nightlife

Tanjong Pagar is home to some of Singapore's most popular cocktail bars, serving drinks well into the early hours. With an abundance of choice in close proximity, it would be easy to fashion your own bar crawl.

Flow Bar

COCKTAIL LOUNGES | Located on the second floor of Restaurant Jag—and run by the restaurant's owners and master mixologist Ricky Paiva—this inviting space specializes in American-style cocktails. Split into four sections, the bar menu offers seasonal, foraged herbs in Garden, playful spins on classics in Living Room, creative concoctions in Playground, or spirit-forward sips in Office. If you're feeling peckish, the food menu is designed by the Michelin-starred kitchen below, with the signature croque monsieur and pulled pork sandwich being particular favorites. ⊠ *Restaurant Jag, 76A Duxton Rd., Level 2, Tanjong Pagar* ☎ *8028–5865* ⊕ *www. flowbarsg.com* Ⓜ *Tanjpong Pagar.*

★ Jigger and Pony

BARS | Yet another of the city's establishments to make the list of the "World's 50 Best Bars," Jigger and Pony serves up exceptional classic cocktails such as negronis and martinis, as well as signature cocktails with an Asian twist (think whiskey sour with a touch of yuzu marmalade). Located in the Amara Hotel, the dimly lit space is cozy and inviting. ⊠ *Amara Hotel, 165 Tanjong Pagar Rd., Chinatown* ☎ *9621–1074* ⊕ *www.jiggerandpony.com* Ⓜ *Tanjong Pagar.*

Night Hawk

COCKTAIL LOUNGES | This small, intimate cocktail bar has the feel of retro Manhattan, complete with leather paneling and low-lit booths. Cocktails are both innovative twists of modern classics and signature creations. Try the signature "Night Hawk," a play on temperature with cold coffee, rum, and vodka layered with warm coconut foam. There's a small menu of nibbles, but the drinks are the real stars of the show. ✉ 43 Tanjongg Pagar Rd., Tanjong Pagar ☎ 9666–0928 ⊕ www.nighthawk.sg Ⓜ Maxwell.

Praelum Wine Bistro

WINE BARS | Top-quality wine needn't be the preserve of stuffy lounges and high-cost tasting menus—at least not according to Duxton Hill-based Praelum. Set in a historic shophouse, this fun, lively wine bar serves great wine and French-inspired plates to share with friends. The team is incredibly knowledgeable and always happy to share with guests, so go with an open mind, and you're sure to drink something new and exciting. ✉ 4 Duxton Hill, Tanjong Pagar ☎ 9022–0141 ⊕ praelum.com.sg Ⓜ Tanjong Pagar.

RPM by D.Bespoke

COCKTAIL LOUNGES | Vinyl records line the walls in specially-built cases at this cool, darkly-lit shochu bar. Unlike its more famous cousin, *sake*, the Japanese spirit *shochu* is a lesser-known clear spirit that can be made by distilling any starchy ingredient, most commonly sweet potato, barley, or rice. Popular in the southern part of Japan, the clear nature of shochu makes it an excellent base for many cocktails, which RPM excels at. If you don't fancy a mix (or if want to get under the skin of this intriguing spirit), you can take a shochu flight or get a recommendation from one of the friendly bartenders for a drink on the rocks. Sip away while listening to a mix of American funk and soul to Japanese jazz. ✉ 16 Duxton Rd., Tanjong Pagar ☎ 8359–1334 ⊕ www.facebook.com/RPMbyDBespoke Ⓜ Tanjong Pagar.

★ SG Taps

BARS | Post-work revelers at this bar on Duxton Hill regularly spill out onto the street. Singaporean brews lead the way on the taps, although there is a rotating cast of beers from Australia, the United States and Japan as well. You'll find a well-stocked fridge to explore if nothing on draft suits you, and a decent selection of spirits on the top shelf. A fun Japanese-Singaporean fusion food menu will help tide you over before dinner. ✉ 13 Duxton Hill, Tanjong Pagar ☎ 6904–8474 ⊕ www.facebook.com/SGTAPS13 Ⓜ Tanjong Pagar.

★ Tippling Club

COCKTAIL LOUNGES | This outstanding mixology bar doubles as an award-winning restaurant where the cocktails are inspired by the food. There are two ways to experience it: the bar, which requires no reservations, or the restaurant, which does. Get a dinner reservation if you can so you can try the innovative cocktails with their excellent modern cooking. ⊠ *38 Tanjong Pagar Rd., CBD* ☎ *6475–2217* ⊕ *www.tipplingclub.com* Ⓜ *Tanjong Pagar.*

👜 Shopping

ANTIQUES

Tong Mern Sern

ANTIQUES & COLLECTIBLES | Housing a large collection of antiques and vintage pieces, the store displays a large banner across Tong Mern Sern, happily proclaiming to "buy junk and sell antiques." Oft-pictured and eminently Instagram-able, this three-story shop-house is home to a wealth of treasures, though you may need to spend an afternoon searching through it to find them. ⊠ *51 Craig Rd., Tanjong Pagar* ☎ *6223–1037* ⊕ *www.facebook.com/tong-mernsern* Ⓜ *Tanjong Pagar.*

BOOKS

Littered with Books

BOOKS | One of the best independent bookstores in Singapore, this cozy Duxton Hill favorite not only curates a fantastic range of books, but the staff are approachable and eager to recommend. ⊠ *20 Duxton Rd., Tanjong Pagar* ☎ *6220–6824* ⊕ *www.facebook. com/lwbsg* Ⓜ *Tanjong Pagar.*

CRAFTS

HULS Gallery

CRAFTS | This quiet gallery showcases fine crafts from artisans around Japan. Browse through traditionally made tea- and sake-ware, fine-dining sets, and larger art pieces made using everything from ceramic and lacquerware to bamboo and woodwork. The gallery also has regular events and exhibitions, exploring the deep history and heritage of Japanese crafts. ⊠ *24 Duxton Hill, Tanjong Pagar* ☎ *9643–8910* ⊕ *huls.com.sg* Ⓜ *Tanjong Pagar.*

PERFUME

Maison 21G

PERFUME | Create your own unique perfume at this Parisian boutique perfumery on Duxton Hill. There are a range of atelier, or workshops, to create the perfect fragrance, including bridal, family, and love. Each is led by an expert scent designer to guide you on your *eau de parfum* discovery. ⊠ *77 Duxton Rd., Tanjong Pagar* ☎ *9477–7818* ⊕ *www.maison21g.com* Ⓜ *Tanjong Pagar.*

RECORDS

Retrophonic Records

RECORDS | Head to this vinyl boutique for all your retro audio needs. Not only is there a large collection of vinyl records sourced from overseas, with everything from Japanese jazz to Britpop, there's also a range of turntables, record players, amplifiers, and speakers to peruse. ⊠ *18A Duxton Rd., Tanjong Pagar* ☎ *6220–8489* ⊕ *www.retrophonicrecords.com* Ⓜ *Tanjong Pagar.*

TEA

Yixing Yuan Teahouse

OTHER FOOD & DRINK | Stock up on high-grade Chinese tea at this traditional teahouse and restaurant, which has a large range of leaves, teaware, and gifts available for purchase. The staff are happy to recommend tea for all palates, or you can sit down to enjoy a freshly-brewed pot to taste. The teahouse also runs tea appreciation workshops for guests to get a deeper understanding of Chinese tea culture. ⊠ *78 Tanjong Pagar Rd., Chinatown* ☎ *6224–6961* ⊕ *www.yixingxuan-teahouse.com* Ⓜ *Maxwell.*

Chapter 5

TIONG BAHRU, SINGAPORE RIVER, AND RIVER VALLEY

Updated by
Olivia Lee

⊙ Sights   🍴 Restaurants   🛏 Hotels   ⚫ Shopping   🍸 Nightlife

★★★☆☆   ★★★★☆   ★★★★☆   ★★★☆☆   ★★★☆☆

NEIGHBORHOOD SNAPSHOT

TOP EXPERIENCES

■ **Brunch like a local:** Tuck into coffee and avocado toast like the athleisure-clad locals in a cool café.

■ **Get active along the river:** Walk, run, or cycle the length of Singapore River.

■ **Try the local food:** The Tiong Bahru Hawker Centre and Zion River Food Court are both excellent spots.

■ **Singapore by boat:** Take a boat ride on the river to admire the colorful shophouses.

GETTING HERE

Tiong Bahru can be reached by both the East–West Line (Tiong Bahru) and Thomson–East Coast Line (Havelock Road). Several buses (including the 5, 16, and 33) also traverse the neighborhood. River Valley is slightly less accessible, although Great World City on the Thomson–East Coast Line is around a 10- to 15-minute walk. The Singapore River can be reached with a short walk from a few MRT stations, including Havelock Road, Clarke Quay, and Raffles Place.

PLANNING YOUR TIME

Spend the morning in Tiong Bahru, taking in the bustle of the Wet Market, before a walk around the art deco buildings, stopping in at a few boutiques. River Valley is also great for a a languid weekend brunch, then an afternoon walk on the river, before finishing at one of the three quays for a drink.

VIEWFINDER

■ Tiong Bahru is one of the most photogenic neighborhoods in Singapore. The red roofs and spiral staircases of the art deco heritage buildings contrast beautifully with the blue skies and leafy palms. Great views are everywhere, but the curved "horse-shoe"-shaped flats at **Moh Guan Terrace** are particularly striking.

PAUSE HERE

■ Get a coffee along Singapore River and watch the joggers and cyclists. There are lots of quiet spots to choose from, but the Robertson Quay stretch has the best cafés, with river views a great side benefit. Weekday mid-mornings are the most peaceful time to visit, before office workers pile out for their lunch breaks.

Both River Valley and Tiong Bahru are considered desirable neighborhoods to live in, especially by expats. This makes the areas feel fairly international, with restaurants and cafés that wouldn't feel out of place in London or New York. At the same time, both retain a traditional charm, especially Tiong Bahru with its well-preserved art deco flats and local *kopitiams* (coffee shops).

Tiong Bahru was built in the 1930s as Singapore's first public housing estate. The low-rise art deco buildings initially housed residents from overcrowded parts of Chinatown, but they were gradually taken over by the city's trendsetters, turning the area into one of the most sought-after residential addresses in Singapore. And as the number of young and wealthy people in the area grew, so too did the number of funky coffee shops, craft breweries, and bookstores. Today, it's one of Singapore's coolest neighborhoods, where indie boutiques and vegetarian cafés are the norm. Still, beneath the hipster veneer, there's a huge amount of history to uncover, including the fact that Tiong Bahru used to be home to the largest Chinese burial site in the country.

Just across the river lies River Valley, a neighborhood well-positioned between Orchard and the Singapore River. Sometimes overlooked as an affluent expat area, it's important to know it's not just fancy condos. The area has some lovely places to eat and drink, as well as hawker centers and national monuments. It stretches down to laid-back Robertson Quay, one of three Quays along the banks of the Singapore River.

The other two quays are Clarke Quay and Boat Quay, both offering a collection of food and drink spots that get especially loud and fun at night. Clarke Quay stands upstream from Boat Quay, which was a trading center during the colonial era. Its once-abandoned warehouses and shophouses have now become part of a brightly colored maze of restaurants, bars, and clubs. Aside from drinking and eating, the Singapore River is also a great place to stretch your legs. The 3.2-km waterway has been the lifeline of Singapore for almost 200 years and remains a central part of the culture today.

Tiong Bahru

Not far from Chinatown is one of Singapore's coolest neighborhoods, a trendy spot to relax at a café, sample craft suds at a bar, or shop at boutiques along mural-lined streets.

Sights

Bird Corner

OTHER ATTRACTION | Now just a metal monument—in the 1980s, this was the site of Tiong Bahru's most loved coffeeshop, where locals could hang their bird cages while they sat and sipped coffee. The shopowner, Wah Heng, devised the concept after seeing how much attention a nearby pet shop was getting from its bird cages. Indeed, many bird owners made a beeline for the shop, and before long, the cacophony of song and colorful cages drew attention from locals, tourists, and journalists alike. Sadly, the coffee shop closed in the early 2000s. ⊠ *3 Seng Poh Rd., Tiong Bahru* Ⓜ *Tiong Bahru.*

Grave of Tan Tock Seng

CEMETERY | This small and unassuming site on the edge of Tiong Bahru marks the final resting place of one of Singapore's most important Chinese pioneers, who founded The Chinese Pauper's Hospital (later to be called Tan Tock Seng Hospital) and established the Thain Hock Keng temple, the oldest Chinese temple in Singapore. He died in 1850 and was moved to this resting place around 1882. The fenced site is surrounded by miniature lions and has a plaque explaining more about his life and achievements. His Tan's daughter-in-law and granddaughter-in-law rest nearby. The site is on the busy Outram Road: cross over the bridge opposite the gas station for access. ⊠ *254 Outram Rd., Tiong Bahru* ✛ *Cross Outram Rd. via the pedestrian walkway next to the gas station* ⊕ *www.roots.gov.sg* ☒ *Free* Ⓜ *Havelock.*

Qi Tian Gong Temple

TEMPLE | The small but elaborate Qi Tian Gong Temple, housed within a simple shophouse, is more popularly known as the Monkey God Temple due to its dedication to Sun Wu Kong, the Monkey King. The monkey, which comes from 16th-century fable *Journey to the West* by writer Wu Chenen, represents human caprice and genius. This temple was founded in 1920 in a small taro garden on Eng Hoon Street but was moved to its current location in 1938. There are more than 40 other Monkey God temples found in Singapore alone. ⊠ *44 Eng Hoon St., Tiong Bahru* ☎ *6220–2469* ☒ *Free* Ⓜ *Tiong Bahru.*

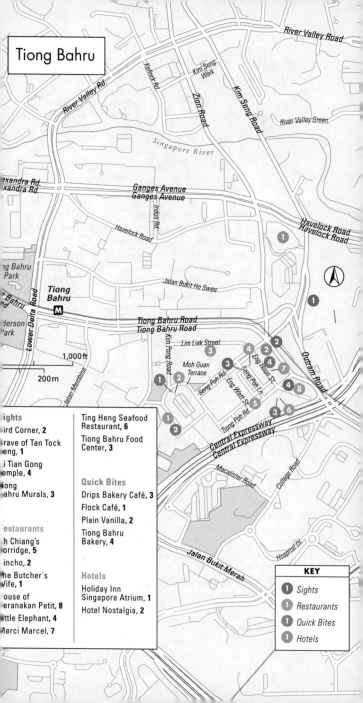

Tiong Bahru

Sights
- Bird Corner, **2**
- Grave of Tan Tock Seng, **1**
- Qi Tian Gong Temple, **4**
- Tiong Bahru Murals, **3**

Restaurants
- Ah Chiang's Porridge, **5**
- Pincho, **2**
- The Butcher's Wife, **1**
- House of Peranakan Petit, **8**
- Little Elephant, **4**
- Merci Marcel, **7**

- Ting Heng Seafood Restaurant, **6**
- Tiong Bahru Food Center, **3**

Quick Bites
- Drips Bakery Café, **3**
- Flock Café, **1**
- Plain Vanilla, **2**
- Tiong Bahru Bakery, **4**

Hotels
- Holiday Inn Singapore Atrium, **1**
- Hotel Nostalgia, **2**

KEY
- 1 Sights
- 1 Restaurants
- 1 Quick Bites
- 1 Hotels

What's in a Name?

The name Tiong Bahru combines the word "Tiong" (meaning "to die" in the Hokkien dialect) and "Bahru" (meaning "new" in Malay). It's thought the name refers to the Chinese burial ground that was here in the 1800s and that no longer exists. By the early 1900s, many of the bodies had already been exhumed to build the neighborhood you see today.

★ Tiong Bahru Murals

PUBLIC ART | There isn't a map to guide you, but hunting for Tiong Bahru's murals is a fun way to spend a few hours. Local artist Yip Yew Chong has painted intricate pictures across the neighborhood: look out for *Pasar and the Fortune Teller* on Block 73 of Eng Watt Street; *Bird Singing Corner* on Block 71 of Seng Poh Lane; and *Home* on Block 74 of Tiong Poh Road. There are more often popping up, though, so keep your eyes open and your camera ready. ⊠ Seng Poh La., Tiong Bahru ⊠ Free Ⓜ Tiong Bahru.

🍴 Restaurants

Ah Chiang's Porridge

$ | **CHINESE** | This true Tiong Bahru classic has been serving neighborhood residents since the 1970s. The porridge served here is a savory Cantonese-style *congee,* usually with slices of pork or fish added. **Known for:** charcoal-cooked congee; mixed pork congee with offal; busy lunchtime lines. ⑤ *Average main: S$5* ⊠ 65 Tiong Poh Rd., Tiong Bahru ☎ 6557–0084 ⊕ www.facebook.com/ahchiangporridgesg ⊟ No credit cards Ⓜ Tiong Bahru.

★ Bincho

$$ | **JAPANESE** | This might be the coolest dinner spot in Singapore. Tucked inside a traditional Singaporean shophouse, this place transforms every night into a Japanese *yakitori,* where dishes are served in a cloak of dry ice; the alluring smell of charcoal fills the air, and the small plates are always colorful, intriguing, and based on what's fresh that day. **Known for:** meat and veggies grilled over charcoal; delicious tasting menus; extensive sake list. ⑤ *Average main: S$40* ⊠ 78 Moh Guan Terr., #01–19, Tiong Bahru ☎ 6438–4567 ⊕ www.bincho.com.sg ⊙ Closed Mon. and Tues. Ⓜ Tiong Bahru.

The Butcher's Wife

$$ | **BRAZILIAN** | One of Singapore's few dedicated gluten-free restaurants is a buzzy Brazilian eatery on hip Yong Siak Street with

Intricately painted murals painted by artist Yip Yew Chong can be found on buildings around the Tiong Bahru neighborhood.

options for vegetarians, vegans, and meat-eaters alike. Comfy sofas and trendy decor lend a relaxing, friendly vibe to the dining space, with outdoor seats hot property in the evening. **Known for:** gluten-free Brazilian fare; approachable natural wines; cool outdoor seating. $ *Average main: S$40* ⊠ *19 Yong Siak St., Tiong Bahru* ☎ *6221–9307* ⊕ *www.thebutcherswifesg.com* ۞ *Closed Mon.* Ⓜ *Tiong Bahru.*

House of Peranakan Petit

$$ | SINGAPOREAN | This intimate, homey spot is an excellent place to try affordable Nonya cuisine. Traditionally the food of Chinese migrants who settled in Singapore, Nonya dishes are marked by their incorporation of Malaysian and Indonesian spices and techniques. **Known for:** ayam buah keluak (chicken in a tamarind sauce and buah keluak nuts); pulot hitam (sticky black rice soup); friendly, attentive service. $ *Average main: S$25* ⊠ *42 Eng Hoon St., Tiong Bahru* ☎ *6222–1719* ⊕ *houseofperanakan.com.sg* ۞ *Closed Tues.* Ⓜ *Tiong Bahru.*

Little Elephant

$$ | THAI | Eclectic decor and cold Chang beer whisk you away from Singapore to the streets of Bangkok at this lively Thai bistro. The menu has all the classics you'd expect, with solid versions of *tom yum* soup, pad Thai, and mango sticky rice. **Known for:** grilled pork neck with homemade sauce; Chang beer on draft; outdoor seats on a quiet street. $ *Average main: S$15* ⊠ *57 Eng Hoon St., #01–72, Tiong Bahru* ☎ *6224–1646* ⊕ *www.littleelephant.sg* Ⓜ *Tiong Bahru.*

Table Manners in Singapore

Thanks to their nation's multiculturalism, Singaporeans are accepting of variations in etiquette, but there are a few things to keep in mind. Traditionally, your food is served family style—placed all at once on the table so everyone can dig in—or, for more formal meals, served a course at a time, again with diners sharing from a single dish. If you're with friends, you can use your chopsticks to serve yourself from the communal dishes, but it's more polite to use a fresh pair of chopsticks if possible. Never leave your chopsticks upright in a rice bowl—this resembles the joss sticks left in incense bowls at graves which is considered a bad omen. It's a sign of respect for a Singaporean to serve you during a family-style meal. It's polite to reciprocate the gesture when their bowl is nearing empty. If you want to be respectful, you should wait for the host or any older people to start eating before you tuck in. Many locals may have religion-based dietary restrictions, such as only eating vegetarian or *halal* (Muslim) food. If you're arranging a meal with Singaporeans be sure to clarify their eating habits before deciding on a restaurant. Smoking is banned in air-conditioned restaurants and banquet/meeting rooms, but many establishments have outdoor patios and seating areas for smokers.

Merci Marcel
$$ | FRENCH FUSION | Rendezvous over a morning coffee, tuck into a light lunch, or sip chilled rosé in the evening breeze at this French-Balinese-style café. The Parisian decor is complete with cozy sofas, plenty of plants, and a lovely outside space strung with fairy lights and cute lanterns. **Known for:** a cheese bar full of European farm selections; wide variety of French wines; lovely outside seating area. ⑤ *Average main: S$30* ⊠ *56 Eng Hoon St., #01–68, Tiong Bahru* ☎ *65/6224–0113* ⊕ *mercimarcelgroup.com* Ⓜ *Tiong Bahru.*

Ting Heng Seafood Restaurant
$$ | SEAFOOD | A lively seafood specialist opposite Qi Tian Gong Temple, Ting Heng's outdoor tables fill up quickly in the evening with locals indulging in the signature fish head steamboat (hot pot). The menu also offers a range of local delicacies, including bamboo clams, salt-baked chicken, and an extensive menu of rice and noodle dishes. **Known for:** lively outdoor seating; large menu of Chinese staples; fish steamboat (hot pot) with house-made fish balls. ⑤ *Average main: S$20* ⊠ *82 Tiong Poh Rd., Tiong Bahru* ☎ *6323–6093* ⊕ *www.facebook.com/TingHengSeafoodRestaurant* ⊗ *No lunch* Ⓜ *Tiong Bahru.*

★ Tiong Bahru Food Center

$ | **ASIAN** | This large, airy upstairs hawker center is busy from morning to night. Highlights include **Loo's Hainanese Curry Rice** (#02–67/68, look for the snaking queue), which serves pork, chicken, prawns, and *chap chye* (cabbage) smothered in traditional Hainanese curry sauce.   **Known for:** wallet-friendly eats; huge variety of local foods; open-air hawker seating. $ *Average main: S$6* ⊠ *30 Seng Poh Rd., Tiong Bahru* �? *No credit cards* Ⓜ *Tiong Bahru.*

☕ Coffee and Quick Bites

Drips Bakery Café

$ | **CAFÉ** | A quiet space to grab a drink after seeing the Qi Tian Gong Temple, this unassuming café is famed for its sweet tarts. Grab a selection box or just try the signature *yuzu*, a tangy, perfumed citrus filling encased in sweet crumbly pastry. **Known for:** fresh fruit tarts; breakfast and brunch menus; quiet coffee spot. $ *Average main: S$7* ⊠ *82 Tiong Poh Rd., #01–05, Tiong Bahru* 📞 *6222–0400* ⊕ *www.drips.com.sg* Ⓜ *Tionig Bahru.*

Flock Café

$$ | **EUROPEAN** | Modern and moodily-lit, this cool little café attracts a young and artsy crowd. The flat whites are excellent—rare in a country where the norm is either strong and black or sugary sweet—the all-day breakfasts feature piles of eggs, sausage, and bacon; and the lunch options include pastas, salads, and burgers. **Known for:** great coffee; all-day breakfast; people-watching from outdoor seating. $ *Average main: S$18* ⊠ *#01–25 Tiong Bahru Estate, 78 Moh Guan Terr., Tiong Bahru* 📞 *6536–3938* ⊕ *flockcafe. com.sg* Ⓜ *Tiong Bahru.*

Plain Vanilla

$ | **CAFÉ** | Famed for fluffy iced cupcakes, the company's flagship Tiong Bahru store is self-described as a "bakery cum café cum retail store." Alongside signature bakes, there is a daily brunch menu and a wide selection of grocery and homeware items for purchase. The alfresco dining area is a quiet space to spend the afternoon. **Known for:** cream-topped cupcakes; daily brunch menu; homewares and grocery items. $ *Average main: S$8* ⊠ *1D Yong Siak St., Tiong Bahru* 📞 *8363–7614* ⊕ *plainvanilla.com.sg* Ⓜ *Tiong Bahru.*

★ Tiong Bahru Bakery

$ | **BAKERY** | Sandwiches, freshly baked breads, quiches, and a variety of sweet and savory pastries make up the menu at this popular café, the perfect spot to grab a quick bite and caffeinate while shopping the area's boutiques. The lighting mounted in wooden boards suspended from the ceiling by rope, the exposed brick and white-washed walls, and the soft, down-tempo beats all make for a relaxing interior. **Known for:** excellent coffee; Kouign-amann pastries; freshly baked bread. $ *Average main: S$14* ⊠ *56 Eng Hoon St., #01–70, Tiong Bahru* ☎ *6220–3430* ⊕ *www.tiongbahrubakery. com* Ⓜ *Tiong Bahru.*

🛏 Hotels

Holiday Inn Singapore Atrium
$$ | **HOTEL** | Less than a five-minute walk from the Singapore River, this enormous hotel—with over 500 rooms, two restaurants, and two pools—is a convenient, spacious choice, especially for families. **Pros:** good views from the higher rooms; directly beside MRT station; halal, vegan, and vegetarian menu options. **Cons:** lacks character (it feels like a chain hotel); location beside two busy roads; limited TV channels. $ *Rooms from: S$240* ⊠ *317 Outram Rd., Tiong Bahru* ☎ *6733–0188* ⊕ *www.ihg.com* ⤳ *512 rooms* ⦿ *No Meals* Ⓜ *Havelock.*

Hotel Nostalgia
$ | **HOTEL** | This boutique-style hotel is furnished to reflect Singapore's colonial heritage, with rooms that are clean, comfortable, and well-designed. **Pros:** great value; outdoor pool; heart of Tiong Bahru. **Cons:** some rooms don't have windows; no parking; rooms are quite small. $ *Rooms from: S$150* ⊠ *77 Tiong Bahru Rd., Tiong Bahru* ☎ *6808–1818* ⊕ *www.hotelnostalgia.com.sg* ⤳ *50 rooms* ⦿ *No Meals* Ⓜ *Tiong Bahru.*

🍸 Nightlife

★ Canjob Taproom
PUBS | This tiny bar specializes in craft beers on tap, including Czech pilsners, pale ales, and IPAs. The decor is very cool, with overturned barrels for tables and fridges full of beer you can buy to takeaway. There's also a range of bar snacks, bratwurst hotdogs, and spam fries. ⊠ *Link Hotel, 50 Tiong Bahru Rd., #01–03, Tiong Bahru* ☎ *9385–3497* ⊕ *www.canjobtaproom.com* Ⓜ *Tiong Bahru.*

Coq & Balls
BARS | Popular with Tiong Bahru locals, this cheekily-named bar is often busy on a Saturday night with revelers piling in for their draft beers, ciders, and ales. The daily happy hour runs until 8 pm, and the menu of bar bites includes grilled cheese sandwiches, truffle fries, and popcorn chicken. ⊠ *Kai Fook Mansion, 6 Kim Tian Rd., Tiong Bahru* ☎ *6276–6609* ⊕ *www.coqnballs.com* Ⓜ *Tiong Bahru.*

★ Lin Rooftop Bar

BARS | On the rooftop of the Link Hotel, this open-air bar is decked out in twinkling fairy lights and has great views of Tiong Bahru. The drink menu is fairly standard—wine, beer, and a selection of signature cocktails—but most people come for the bird's eye location and regular live music. The bar is not well sign-posted: to reach it, go into the Link Hotel lobby, and take the elevator to the roof (R). ✉ *Link Hotel, 50 Tiong Bahru Rd., Tiong Bahru* ✛ *Level R of the hotel, use the elevators in the hotel lobby.* ☎ *8792–8831* ⊕ *www.lin.com.sg* Ⓜ *Tiong Bahru.*

🛍 Shopping

Known for its quaint boutiques, art shops, and knick-knacks, Tiong Bahru is a great place to shop if you're looking for tasteful gifts or pretty souvenirs.

BOOKS

Woods in the Books

BOOKS | FAMILY | Home to one of Singapore's best selections of picture books, Woods in the Books is a small independent bookstore that prides itself on its unique offerings. Staff are always willing to recommend an age-appropriate book, and you'll also find a selection of greeting cards and other gifts for a range of occasions. ✉ *3 Yong Siak St., Tiong Bahru* ☎ *6222–9980* ⊕ *www.woodsinthebooks.sg* Ⓜ *Tiong Bahru.*

CLOTHING

Nana & Bird

WOMEN'S CLOTHING | Stepping into this independent women's clothing boutique is like stepping inside the wardrobe you've always wanted. It's no wonder, as the store was set up by two school friends whose aim was to sell only clothes they would want to buy themselves. Colorful, bold patterns are their style, with both local and international brands for sale. ✉ *1 Yong Siak St., Tiong Bahru* ☎ *9117–0430* ⊕ *shop.nanaandbird.com* Ⓜ *Tiong Bahru.*

CRAFTS

Yenidraws & Friends

CRAFTS | Self-taught Singaporean illustrator Yeni creates unique homewares and gifts with iconic local motifs. Her small shop stocks a wealth of interesting souvenirs and keepsakes that are distinctly Singaporean. ✉ *55 Tiong Bahru Rd., #01–53, Tiong Bahru* ⊕ *yenidraws.com* Ⓜ *Tiong Bahru.*

HOUSEWARES
★ Cat Socrates
HOUSEWARES | From cute plant pots to mindfulness books, Cat Socrates is the shop to go to for all your gift-giving needs. It's particularly good if you are looking for souvenirs: you'll find Singapore-themed puzzles, books, cards, tea towels, and more, as well as postcards and stationery. Friendly reminder: don't pet the cat! ⊠ 78 Yong Siak St., #01–14, Tiong Bahru ☎ 6333–0870 ⊕ catsocrates.myshopify.com Ⓜ Tiong Bahru.

★ Tan Boon Liat
FURNITURE | This aging, imposing blue building on the outskirts of Tiong Bahru hides a treasure trove of furniture and housewares stores. Don't be fooled by the building's exterior; some of Singapore's most stylish and sought-after furniture brands have stores somewhere in the vast block. While the majority of the stores focus on larger pieces, you'll find many small pieces, artworks, and keepsakes as you browse. Highlights include vintage treasures at **Journey East**, Asian gifts and home products at **Singapore Trading Post**, and Chinese antiques at **Emperor's Attic**. Handy tip: if you can't find the store you are looking for, ask the friendly parking assistants. ⊠ 315 Outram Rd., Tiong Bahru ☎ 8683–3880 ⊕ www.tanboonliat.com Ⓜ Havelock.

SHOPPING CENTERS AND MALLS
Tiong Bahru Plaza
MALL | Conveniently located around the Tiong Bahru MRT station, this six-level mall has more than 160 stores selling everything from fashion to kitchenware. There's a number of great places to eat, with a food court in the basement and a selection of slick restaurants on level two. ⊠ 302 Tiong Bahru Rd., Tiong Bahru ☎ 6276–4686 ⊕ www.tiongbahruplaza.com.sg Ⓜ Tiong Bahru.

🏃 Activities

WALKING TOURS
Heritage Tour
SELF-GUIDED TOURS | Take yourself on a heritage tour around Tiong Bahru using the National Heritage Board's map that you can download to your phone. Ten informative signs throughout the neighborhood help to guide you along as you learn about the area's history, including how it once used to be a swampy cemetery. The full trail is around 2.5 km (1.5 miles). ⊠ Tiong Bahru Food Centre, 30 Seng Poh Rd., Tiong Bahru ⊕ www.roots.sg ⊠ Free Ⓜ Tiong Bahru.

Singapore River

The Singapore River stretches 3.2 kilometers from Tanglin Road down to Marina Bay, home to three distinct quays. Once the center of commercial Singapore, this area hummed with energy from bumboats that transported goods to and from its warehouses along the water. Now, Clarke Quay and Boat Quay are best visited at night, when herds of partygoers descend on the area. The more laid-back Robertson Quay neighborhood is good for weekend brunch or a riverside run. A river cruise on a bumboat is a good way to get another perspective on this busy area.

◉ Sights

Boat Quay

BUSINESS DISTRICT | Local entrepreneurs have created a mélange of eateries and bars to satisfy diverse tastes at this dining and drinking stretch along the Singapore River, the country's trading hub from colonial times to the 1970s. Between 7 pm and midnight, the area swells with an after-work crowd enjoying drinks along the water. At the end of Boat Quay and named after Lord Elgin, a British governor-general of India, **Elgin Bridge** links the colonial quarter to Chinatown. The original rickety wooden structure was replaced in 1863 with an iron bridge imported from Calcutta. The current concrete bridge was installed in 1926. ⊠ *Boat Quay, Boat Quay* Ⓜ *Raffles Place.*

★ Clarke Quay

PEDESTRIAN MALL | Stretching along the riverfront, Clarke Quay is canopied by space-age umbrellas and filled with a smorgasbord of entertainment venues, restaurants, bars, and clubs. Come nightfall, the pedestrian-only streets are packed with a mix of visitors and locals hitting up the latest eateries and bars. With its bright lights and festive nightlife, the river along the quay is a world away from the sleepy waterway it was when Sir Stamford Raffles first arrived. Get a view from the river by boarding one of the many bumboats that offer daily 30-minute cruises. Thrill seekers will love the GX5 Extreme Swing, a ride at the river's edge, open from 4:30 pm. ⊠ *3 River Valley Rd., Clarke Quay* ☎ *6337–3292* ⊕ *www. capitaland.com* Ⓜ *Clarke Quay.*

Slingshot Singapore

AMUSEMENT RIDE | Grab an adrenaline-fuelled view of Clarke Quay at the riverside Slingshot ride. Accelerate towards the city skyline on the 70-meter, 5-Gs-inducing **Slingshot**, or plummet down to earth on the 40-meter, 120 km/h **GX-5 Extreme** freefall. Note that

Singapore River and River Valley

KEY

1 *Sights*
1 *Restaurants*
1 *Quick Bites*
1 *Hotels*

Sights

Boat Quay, **9**
Clarke Quay, **7**
Hong San See Temple, **3**
Robertson Quay, **1**
The Singapore Buddhist Lodge, **2**
Slingshot Singapore, **8**
Sri Thendayuthapani Temple, **4**
STPI Creative Workshop and Gallery, **5**
Tan Si Chong Su, **6**

Restaurants

Braci, **14**
Brewerkz, **9**
The Dragon Chamber, **12**
Dumpling Darlings, **13**
8picure, **1**
Esora, **5**
Feng Ji Chicken Rice, **6**
Fook Kin, **4**
Hai Di Lao at Clarke Quay, **11**
Jumbo Seafood, Riverside Point, **10**
Kubo, **7**
Long Beach Seafood, **8**
Po, **3**
Zion Riverside Food Centre, **2**

Quick Bites

Common Man Coffee Roasters, **4**
DOPA, **5**
Grace Espresso, **2**
Pantler, **1**
Sonny's Pizza, **6**
Thong Aik Coffee, **3**

Somerset Rd
Orchard Road

M Dhoby Ghaut
Dhoby Ghaut M

Bras Basah M

Killiney Road

Lloyd Road

River Valley Road
River Valley Road

Kim Yam Road

Dover Rd

Oxley Rise

Fort Canning Link

Fort Canning Park

Fort Canning Reservoir

M Fort Canning

Canning Rise

Armenian St.

Hill Street
Hill Street

Coleman St.

Martin Rd.

Mohamed Sultan Rd.

Unity Street

Merbau Rd.

River Valley Road
River Valley Road

Clarke St.

Tan Tye Pl.

High Street

Nanson Rd.

Clemenceau Avenue

Central Expressway Tunnel

Singapore River

Merchant Road
Merchant Road

Havelock Road

Clarke Quay M

Eu Tong Sen St.
New Bridge Rd.

Upper Circular Rd

Carpenter St.

Hongkong St.

North Canal Rd.
North Canal Rd.

Circular Rd

Central Expressway

Park Crescent

Upper Hokien St.

S. Bridge St.

Upper Pickering St.

M Chinatown

Chutia St.

Market St.

Eu Tong Sen Street
New Bridge Road

Kreta Ayer Road

Keong Saik Rd.

Smith St.

Neil Road

Hotels

Grand Copthorne Waterfront Hotel, **2**

Great World Serviced Apartments, **1**

Heritage Collection on Boat Quay, **9**

Holiday Inn Express Clarke Quay, **7**

InterContinental Singapore Robertson Quay, **5**

Lloyd's Inn, **6**

M Social Singapore, **3**

Paradox Singapore Merchant Court at Clarke Quay, **8**

The Warehouse Hotel, **4**

there is a 125 cm (50 inches) height restriction for riders. ✉ *3E River Valley Rd., Clarke Quay Block E, Clarke Quay* ☎ *9755–3310* ⊕ *slingshot.sg* 🎫 *From $45* ☞ *Min. height requirement: 125 cm (50 inches)* Ⓜ *Clarke Quay.*

Robertson Quay

PEDESTRIAN MALL | Often quieter and more laid-back than its smaller quay cousins (Boat Quay and Clarke Quay), Robertson Quay (known by locals as "Rob Quay") is a relatively tranquil space that is home to great hotels, bars, cafés, and restaurants. Mornings see joggers and cyclists shooting past couples having lazy-morning brunches and families enjoying the wide-open walkways. Evenings tend to be a little louder, from busy Aussie bar Boomarang down to sophisticated dining spots like Kubo. The quay is easily accessed from Fort Canning MRT (Downtown Line), as well as Great World MRT and Havelock MRT (Thomson-East Coast Line) further up the river. Keep your eyes open, as you may spot Singapore's famous otter families fishing in this quieter section of the river. ✉ *Robertson Quay, Robertson Quay* Ⓜ *Fort Canning.*

STPI Creative Workshop and Gallery

ART GALLERY | Explore the mediums of print and paper at this creative workshop and art gallery by Robertson Quay. Exhibitions and work from visiting international artists change regularly, so check their website for further information. There are also works from leading artists available for purchase. ✉ *41 Robertson Quay, Robertson Quay* ☎ *6336–3663* ⊕ *www.stpi.com.sg* Ⓜ *Fort Canning.*

★ Tan Si Chong Su

TEMPLE | Also known as Po Chiak Keng, meaning "protection of the innocent," the ancestral hall of the Tan Clan is a well-preserved example of traditional Hokkien architecture. Colorful ceramics were used to create sculptures of dragons, tigers, and flowers, and the intricately carved granite columns at the main entrance are rare among temples in Singapore. Tradition dictates visitors enter from the Dragon's Door (🔲🔲🔲) gate and leave via the Tiger's Gate (🔲🔲🔲) to ensure the deity's blessings are bestowed. ✉ *15 Magazine Rd., Clarke Quay* ☎ *6533–2880* ⊕ *www.pck.org.sg* 🎫 *Free* Ⓜ *Clarke Quay.*

 Restaurants

Braci

$$$$ | MODERN ITALIAN | When you have a meal at this cozy, open-kitchen restaurant with a rooftop bar, it feels like you're dining at a friend's—a friend with one-Michelin-star culinary chops. Here, the flame-kissed grilled mains are the draw, but you should also leave room for popular starters like the foie gras semifreddo and the house-made charcoal-baked bread. **Known for:** riverside views; homey but refined food; amazing bread. $ *Average main: S$258* ⊠ *52 Boat Quay, Level 5/6, Boat Quay* ☎ *6866–1933* ⊕ *www.braci.sg* ☾ *Closed Sun.* Ⓜ *Clarke Quay.*

Brewerkz

$$ | **AMERICAN** | **FAMILY** | This buzzy, breezy microbrewery, sprawling along a prime stretch of real estate on the Singapore River, across from Clarke Quay, serves Western-friendly favorites like burgers and pizzas, buffalo wings, beer-battered fish-and-chips, and chargrilled steaks, along with lighter fare like grilled fish and soups. The portions are hearty—perfect for soaking up pours of Brewerkz's award-winning craft beers. **Known for:** locally brewed beers; hearty portions; casual business lunches. $ *Average main: S$30* ⊠ *Riverside Point, 30 Merchant Rd., #01–07, Clarke Quay* ☎ *9011–9048* ⊕ *www.brewerkz.com* Ⓜ *Clarke Quay.*

The Dragon Chamber

$$$ | **CHINESE** | A fridge tucked away in the corner of an unassuming *kopitiam* (coffee shop) hides this ultra-cool restaurant in the heart of Boat Quay. Serving "guerilla-style" Chinese food, the restaurant has an atmosphere to match, with the dark entrance corridor giving way to a Chinese-style speakeasy, where old-school crockery and medicine counter drawers clash with comic-book wallpaper. **Known for:** speakeasy-style hidden entrance; unique ingredients like crocodile foot; creative approaches to traditional Chinese dishes. $ *Average main: S$45* ⊠ *2 Circular Rd., Boat Quay* ☎ *6950–0015* ⊕ *www.thedragonchamber.com* ☾ *Closed Mon.* Ⓜ *Clarke Quay.*

Dumpling Darlings

$$ | **ASIAN FUSION** | Follow the neon dumpling sign and giant dumpling mural to get to this intimate, fun restaurant in Boat Quay, which serves a range of dumplings and noodle dishes. Original dumplings are pot-sticker style with pork, ginger, and cabbage filling, but the menu offers many other varieties, all of which pack a punch. **Known for:** creative dumpling flavors; great-value lunch set menus; small, busy space. $ *Average main: S$15* ⊠ *86 Circular Rd., Boat Quay* ☎ *8889–9973* ⊕ *www.dumplingdarlings.com.sg* ☾ *Closed Sun.* Ⓜ *Clarke Quay.*

Hai Di Lao at Clarke Quay

$$ | **CHINESE** | Robust soup bases, gourmet ingredients, and hand-pulled noodles aside, what makes this hotpot joint one of the most popular in Singapore is its next-level service. Free manicures, a children's playroom, and complimentary drinks and snacks are offered even as you wait for your table—a nice move

to placate customers stuck in the notoriously long lines. **Known for:** satisfying hotpot; above-and-beyond service; freebies like take-away popcorn and crackers. $ *Average main: S$40 ⊠ Clarke Quay, 3D River Valley Rd., #02–04, Clarke Quay* ☎ 6337–8627 ⊕ *www.haidilao-inc.com/sg* Ⓜ *Clarke Quay.*

Jumbo Seafood, Riverside Point
$$$ | CHINESE | FAMILY | As the crowds that permanently pack it show, Jumbo Seafood is the place to get your hands dirty while savoring award-winning chilli and black-pepper crab, freshly snapped up from on-site seafood tanks. There's an extensive menu besides crab, including signature beef fillet with black pepper sauce and braised lobster. **Known for:** chilli crab; live seafood; big-group gatherings. $ *Average main: S$50 ⊠ Riverside Point, 30 Merchant Rd., #01–01/02, Clarke Quay* ☎ 6532–3435 ⊕ *www.jumboseafood.com.sg* Ⓜ *Clarke Quay.*

Kubo
$$$ | FILIPINO | Woodfired Filipino-inspired food isn't necessarily what you'd expect along Robertson Quay, but this classy restaurant delivers exciting cooking in a laid-back atmosphere. Taking inspiration from Pinoy barbecue, the open kitchen-led space is roomy and attractive, centered by the sounds of cooking in the *pugon* (traditional brick oven). **Known for:** house-aged duck and crab fat risotto; head chef from well-known Burnt Ends and Meatsmith restaurants; Filipino-style halo halo for dessert. $ *Average main: S$45 ⊠ 80 Mohamed Sultan Rd., Robertson Quay* ☎ 9645–8436 ⊕ *www.kubo.com.sg* ☉ *Closed Mon. No lunch Tues.–Fri.* Ⓜ *Fort Canning.*

Long Beach Seafood
$$ | SEAFOOD | This bright spot by the river at Robertson Quay offers outdoor tables and a large menu of seafood and other Chinese dishes. The signatures here are the iconic Singaporean dishes of chilli crab and black pepper crab, which the restaurant invented in the 1950s. **Known for:** good set menus; outdoor riverside location; black pepper and chilli crab (both invented here). $ *Average main: S$35 ⊠ 60 Robertson Quay, #01–14, Robertson Quay* ☎ 6336–3636 ⊕ *longbeachseafood.com.sg* Ⓜ *Fort Canning.*

★ Po
$$$ | SINGAPOREAN | Housed in the historic Warehouse Hotel, this modern restaurant is named after the founder's *popo* (grandmother), from whom their famed *popiah* (fresh spring rolls) recipe is said to have originated. Classic hawker dishes are given a refined update here with high-quality ingredients and impeccable service. **Known for:** hand-rolled popiah; kueh pie tee (pastry shells with spicy turnip, pork, and prawn filling); creative cocktail menu.

$ Average main: S$50 ⊠ The Warehouse Hotel, 320 Havelock Rd., Robertson Quay ☎ 6828–0007 ⊕ www.po.com.sg Ⓜ Havelock.

☕ Coffee and Quick Bites

Common Man Coffee Roasters

$$ | **CAFÉ** | A dedicated specialty Arabica coffee roaster just off Robertson Quay, Common Man Coffee Roasters is better known for its exceptional brunch, featuring fluffy pancakes, avocado toasts, and full fry-ups. Many come for the brilliant range of vegetarian, vegan, and gluten-free breakfast options. **Known for:** all-day brunch; expertly-roasted coffee; shaded outdoor seating. $ Average main: S$25 ⊠ 22 Martin Rd., #01–00, Robertson Quay ☎ 6836–4695 ⊕ commonmancoffeeroasters.com Ⓜ Fort Canning.

DOPA

$ | **ICE CREAM** | This trendy coffee and ice-cream joint may be a little out of the way, but it's the perfect spot to cool off after a stroll down the river. The nut-based gelato delivers big flavor (the home-roasted pistachio is a rightful crowd-favorite), and single-origin coffee is bold and smooth. **Known for:** cozy space in old shophouse; addictive flavours, like home-roasted pistachio; smooth, nut-based artisanal gelato. $ Average main: S$9 ⊠ 29 South Bridge Rd., Clarke Quay ☎ 6535–3539 ⊕ www.dopadopacreamery.com Ⓜ Clarke Quay.

Sonny's Pizza

$ | **PIZZA** | This uber-hip neighborhood joint serves New York–style slices and craft beers. A great place to grab a bite before exploring the bars around Boat Quay. **Known for:** New York–style pizza by the slice; bottles of ice-cold craft beer; fully loaded fries and buffalo chicken wings. $ Average main: S$8 ⊠ 17 Circular Rd., Boat Quay ☎ 9822–4825 ⊕ www.sonnyspizzas.com ⊙ Closed Sun. Ⓜ Raffles Place.

🛏 Hotels

Grand Copthorne Waterfront Hotel

$$ | **HOTEL** | Large windows throughout this hotel give full focus to the Singapore River, and the rooms bring to mind those of a resort, with parquet floors and rattan furniture. **Pros:** family-friendly; filtered water in room; central location. **Cons:** small pool for such a large hotel; bathrooms have no tubs; rooms could be bigger. $ Rooms from: S$310 ⊠ 392 Havelock Rd., Robertson Quay ☎ 6733–0880 ⊕ www.millenniumhotels.com ⇄ 574 rooms ❗ Free Breakfast Ⓜ Havelock.

Heritage Collection on Boat Quay

$$ | APARTMENT | These compact studio apartments with kitch-enettes (though some without windows) require check-in via a mobile app, which later becomes your key. **Pros:** riverside location near Clarke Quay MRT; complimentary laundry facilities on-site; all units have kitchenettes. **Cons:** some rooms get street noise; no elevator; units can be quite small. $ Rooms from: S$200 ⊠ 80 Boat Quay, Clarke Quay ☎ 6223–7155 ⊕ hericoll.com ⪢ 41 rooms ⊘ No Meals ☞ 5-night min. stay Ⓜ Clarke Quay.

Holiday Inn Express Clarke Quay

$$ | HOTEL | One of the more sophisticated Holiday Inn Express options around (the building was initially constructed for a four-star hotel until the Holiday Inn chain took over), this comfortable lodg-ing provides great amenities like a free breakfast, 24-hour rooftop fitness center, and a rooftop pool complete with whirlpools and views of Clarke Quay and Robertson Quay. **Pros:** rooftop pool; great views from fitness center; guide dogs allowed. **Cons:** lack of storage space in rooms; parking is expensive; common areas can get crowded. $ Rooms from: S$215 ⊠ 2 Magazine Rd., Clarke Quay ☎ 6589–8000 ⊕ www.ihg.com/holidayinnexpress ⪢ 442 rooms ⊘ Free Breakfast Ⓜ Clarke Quay.

InterContinental Singapore Robertson Quay

$$ | HOTEL | This stylishly masculine hotel has ultra-modern rooms that are smaller than at most InterContinental hotels but have well-utilized spaces and floor-to-ceiling windows with views of the Robertson Quay area. **Pros:** great dining options at the hotel and nearby; beautiful pool; right next to the Singapore River. **Cons:** location isn't the most accessible; some rooms are on the small side; design is not the most suitable for families. $ Rooms from: S$315 ⊠ 1 Nanson Rd., Robertson Quay ☎ 6826–5000 ⊕ www.ihg.com/intercontinental ⪢ 225 rooms ⊘ No Meals Ⓜ Fort Canning.

M Social Singapore

$$ | HOTEL | It's clear this mod boutique hotel designed by Philippe Starck is for the digital nomad generation: each loft-style room includes a snug workspace on the mezzanine, and the common spaces feature interactive elements like iPads on the walls and a robot to cook your breakfast eggs for you. **Pros:** compact design; unique swimming pool; features for solo travelers, like single rooms and single-portion bottled wines. **Cons:** rooms are small; not family-friendly; gym and pool not open until 8 am. $ Rooms from: S$200 ⊠ 90 Robertson Quay, Robertson Quay ☎ 6206–1888 ⊕ www.millenniumhotels.com ⪢ 293 rooms ⊘ No Meals Ⓜ Clarke Quay.

Paradox Singapore Merchant Court at Clarke Quay

$$ | HOTEL | At this older, but well-located, hotel, standard rooms are comfortable; larger suites have a few more amenities and balconies overlooking Clarke Quay. **Pros:** great location; balcony rooms available overlooking Clarke Quay; family-friendly facilities like the kids pool. **Cons:** hotel needs a refresh; some rooms don't have views; standard rooms are small for the price. $ *Rooms from: S$310* ⊠ *20 Merchant Rd., Clarke Quay* ☎ *6337–2288* ⊕ *www.paradoxhotels.com/singapore* ⤴ *476 rooms* ⦿ *No Meals* Ⓜ *Clarke Quay.*

★ The Warehouse Hotel

$$$ | HOTEL | Occupying a restored warehouse by the river, this progressive, distinctively designed boutique hotel partners with local makers and creators to showcase environmentally sound Singapore amenities. **Pros:** eco-friendly environment; hip local flavor; riverside location. **Cons:** some rooms are windowless; curtains used for privacy in some bathrooms; no on-site gym. $ *Rooms from: S$430* ⊠ *320 Havelock Rd., Clarke Quay* ☎ *6828–0000* ⊕ *www.thewarehousehotel.com* ⤴ *37 rooms* ⦿ *Free Breakfast* Ⓜ *Havelock.*

Ⓨ Nightlife

Boomarang

PUBS | This Aussie hangout is one of the more popular weekend spots on Robertson Quay, often with a lively expat crowd enjoying cold beers and live Australian sports. The evenings can get a bit raucous (the pub stays open until 3 am) but is often a laid-back place to drink. The restaurant is open all day and is a nice spot by the river for a brunch or afternoon bite. ⊠ *60 Robertson Quay, #01–15, Robertson Quay* ☎ *6738–1077* ⊕ *www.boomarang.com.sg* Ⓜ *Fort Canning.*

Headquarters

DANCE CLUBS | The music takes center stage at this underground club, where you can dress down and party alongside a like-minded community to sub-genres like acid house, techno, and disco. ⊠ *66A Boat Quay, Boat Quay* ⊕ *www.thugshopsg.com/headquarters* Ⓜ *Clarke Quay.*

Molly Malone's Irish Pub & Brasserie

PUBS | Classic fish-and-chips join the beers, cocktails, and whiskeys at this friendly Irish bar, which was originally built in Ireland before being transported in full to Singapore in 1995. The bar is full of interesting characters and is the closest you'll come to a local joint in the area. There's also live music most nights,

The quays along the Singapore River come alive at night, when crowds pack the bars and restaurants.

TVs screening live sports, and a full menu of pub classics. ✉ *56 Circular Rd., Boat Quay* ☎ *6536–2029* ⊕ *www.molly-malone.com* Ⓜ *Raffles Place.*

Southbridge

BARS | Boasting one of the best downtown views of Marina Bay in Singapore, this rooftop bar is semi-hidden in a nondescript shophouse on the edge of Boat Quay. There are generous happy hour deals, including 2-for-1 gin and tonics, a decent menu of nibbles and platters (the oysters are a must), and, when the lights go down, a buzzing crowd soaking up the brilliant vista. Ask for seats by the edge when you book to get the best views. ✉ *80 Boat Quay, Level 5, Boat Quay* ✛ *Take the lift to the rooftop* ☎ *6877–6965* ⊕ *www.southbridge.sg* Ⓜ *Clarke Quay.*

TAP Craft Beer

BARS | This relaxed bar along the edge of the Singapore River has up to 20 Singaporean and international craft beers on draft each month and a small menu of bar snacks. The shaded spots outside, under the canopy of large rain trees, are a great place to people-watch as the evening arrives. ✉ *86 Robertson Quay, #01–02, Robertson Quay* ☎ *6694–2885* ⊕ *www.tapthat.com.sg* Ⓜ *For Canning.*

★ 28 Hong Kong Street

BARS | Don't be fooled by the fact that the name of this bar is its address—it can still be easy to miss. Opened in 2011 as one of the early pioneers of Singapore's speakeasy cocktail scene, it's a regular on Asia's 50 Best Bars list. Inside the laid-back space, you'll find American-style craft cocktails, a decent menu of bar snacks, and an ever-changing soundtrack of 1990s U.S. hip-hop. ⊠ *28 Hong Kong St., Boat Quay* ☎ *8318–0328* ⊕ *www.28hks.com* Ⓜ *Clarke Quay.*

★ Wine RVLT

WINE BARS | Founded by two veteran Singaporean sommeliers, this self-proclaimed "ridiculously fun" wine bar has a focus on easy-drinking sustainable wines and a punky, underground atmosphere. The bar stocks around 170 different labels, and wines by the glass regularly rotate. There's no list, so amble up to the bottles displayed in the corner and take your pick (the prices are written on the bottle, and there's always a friendly sommelier to help you choose). The exceptional food menu, with popular favorites like chicken nuggets with sriracha, and beef tartare with smoked egg yolk, is worth the trip alone. ⊠ *38 Carpenter St., #01–01, Boat Quay* ☎ *6909–5709* ⊕ *www.winervlt.sg* Ⓜ *Clarke Quay.*

★ Zouk

DANCE CLUBS | The long-running Zouk always manages to reinvent itself. The huge dance club, carved out of renovated riverside warehouses, is four venues in one: Zouk, the main dance room that specializes in all genres of electronic music; the more sophisticated and intimate Capital; and Phuture for hip hop lovers; and Red Tail Bar for cocktails and sharing bites. Visiting international DJs take the decks weekly, and the club consistently gets rave reviews overseas. ⊠ *The Cannery, 3C River Valley Rd., Clarke Quay* ☎ *9006–8549* ⊕ *www.zoukclub.com.sg* Ⓜ *Clarke Quay.*

🎭 Performing Arts

Singapore Repertory Theatre

THEATER | **FAMILY** | The popular Singapore Repertory Theatre stages plays and musicals at the KC Arts Center. Its subsidiary, The Little Company, produces children's plays for two age groups (under-5s and 6 to 12 year-olds). ⊠ *Robertson Walk, 20 Merbau Rd., Robertson Quay* ☎ *6733–8166* ⊕ *www.srt.com.sg* Ⓜ *Fort Canning.*

🛍 Shopping

SHOPPING CENTERS AND MALLS

Clarke Quay Central

MALL | The Singapore River is more known for its bars and restaurants, so isn't somewhere locals usually come to shop. If you do need something, though, this large mall has the usual brands, including eateries and amenities from fast food restaurants to drug stores. Japanese superstore Don Don Donki has a large space in the basement with a good range of Japanese food stalls. ✉ *6 Eu Tong Sen St., Clarke Quay* ☎ *6532–9922* ⊕ *www.fareast-malls.com.sg* Ⓜ *Clarek Quay.*

🏃 Activities

BOAT TOURS

★ Singapore River Cruise

BOAT TOURS | FAMILY | Early in Singapore's history, bumboats were used to transport goods up and down the Singapore River, from the businesses in Boat Quay to warehouses in Clarke Quay. These days, there's no better way to see the river and modern Singapore than from one of these retrofitted barges. You can take a bumboat from the Clarke Quay jetty for a 40-minute fixed-route cruise that will take you through Boat Quay, Clarke Quay, and Marina Bay. Bookings can be made online or at kiosks along the river. ✉ *Clarke Quay, Clarke Quay* ☎ *6336–6111* ⊕ *rivercruise.com.sg* ✆ *From S$26* Ⓜ *Clarke Quay.*

SPAS

Sabaai Sabaai

SPAS | This small boutique spa specializes in Thai massage and other therapeutic treatments. Highlights include the rhythmic Thai signature massage, which is perfect for those with muscle tension, and the Thai Herb massage, which uses herbal compress and essential oils to relieve pain and inflammation. There's a full menu of massage and spa therapy to choose from, all completed by expert masseurs in peaceful massage rooms. ✉ *49A Boat Quay, Clarke Quay* ☎ *9337–3715* ⊕ *www.sabaaisabaai.com* ✆ *Thai massage from S$88 (60 mins), head and shoulder massage from S$58 (30 mins).* Ⓜ *Clarke Quay.*

River Valley

River Valley is primarily a residential neighborhood, home to a lot of the city's expats. Even so, it's an interesting place to walk around, taking in the extravagant mansions, uniquely designed houses and shiny condos. Enjoy a morning yoga class, have a leisurely brunch, or stop for a glass of wine at one of the small bistros on River Valley road.

◉ Sights

Hong San See Temple

TEMPLE | Once overlooking the sea, Hong San See Temple is now swamped by high-rise buildings on Institution Hill. Established by Hokkien immigrants in the early 20th century, the Hong San See translates as "Temple on Phoenix Hill," carvings of which you'll see amongst dragons in the large granite columns. Dedicated to the deity Guang Ze Zun Wang, the temple was designed in traditional Hokkien style, with upturned swallow-tails on the curved roofs and decorations made with colorful ceramics. The temple is now a national monument after years of restoration work. ⊠ *31 Mohamed Sultan Rd., River Valley* ⊕ *www.roots.gov.sg* ☒ *Free* Ⓜ *Fort Canning.*

The Singapore Buddhist Lodge

TEMPLE | Home to the Buddhist charitable organization by the same name, this striking building on Kim Yam Road houses multiple intricate Buddha statues and calm open spaces for peaceful reflection. The foundation offers talks on Buddhism (some in English, others in Chinese), traditional Chinese medicine clinics, and free vegetarian food cooked by volunteers daily. Note there can be queues on Buddhist holidays. The website is in Chinese, but the information at the lodge is in English. ⊠ *17–19 Kim Yam Rd., River Valley* ☎ *6737–2630* ⊕ *www.sbl.org.sg* ☒ *Free* Ⓜ *Fort Canning.*

Sri Thendayuthapani Temple

TEMPLE | Also known as Chettiars' Temple, this southern Indian temple, a national monument that's home to numerous shrines, is a replacement for the original, which was built in the 19th century. The 75-foot-high gopuram, with its many colorful sculptures of godly manifestations, is astounding. The chandelier-lighted interior is lavishly decorated; 48 painted-glass panels are inset in the ceiling and angled to reflect the sunrise and sunset. The temple is the main gathering point for devotees during the Tamil festival Thaipusam and a sight to watch, as attendees pierce their bodies with metal spikes and hooks and walk over burning coals as part of the festival's pilgrimage. ⊠ *15 Tank Rd., River Valley* ☎ *6737–9393* ⊕ *www.sttemple.com* ☒ *Free* Ⓜ *Fort Canning.*

🍴 Restaurants

8picure

$$$ | ITALIAN | An unpretentious Italian fusion restaurant, 8picure belies its understated look with excellent cooking and a warm, cozy atmosphere. Chef Gabriel explains each of the meticulously crafted dishes in person, with quality ingredients like Iberico pork

The elaborately decorated Sri Thendayuthapani Temple is one of the most colorful Indian temples in Singapore.

and New Zealand lamb used throughout the set and à la carte menus. **Known for:** intimate dining space; explanations of the dishes by the head chef; black garlic pesto sardines capellini and crab cake with chilli crab sauce. $ *Average main: S$40* ✉ *Loft@ Nathan, 428 River Valley Rd., #01–04, River Valley* ☎ *6677–1075* ⊕ *www.8picure.com.sg* ⊗ *Closed Sun. and Mon. No lunch Tues., Wed., and Sat.* Ⓜ *Great World.*

Esora

$$$$ | **JAPANESE** | You can get excellent kappo-style, modern Japanese food in this serenely-converted shophouse, where you sit at a counter while the omakase menu is cooked before you. Menus are seasonal, with dishes, ingredients, and floral arrangements changing over the course of the year. **Known for:** need to reserve far in advance; exceptional tea-pairing program; seasonal food. $ *Average main: S$368* ✉ *15 Mohamed Sultan Rd., River Valley* ☎ *8533–7528* ⊕ *www.restaurant-esora.com* ⊗ *Closed Mon. and Tues. No lunch Wed. and Fri.–Sun.* Ⓜ *Fort Canning.*

Feng Ji Chicken Rice

$$ | **CHINESE** | Originally founded as a hawker stall in Woodlands, Feng Ji Chicken Rice is now a much-loved *tze char* (small, affordable plates) restaurant in River Valley. Of course, the signature here is Hainanese chicken rice, with tender chicken, aromatic rice, and flavorful broth. **Known for:** range of meat and veg dishes for sharing; succulent chicken and rice with light broth; historic former-hawker-stall-turned-restaurant. $ *Average main: S$15* ✉ *225*

River Valley Rd., River Valley 🕾 *9724–9692* ⊕ *www.facebook.com/ FengJiChickenRice* Ⓜ *Fort Canning.*

★ Fook Kin

$$ | CHINESE | Based on the old-school eateries of Hong Kong, Fook Kin specializes in *char siew* (Cantonese-style barbecued pork), crispy pork belly, and other roast meats. Aside from the much-loved meat, the menu features a good selection of soups, dim sum, and rice bowls. **Known for:** expertly roasted meats; craft beer and sake fridge; lively, canteen-style dining. ⑤ *Average main: S$25* ✉ *111 Killiney Rd., River Valley* 🕾 *6737–3488* ⊕ *www.facebook. com/fookkinsg* Ⓜ *Somerset.*

★ Zion Riverside Food Centre

$ | SINGAPOREAN | Standing on the Singapore River with waterside views, this breezy food center is well-known for the quality of its hawker stalls. Famous stalls include No. 18 Zion Road Fried Kway Teow (#01–17), serving smoky noodles with cockles, fish cake, and Chinese sausage; and Michelin-rated Zion Road Big Prawn Noodle (#01–17), serving spicy noodles with large prawns, pork rib, and fried onions. **Known for:** wallet-friendly local eats; Michelin-rated hawkers; riverside seating. ⑤ *Average main: S$7* ✉ *70 Zion Rd., River Valley* ⊟ *No credit cards* Ⓜ *Great World.*

☕ Coffee and Quick Bites

Grace Espresso

$ | CAFÉ | This cozy neighborhood café has good coffee and plenty of brunch options. The space is fairly small and gets busy on weekends, so if there are no seats, take your coffee down to the river. **Known for:** busy weekend brunch crowd; cute spot with outdoor seats; well-roasted coffee. ⑤ *Average main: S$6* ✉ *Loft@ Nathan, 428 River Valley Rd., #01–14, River Valley* 🕾 *8501–2693* ⊕ *www.facebook.com/Graceespressosg* Ⓜ *Great World.*

Pantler

$ | BAKERY | This quiet café and bakery specializes in Japanese-style cakes and pastries. **Known for:** delicate, Japanese-inspired pastries; light, indulgent cream puffs; serene café space. ⑤ *Average main: S$10* ✉ *474 River Valley Rd., River Valley* 🕾 *6221– 6223* ⊕ *www.pantler.com.sg* 🕙 *Closed Mon.* Ⓜ *Great World.*

Thong Aik Coffee

$ | CAFÉ | Hidden in an older housing estate just off the river, Thong Aik Coffee serves traditional *kopi* and local breakfast options in a casual setting. However, the real star is the affordable, homely Thai food, which makes for an unexpectedly delicious lunchtime bite. **Known for:** quiet space in residential area; authentic Thai dishes at lunch; strong local coffee with kaya toast. **⑤** *Average main: S$5* ✉ *78 Indus Rd., #01–495, River Valley* ☎ *8265–4922* ⊕ *www.facebook.com/thongaikcoffee* 𝌑 *Closed Sun.* **Ⓜ** *Havelock.*

🛏 Hotels

Great World Serviced Apartments

$$$ | APARTMENT | A good option for longer stays, these fully furnished one- to four-bedroom apartments offer the conveniences of home (including full kitchens) with some perks of full-service hotel living. **Pros:** pet-friendly; monthly rates available for long stays; free parking. **Cons:** expensive; no complimentary breakfast; minimum six-night stay. **⑤** *Rooms from: S$470* ✉ *Great World, 2 Kim Seng Walk, River Valley* ☎ *6722–7000* ⊕ *stay.greatworld. sg* 🛏 *304 apartments* |◯| *No Meals* ☞ *6-night min.* **Ⓜ** *Great World.*

Lloyd's Inn

$ | HOTEL | If you're looking for an affordable stay near Orchard Road, Lloyd's Inn—located on a quiet residential street—is only a 10-minute walk away. **Pros:** good selection of room types; quiet location; outdoor rain showers and bathtubs. **Cons:** minimal facilities (small pool, no gym); cheaper room categories are small; breakfast is not on-site. **⑤** *Rooms from: S$170* ✉ *2 Lloyd Rd., River Valley* ☎ *6737–7309* ⊕ *www.lloydsinn.com/singapore* |◯| *Free Breakfast* **Ⓜ** *Somerset.*

🍸 Nightlife

Partners in Crime

BARS | A busy neighborhood bar perched on the corner of Zion and River Valley roads fills up every evening. Inside tables are good for watching live sports, but the sought-after outside tables are much better for enjoying the evening atmosphere. Regular free-flow drinks promotions are very good value, plus the food menu features a solid choice of bar classics. ✉ *397 River Valley Rd., River Valley* ☎ *6909–2503* ⊕ *www.partnersincrime.com.sg* **Ⓜ** *Great World.*

★ Revival

BARS | This bar is a sophisticated loft-style space that creates elegant cocktails inspired by iconic art, such as the "Pathway in Monet's Garden," featuring gin, elderflower, and honeysuckle. Sit in the green and earth-hued art deco main room with its long marble countertop, or head to the patio for cocktails in the evening air. The kitchen regularly rotates local chefs, creating an interesting and varied bar snack menu. ✉ *UE Square, 205 River Valley Rd., #01–76, River Valley* ☎ *9488–3726* ⊕ *www.revivalbarsg.com* **Ⓜ** *Fort Canning.*

Temple Cellars

BARS | Hip bottle shop Temple Cellars is a haven for craft beer enthusiasts and low-intervention wine lovers. Large stocked fridges and shelves line the walls of the small space in UE Square, with a particularly good selection of low-alcohol offerings. You'll find a focus on small, independent producers of spirits, sake, wines, and more here, with a large collection of beers from Singapore's craft brewers. The outdoor seats are a great place to grab a draft beer or sample some of the bottles on offer. ⊠ *UE Square, 81 Clemenceau Ave., #01–12, River Valley* ☎ *8800–2975* ⊕ *www.templecellars.com* Ⓜ *Fort Canning.*

🛍 Shopping

ANTIQUES

Shang Antique

ANTIQUES & COLLECTIBLES | One of Singapore's most respected antique stores specializes in Southeast Asian pieces, which are selected from neighboring regions including Cambodia, Vietnam, and Thailand. The collection offers items dating from as early as the 7th century, with a fascinating range of furniture, art, sculptures, and more. All pieces come with certificates of authenticity and can be shipped overseas. ⊠ *296 River Valley Rd., River Valley* ☎ *6388–8838* ⊕ *www.shangantique.com.sg* Ⓜ *Fort Canning.*

CLOTHING

Our Second Nature

WOMEN'S CLOTHING | Found in Great World City, this local boutique label creates comfortable everyday wear inspired by nature. Working closely with local artists, the patterns and prints are unique, and create a distinct look for their signature dresses. ⊠ *Great World, 1 Kim Seng Promenade, #01–159, River Valley* ⊕ *oursecondnature.com* Ⓜ *Great World.*

FOOD

Little Farms

FOOD | This boutique grocer specializes in sourcing high-quality produce from independent suppliers in Australia and Europe. The shelves are lined with everything from Barossa Valley wine to artisanal French cheeses and breads. The store also works with local Singaporean growers and food artisans, so it's a good spot to look for some quality food souvenirs. Aside from the grocer's, there's a café with outdoor seats here, which makes a great place to stop for brunch or an afternoon drink. ⊠ *Valley Point, 491 River Valley Rd., #01–20, River Valley* ☎ *3105–1154* ⊕ *www.littlefarms.com* Ⓜ *Great World.*

SHOPPING CENTERS AND MALLS

Great World

MALL | This large mall used to be the site of Great World Amusement Park, which provided entertainment to local Singaporeans up until the 1970s. Now home to some of Singapore's most popular chain stores, the mall is often frequented by families exploring the shops and activities aimed at kids. There are two high-quality supermarkets here as well as several delicatessens and specialty grocers, so it's a good place to shop for food souvenirs. As with all malls in Singapore, there's a wide range of options for eating and drinking throughout; highlights include Malaysian hawker stalls at Malaysia Chiak!; Japanese food court &JOY Dining Hall; and branches of dim sum favorite Imperial Treasure. ⊠ *1 Kim Seng Promenade, River Valley* ☎ *6737–3855* ⊕ *shop.greatworld.com.sg* Ⓜ *Great World.*

🏃 Activities

BOXING

9Round River Valley

BOXING | Get an awesome full-body workout in 30 minutes at this kickboxing gym that welcomes everyone from beginners to pros. You'll spend 3 minutes at a time at 9 training stations, with a semi-private instructor on hand to help your technique. The best part: they offer a full workout for free with no obligations to all first-timers. ⊠ *460 River Valley Rd., River Valley* ☎ *8383–9460* ⊕ *www.9round.sg* 🖭 *First session free; rates from S$60 per week* Ⓜ *Great World.*

YOGA

★ Hom Yoga

YOGA | There are two Hom Yoga locations in Singapore, but the River Valley one is by far the better outlet. Beautiful and minimalist, in bright white with leafy greenery, it's the perfect place to relax with a Vinyasa flow or Yin meditation class. They offer one-off classes or a seven-day trial for unlimited classes. ⊠ *491 River Valley Rd., #01–18/19, River Valley* ☎ *6219–0330* ⊕ *homyoga.com* 🖭 *Classes from S$38* Ⓜ *Great World.*

Chapter 6

LITTLE INDIA AND KAMPONG GLAM

Updated by
Charlene Fang

⦿ Sights   🍴 Restaurants   🛏 Hotels   🛍 Shopping   🍸 Nightlife
★★★★☆   ★★★☆☆   ★★☆☆☆   ★★★☆☆   ★★★☆☆

NEIGHBORHOOD SNAPSHOT

TOP EXPERIENCES

■ **Explore Tekka Market:** Take in the sights, sounds, and aromas of Little India's vibrant market full of food stalls.

■ **See the Sultan Mosque:** Learn more about this magnificent mosque (the largest in Singapore), built in 1824.

■ **Search for colorful murals:** Snap some photos against the backdrop of Little India's colorful masterpieces or of Kampong Glam's Gelam Gallery.

■ **Shop the boutiques:** Away from Singapore's splashy shopping malls, this area offers a more personal experience, where you can buy local textiles or make your own perfume.

■ **Have a night out:** Kampong Glam is home to some of the coolest bars in Singapore, including the famed Atlas.

GETTING HERE

Kampong Glam and Little India are north and east of the Singapore River and conveniently situated close to MRT stations—Bugis and Jalan Besar for Kampong Glam, Little India and Farrer Park for Little India. Both neighborhoods are best explored on foot; however, hailing a taxi or ordering a ride share is easy. Note that Little India is particularly crowded on Sunday.

PLANNING YOUR TIME

The area can be covered in one day. Spend the morning in Little India, exploring its colorful streets and temples at leisure. In the mid-afternoon, make your way to Kampong Glam via taxi or MRT. Reach the Sultan Mosque by sunset for a breathtaking view of the golden dome.

VIEWFINDER

■ Insert yourself in the large-scale mural by Psyfool depicting the different trades of Little India, including a dhobi, parrot astrologer, milk seller, and more. The mural is located between Belilios Lane and Belilios Road. 🚇 *Little India.*

■ In Kampong Glam, stop outside of Konditori Artisan Bakes, and you'll find the perfect spot to take a photo with the majestic Sultan Mosque and its golden domes in the backdrop. The view is between Bussorah and Baghdad street.

PAUSE HERE

■ The little park at 5 Hindoo Rd. does double duty. It's a great photo-opp, with its large and small colorful elephant sculptures, but there are also activities to entertain the little ones.

The culturally rich and historically significant neighborhoods of Little India and Kampong Glam, with their charming mix of old and new, are well worth exploring. Here, the vibrant streets are never quiet, hip cafes sit next to religious monuments, and chic watering holes and century-old eateries can be enjoyed in a single visit.

One of the most easily recognized parts of the city, Little India—designated as such during colonial rule—is the area east of the Singapore River and across from Chinatown. What is still the cultural center for Singapore's large Indian community is also one of the most vibrant parts of the city. You'll find shops selling saris, flower garlands, and all the necessary ingredients for an Indian meal; hip restaurants and bars sharing space with traditional eateries; locals off to visit temples; and streets just generally bustling with people. Many backpackers stay in the budget hostels along Dunlop Road. Recently, boutique hotels have also began to appear in the area.

The Kampong Glam neighborhood was the home of Malay groups before British colonization began in the early 1800s. Following the reallocation of ethnic groups, Kampong Glam was designated for the sultan, along with other Malays, as well as Arabs. Over the years, it served as a gathering point for local Muslims as well as Muslim immigrants from Malaysia, Indonesia, and the Middle East. Some street names, such as Arab Street, Baghdad Street, and Kandahar Street, reflect that history.

These days, this area north of the Singapore River remains composed of ethnic Malays, Arabs, Chinese, and Indians. "Glam" prononunced "glum" refers to a tree that grew in abundance in the area in early Singapore and was used for boat-making, as a seasoning, and as medicine. "Kampong" just means "village." Now a lively shopping and lifestyle destination, Kampong Glam has standout streets like Haji Lane and Khandahar Street, which is a good place to pick up local designs or to grab a bite. Bordering Kampong Glam is the Bugis area, once a red-light district and now a thriving retail area.

Little India

A wander around the streets of Little India should probably include a stop at one of the restaurants along Serangoon Road or Tekka Market for a bite. Make time to visit to one of its temples. The Mustafa Centre, which should also be on the itinerary, is open 24 hours, seven days a week. The neighborhood gets very crowded on Sundays, so that's not the best day if you don't like crowds. A visit of a few hours should suffice.

Sights

Abdul Gaffoor Mosque

MOSQUE | This mosque was completed in 1910 and has recently been restored. Though it has none of the exotic, multicolor statuary of the Hindu temples, it still woos you with its intricately detailed Moorish facade in the Muslim colors of green and gold and its unusual architectural symmetry. Shorts are not allowed, and remember to take off your shoes. Only worshipers should enter the prayer hall, and visitors should avoid evening prayer sessions and Fridays. ✉ *41 Dunlop St., Little India* ☎ *6295–4209* ⊕ *www.facebook.com/masjidabdulgafoor* ✆ *Free* Ⓜ *Little India.*

★ Indian Heritage Centre

HISTORY MUSEUM | Following the colonization of Singapore in 1819, Indians began to make their way over to Singapore, and today they form the country's third-largest ethnic group. Inside the stunning Indian Heritage Centre, the history of the Indian and South Asian communities is detailed through five permanent exhibitions. Other showcases include opulent gold jewelry from the Saigon Chettiars' Temple Trust, personal heirlooms, and intricately carved doorways and frames, one holding as many as 5,000 carvings. Free guided tours in English, Tamil, and Chinese are offered. Before leaving, take time to admire the building, modeled after a *baoli* (Indian stepwell)—it's especially eye-catching at sunset. ✉ *5 Campbell La., Little India* ☎ *6291–1601* ⊕ *www.indianheritage.org. sg/en* ✆ *$8* ⊘ *Closed Mon.* Ⓜ *Little India.*

Leong San See Temple

TEMPLE | This temple's main altar is dedicated to Kuan Yin (Goddess of Mercy)—also known as Bodhisattva Avalokitesvara—and is framed by beautiful, ornate carvings of flowers, a phoenix, and other birds. The temple, also called Dragon Mountain Temple, was built in 1926. To the right of the main altar is an image of Confucius to which many parents bring their children to pray for intelligence and filial piety. If you enter from the prayer hall's side doors,

Little India

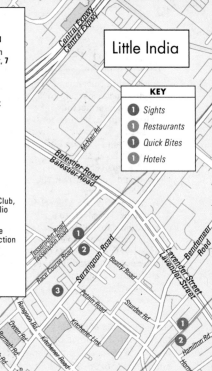

KEY

1 *Sights*

1 *Restaurants*

1 *Quick Bites*

1 *Hotels*

1,000 ft

200 m

Little India's Murals

Little India's colorful murals can be used as markers on your own informal tour of this vibrant neighborhood. Located sporadically on Clive Street, Upper Dickson Road, Starlight Road, Serangoon Road, Kerbau Road, Hindoo Road, and Dunlop Street, the murals depict everything from cheeky cows on bicycles to parrot astrologers to traditional Indian dancers. You'll have to keep an eye out as some are plastered on the sides of buildings while others are located along narrow alleyways.

A good resource to use when planning your walk is Art Walk Little India (⊕ www.artwalklittleindia.sg), which hosts an annual art walk in January. Their map marks 18 murals in the neighborhood using top sights like Tekka Market, the Indian Heritage Centre, and the House of Tan Teng Niah as landmarks to guide you. Try to spot "A Ride Through Race Course Road" on 74 Race Course Rd. to reflect on the neighborhood's beginnings in the 1840s as a hub for horse racing.

you'll reach the ancestral hall in the rear, where you can see tablets with the names of deceased worshippers. When you visit, be sure to observe a modest dress code. ⊠ 371 Race Course Rd., Little India ☎ 6298–9371 Ⓜ Farrer Park.

★ Sri Srinivasa Perumal Temple

TEMPLE | Dedicated to Vishnu the Preserver, the temple is easy to recognize by its 60-foot-high monumental gopuram, with tiers of intricate sculptures depicting Vishnu in the nine forms in which he has appeared on Earth. Especially vivid are the depictions of Vishnu's manifestations as Rama, on his seventh visit, and as Krishna, on his eighth. Inside, you'll find devotees making offerings of fruit to one of the manifestations of Vishnu. This is done either by handing coconuts or bananas, along with a slip of paper with your name on it, to a temple official, who'll chant the appropriate prayers to the deity and place holy ash on your head, or by walking clockwise while praying, coconut in hand, around one of the shrines a certain number of times, then breaking the coconut (a successful break symbolizes that Vishnu has been receptive to the incantation). Dress conservatively and remove your shoes before you enter. ⊠ 397 Serangoon Rd., Little India ☎ 6298–5771 ⊕ www.sspt.org.sg 🎟 Free ⊘ Closed Sat. Ⓜ Farrer Park.

Sri Veeramakaliamman Temple

TEMPLE | Dedicated to Kali the Courageous, a ferocious incarnation of Shiva's wife, Parvati the Beautiful, this temple was built in 1881

Locals shop for fruits and veggies at the famous Tekka Market.

by indentured Bengali laborers working at nearby lime pits. Inside is a jet-black statue of Kali, the fiercest of the Hindu deities, who demands sacrifices and is often depicted with a garland of skulls. More cheerful is the shrine to Ganesh, the elephant-headed god of wisdom and prosperity. Perhaps the most popular Hindu deity, Ganesh is the child of Shiva and Parvati. During the temple's opening hours you will see Hindus going in to receive blessings: the priests streak devotees' foreheads with *vibhuti,* the white ash from burned cow dung. ⊠ *141 Serangoon Rd., Little India* ☎ *6295–4538* ⊕ *www.srivkt.org* Ⓜ *Farrer Park.*

★ Tekka Market
MARKET | Renovated in 2023, this is one of the city's largest and busiest wet markets (where meat and fish are sold). Tekka also has a staggering array of fruits, vegetables, herbs, and spices for sale. On the Sungei Road side of the ground floor are stalls selling Chinese, Indian, Malay, and Western foods. Many of the stalls are run by second- or third-generation hawkers, making this an excellent place to sample Singapore's famed hawker food. Upstairs shops sell hardware, shoes, luggage, textiles, and Indian clothing. ⊠ *665 Buffalo Rd., Little India* ⊕ *www.singapore-guide. com/food-dining/tekka-centre.htm* Ⓜ *Little India.*

Temple of 1,000 Lights
TEMPLE | The Sakya Muni Buddha Gaya is better known by its pop-ular name because of its lightbulbs surrounding a 50-foot Buddha. Sporting a fusion of Indian, Thai, and Chinese influences, the entire temple as well as the Buddha statue, was built by the Thai

monk Vutthisasala. Until he died at the age of 94, he was always in the temple, ready to explain Buddhist philosophy. Among the relics he procured: a mother-of-pearl-inlaid cast of the Buddha's footprint and a piece of bark from the bodhi tree under which the Buddha is believed to have received enlightenment. Around the pedestal supporting the great Buddha statue is a series of scenes depicting the story of his search for enlightenment; inside a hollow chamber at the back is a re-creation of the scene of the Buddha's last sermon. ⊠ *336 Race Course Rd., Little India* ☎ *6294–0714* Ⓜ *Farrer Park.*

🍴 Restaurants

★ Allauddin's Briyani

$ | **INDIAN** | Of the Tekka Market's many tantalizing eateries, this spot, in business since the 1950s, comes highly recommended—as evidenced by lines that are particularly long at lunchtime. It's worth the wait, though, to enjoy a comfort meal of aromatic biryani rice combined with fork-tender chicken or mutton chunks, and all the orders come with a side of vegetable dhal and pickled vegetables. **Known for:** mutton biryani; fluffy rice; affordable local favorite. ⑤ *Average main: S$5* ⊠ *666 Buffalo Rd., #01–232 Tekka Market and Food Centre, Little India* ☎ *6296–6786* ▭ *No credit cards* Ⓜ *Little India.*

★ The Banana Leaf Apolo

$$ | **INDIAN** | This casual, cafeteria-style, Indian restaurant is one of the best (and busiest) of its kind in Little India. Standout dishes include the signature fish-head curry, as well as the fish tikka, mutton mysore, and prawn masala, but choose whatever sounds good, and you'll still do well. **Known for:** authentic Indian served on banana leaves; affordable prices; fish-head curry. ⑤ *Average main: S$16* ⊠ *54 Race Course Rd., Little India* ☎ *6293–8682* ⊕ *www. thebananaleafapolo.com* Ⓜ *Little India.*

Komala Vilas Restaurant

$ | **INDIAN** | In operation since 1947, this is one of Little India's best-known stops for northern and southern Indian vegetarian cuisine. Most plates come with curries, rice, dhal, condiments, Indian breads, or special sauces; for dessert there's a well-stocked counter of sweets. **Known for:** paper thin dosais (lentil and rice flour pancakes); Indian sweets; busy downstairs, quieter upstairs. ⑤ *Average main: S$7* ⊠ *76–78 Serangoon Rd., Little India* ☎ *6293–6980* ⊕ *www.komalavilas.com.sg* Ⓜ *Little India.*

Madras New Woodlands Restaurant

$ | INDIAN | This no-frills vegetarian restaurant is a long-running local favorite and one of the better south Indian restaurants in vibrant Little India. Opt for the *thali* if you're hungry: it's a large platter of *dosai* (pancakes) with three spiced vegetables, curd, dhal, *rasam* (hot and sour soup), papadam, and Indian-style condiments. **Known for:** south Indian cuisine; paper dosai; masala tea. $ *Average main: S$6* ⊠ *12–14 Upper Dickson Rd., Little India* ☎ *6297–1594* ⊕ *www.madrasnewwoodlands.com* ▭ *No credit cards* Ⓜ *Little India.*

★ Meatsmith Little India

$$ | INDIAN | Give into the heady aromas wafting out of this Indian-influenced barbecue joint, and you won't regret it. Although a meal here is pricier than those at its more casual neighbors, the cost difference is easily justified by the intense, mouthwatering flavors and creative menu. **Known for:** juicy suckling pig biryani; spice-heavy meats; cool, grungy spot for a meal. $ *Average main: S$26* ⊠ *21 Campbell La., Little India* ☎ *9625–9056* ⊕ *www. meatsmith.com.sg* ⊘ *Closed Mon. and Tues.* Ⓜ *Jalan Besar.*

Muthu's Curry

$ | INDIAN | FAMILY | You'll be spoiled for choice when it comes to Indian food on Race Course Road, but this restaurant established in 1969), along with the similarly popular Banana Leaf Apolo a few blocks down, is widely considered the best of the lot. There's a full range of North and South Indian options here, but the fish-head curry with okra and pineapple, the *milagu kozhi varuval* (chicken with pepper and coriander seeds), and the masala prawns are some of the standouts. **Known for:** wide variety of Indian dishes; fish-head curry; contemporary space. $ *Average main: S$12* ⊠ *138 Race Course Rd., #01–01, Little India* ☎ *6392–1722* ⊕ *www.muthuscurry.com* Ⓜ *Little India.*

Swee Choon Tim Sum Restaurant

$ | CANTONESE | A local favorite for late night dim sum, this low-frills supper spot has been known to have a line well into the wee hours of the morning. Order the usual suspects—siew mai, bean-curd prawn roll, or pork congee with century egg—but save space for signature dishes like the *mee sua kueh*, a deep-fried vermicelli cake, and Shanghainese favorites like the Sichuan chilli wantons and juicy xiao long bao. **Known for:** affordable dim sum; deep-fried vermicelli cake; mouthwatering chilli wantons. $ *Average main: S$7* ⊠ *183–193 Jalan Besar, Little India* ☎ *6225–7788* ⊕ *www. sweechoon.com* ⊘ *Closed Tues.* Ⓜ *Jalan Besar.*

☕ Coffee and Quick Bites

Chye Seng Huat Hardware

$ | CAFÉ | Singapore's vibrant third-wave coffee scene owes a lot to to Chye Seng Huat Hardware, one of the first specialty coffee spots in the area. The former hardware store turned hip coffee space is rarely empty, and regulars swear by both the brews and the robust brunch menu. **Known for:** flat white; lively weekend brunch crowd; ethically sourced coffee beans. $ *Average main: S$6* ✉ *150 Tyrwhitt Rd., Little India* ☎ *6299–4321* ⊕ *www.cshhcoffee.com* ☾ *Closed Mon.* Ⓜ *Farrer Park.*

★ Le Café Confectionary and Pastry

$ | BAKERY | The trademark shortbread-like crust, which has a light almond flavor, puts this bakery's pastries in a class above those made elsewhere; it's also why the take-out shop's buttery, golf ball–sized pineapple tarts and silky smooth bean curd tarts are often sold out. Luckily, Le Café sells a bunch of other goodies, including traditional moon-pie pastries filled with lotus-seed paste, prawn-roll snacks, and mao shan wang–filled durian puffs that are downright addictive. **Known for:** arguably the best pineapple tarts in Singapore; traditional moon pies; silky smooth bean-curd tarts. $ *Average main: S$7* ✉ *Blk 637 Veerasamy Rd., #01–111, Little India* ☎ *6294–8813* ⊕ *www.lecafe.com.sg* ☾ *No dinner* Ⓜ *Jalan Besar.*

The Patissier

$$ | BAKERY | This homegrown takeaway patisserie melds intricate French baking techniques with innovative flavor combinations to create unique treats. It's famous for its passion fruit meringue—meringue sponge cake filled with passion fruit mousse and fruit—but other easier-to-transport goodies like cookies and tarts are also available. **Known for:** French-influenced local bakery; signature passion fruit meringue; pre-order waiting lists. $ *Average main: S$15* ✉ *166 Tyrwhitt Rd., Little India* ☎ *6737–3369* ⊕ *www.thepatissier.com.sg* Ⓜ *Bendemeer.*

🛏 Hotels

The Vagabond Club, a Tribute Portfolio Hotel

$$ | HOTEL | Designed by French designer Jacques Garcia, this small boutique hotel (now part of the Marriot group) stands out with its velvet furnishings, opulent decor, and rotational Artist-in-Residence program. **Pros:** tasteful decor and art; personalized service and local experiences; club lounge privileges. **Cons:** standard rooms are on the small side; a bit far from the MRT station; street noise. $ *Rooms from: S$320* ✉ *39 Syed Alwi Rd.,*

Little India ☎ *6291–6677* ⊕ *www.marriott.com* 🛏 *41 rooms* ⏹⃝ *No Meals* Ⓜ *Jalan Besar.*

Wanderlust, The Unlimited Collection by Oakwood

$$ | HOTEL | Located minutes away from the Downtown MRT line, this newly refurbished hotel, housed in a 1920s art deco building, has some rooms equipped with kitchenettes. **Pros:** slick, modern design; hip on-site restaurant Kotuwa; loft rooms. **Cons:** some rooms are small; no swimming pool; not all rooms have kitchenettes. ⑤ *Rooms from: S$200* ✉ *2 Dickson Rd., Little India* ☎ *6396–3322* ⊕ *www.discoverasr.com* 🛏 *29 rooms* ⏹⃝ *No Meals* Ⓜ *Jalan Besar.*

🍸 Nightlife

The Whiskey Library & Jazz Club

BARS | Hidden in a corner of the Hotel Vagabond Club, this bar houses a collection of 1,000 rare, single-cask, limited-edition whiskies that would impress even the most seasoned connoisseur. It's styled like a typical whiskey den, with lots of wood, velvet, and a glass showcase. The cigar menu is up to par, and there's live jazz starting at 5 pm from Wednesday to Saturday. ✉ *Hotel Vagabond Club, 39 Syed Alwi Rd., Little India* ☎ *8866–0896* ⊕ *www.whiskey-libraryandjazzclub.sg* Ⓜ *Jalan Besar.*

Olibier Rooftop Bar

BREWPUBS | Singapore's love of rooftop bars extends beyond the Central Business District and into Little India with this no-frills, homestyle watering hole decorated with lawn chairs and unvarnished wooden tables. Browse their rotating menu of craft beers from Beijing-style witbiers to classic Belgian pilsners. Keep your stomach lined with local snacks like fishball *keropok,*and if you're lucky a tarot card reader might be in residence for the evening. ✉ *70A Dunlop St., Little India* ☎ *9769–8202* ⊕ *www.facebook. com/Olibier.sg* Ⓜ *Jalan Besar.*

🎭 Performing Arts

TRADITIONAL DANCE

Sri Warisan Som Said Performing Arts

FOLK/TRADITIONAL DANCE | This popular troupe—founded by renowned cultural Medallion recipient Madam Som Said—offers traditional Malay performances in town several times a year. ✉ *47 Kerbau Rd., Little India* ☎ *6225–6070* ⊕ *www.sriwarisan.com* Ⓜ *Little India.*

🛍 Shopping

HOUSEWARES

Jothi Store & Flower Shop

FLORIST | Around since 1963, this bustling, family-owned shop is hard to miss, thanks to the dozens of fragrant garlands decorating the store front. Inside, the shelves stock Indian household goods (prayer items, cosmetics, copperware, henna), so even if you don't end up buying anything, you'll leave with a better understanding of Indian culture. ✉ *1 Campbell La., Little India* ☎ *6338–7008* ⊕ *www.jothi.com.sg* Ⓜ *Little India.*

Mud Rock Ceramics

HOUSEWARES | Handmade and beautifully imperfect, the ceramics from this shop make perfect mementos. The bowls, plates, vases, and other items are so popular that even local eateries—including Burnt Ends, Le Binchotan, The Ottomani—use them. You can plan ahead to attend one of their classes, or get a piece delivered to your hotel. Custom orders are accepted, but all visits must be scheduled. ✉ *85 Maude Rd., Little India* ✉ *mudrockedu@gmail.com* ⊕ *www.mudrockceramics.com* ☉ *By appointment only* Ⓜ *Jalan Besar.*

SHOPPING CENTERS AND MALLS

Little India Arcade

SHOPPING CENTER | You'll find plenty of colorful eye candy at this cluster of shops near the Little India MRT. Jewelry, music, Indian-style sweets and snacks, and fabrics are all available. Across the street at the Tekka Market, you can also walk through a bustling food market and feast on cheap Indian eats at the hawker stalls. ✉ *48 Serangoon Rd., #02–07, between Campbell La. and Hastings Rd., Little India* ☎ *6295–5998* ⊕ *www.littleindiaarcade.com.sg* Ⓜ *Little India.*

★ Mustafa Centre

SHOPPING CENTER | This used to be a humble store frequented only by local shoppers—until word spread about its low prices and mind-boggling variety of goods. A visit to this sprawling, 24/7 complex just might be your most memorable Singapore shopping experience, provided you don't mind patiently navigating the sometimes overwhelming crowds. Surrounded by scores of Indian restaurants, some of which are similarly open all day and night, Mustafa Centre carries just about any manufactured product you can imagine—and they're often sold at cut-rate prices. It's great fun to wander and see what kind of treasures you can turn up. Be

Shop for everything from jewelry to perfume to chocolate on a trip to the Mustafa Centre.

sure to check out the massive supermarket, and, if you have spare money to change, do it here as the foreign-exchange rates (available online) are competitive. ✉ *Mustafa Centre, 145 Syed Alwi Rd., Little India* ☎ *6295–5855* ⊕ *www.mustafa.com.sg* Ⓜ *Farrer Park.*

TEXTILES
Haniffa Textiles
FABRICS | Spread across eight shop spaces, Haniffa Textiles has made a name for itself with its stock of saris. Try this silk shop for a cornucopia of richly colored and ornamented fabrics, scarves, bedspreads, and the like, often at surprisingly affordable prices. ✉ *60 Serangoon Rd., Little India* ☎ *6299–3709* ⊕ *www.haniffa. com.sg* Ⓜ *Little India.*

Kampong Glam

The Sultan Mosque serves as the unofficial center of the neighborhood, with the many shops of Arab Street a short walk away. A visit here would pair well with one to Little India, a few blocks to the north. With so many shops worth exploring, you'll probably want to come during business hours. A couple of hours is probably enough time to explore and to have a bite at one of the restaurants in the area toward the evening when things comes alive.

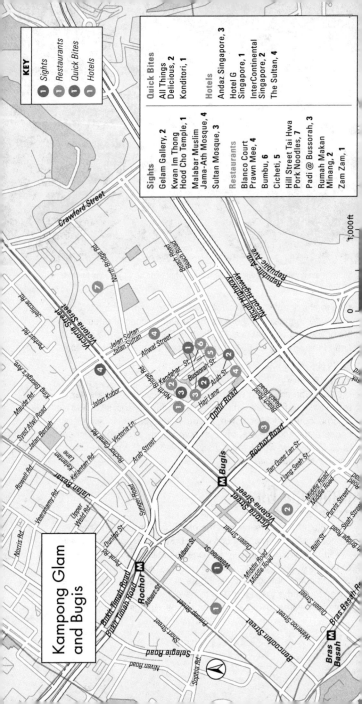

Kampong Glam and Bugis

KEY

- Sights
- Restaurants
- Quick Bites
- Hotels

Sights
Gelam Gallery, **2**
Kwan Im Thong
Hood Cho Temple, **1**
Malabar Muslim
Jama-Ath Mosque, **4**
Sultan Mosque, **3**

Restaurants
Blanco Court
Prawn Mee, **4**
Bumbu, **6**
Cicheti, **5**
Hill Street Tai Hwa
Pork Noodles, **7**
Padi @ Bussorah, **3**
Rumah Makan
Minang, **2**
Zam Zam, **1**

Quick Bites
All Things
Delicious, **2**
Konditori, **1**

Hotels
Andaz Singapore, **3**
Hotel G
Singapore, **1**
InterContinental
Singapore, **2**
The Sultan, **4**

0   1,000 ft

👁 Sights

Gelam Gallery

PUBLIC ART | Singapore's "outdoor art gallery" is open 24/7 amid the back alleyways off Muscat Street. Here, more than 30 colorful murals have been drawn by artists like local graffiti pioneer Slacsatu, international artists, and graduates from Singapore's LASALLE College of the Arts and the Nanyang Academy of Fine Arts. ✉ *80 Arab St., Kampong Glam* ⊕ *www.facebook.com/OneKampong-Gelam* Ⓜ *Bugis.*

Malabar Muslim Jama-Ath Mosque

MOSQUE | The only mosque in Singapore built and managed by the Malabar Muslim community (immigrants to Singapore from Kerala) was rebuilt in 1962 and has striking blue geometric tiles and a golden dome. Friday prayers are conducted in Arabic and translated into several languages including Malayalam and Urdu. Note that photographs shouldn't be taken here after 1 pm. ✉ *471 Victoria St., Kampong Glam* ☎ *6294–3862* ⊕ *www.malabar.org.sg* Ⓜ *Bugis.*

★ Sultan Mosque

MOSQUE | The first mosque on this site was built in the early 1820s with a grant from the East India Company. The current structure, built in 1928 by Denis Santry of Swan & Maclaren—the architect who designed the Victoria Memorial Hall—is a dramatic building with golden domes and minarets that glisten in the sun. The walls of the vast prayer hall are adorned with green and gold mosaic tiles on which passages from the Koran are written in Arabic. The main dome has an odd architectural feature: hundreds of bottle ends are jammed in between the dome and base. This unusual feature originated as a way for lower-income Muslims to donate during the mosque's construction so that all could contribute. At midday on Friday, the Islamic Sabbath, Muslims from all over Singapore enter through one of the Sultan Mosque's 14 portals to recite the Koran. The best view of the Sultan Mosque is at the junction of Bussorah Street and Beach Road. ■**TIP→ Walk-ins are welcome Saturday through Thursday from 10 am to 12 pm and from 2 pm to 4 pm.** ✉ *3 Muscat St., Kampong Glam* ☎ *6293–4405* ⊕ *www.sultanmosque.sg* ⊙ *Closed Sun.* Ⓜ *Bugis.*

🍴 Restaurants

Blanco Court Prawn Mee

$ | ASIAN | Arguably one of Singapore best spots for a bowl of prawn noodles, this humble establishment draws regulars who love its slow-simmered umami broth with fresh prawns and fork-tender pork ribs. The line for a bowl can be long, so come early to avoid an unnecessary wait. **Known for:** prawn noodles in a hearty broth; jumbo option; flavorful chilli. $ *Average main: S$5* ✉ *243 Beach Rd., #01–01, Kampong Glam* ☎ *6396–8464* ▭ *No credit cards* ◷ *Closed Tues.* Ⓜ *Bugis.*

Bumbu

$ | INDONESIAN | Coffee chicken, butter-oat soft-shell crab, and beef green curry are among the halal Thai–Indo fusion dishes at this homey shophouse. Salads, particularly the Thai-style pomelo, are great sides, and portions are generally small, so this is an easy place to taste a number of different dishes. **Known for:** pretty Peranakan decor; affordable buffet; butter-oat soft-shell crab. $ *Average main: S$12* ✉ *44 Kandahar St., Kampong Glam* ☎ *6392–8628* ⊕ *www.bumbu.com.sg* ◷ *Closed Mon.* Ⓜ *Bugis.*

★ Cicheti

$$ | ITALIAN | Expect good vibes and authentic food at this hip Italian eatery, known for its pizzas baked in a signature wood-fired oven imported from Naples itself. The 10-inch Neopolitan pies are a favorite, but for a well-rounded meal, don't ignore the handmade pastas and small selection of desserts. **Known for:** 10-inch Neopolitan pies; handmade pastas; cool vibe. $ *Average main: S$24* ✉ *52 Kandahar St., Kampong Glam* ☎ *9725–6255* ⊕ *www.cicheti.com* Ⓜ *Bugis.*

★ Hill Street Tai Hwa Pork Noodles

$ | CHINESE | Be warned: The line for this one-Michelin-star eatery rarely lets up, but the wait is worth it. After just one spoonful of the juicy minced meat and springy egg noodles dressed in a secret recipe of chilli and black vinegar, you'll understand why locals have kept this no-frills eatery a well-guarded secret for years. **Known for:** well-regarded eatery; long lines, but it's cheap; heritage hawker. $ *Average main: S$6* ✉ *466 Crawford La., #01–12, Kampong Glam* ▭ *No credit cards* ◷ *Closed Mon.* Ⓜ *Lavender.*

Padi @ Bussorah

$$ | INDONESIAN | FAMILY | Tuck into a communal meal of *nasi ambeng* (a Javanese rice dish with meat and vegetables) at this popular Kampong Glam eatery. The celebratory dish, commonly served during festive occasions, can be customized to fit the size of your dining party (from one to five diners). **Known for:** full flavored nasi ambeng, a Javanese rice dish; group dining; tender beef rendang. $ *Average main: S$18* ✉ *53 Bussorah St., Kampong Glam* ☎ *6291–3921* ⊕ *www.padibussorah.com* Ⓜ *Bugis.*

★ Rumah Makan Minang

$ | **INDONESIAN** | **FAMILY** | A second generation business that started out as a wooden stall, this authentic *nasi padang* (Padang steamed rice served with various pre-cooked dishes) serves a fork-tender *beef rendang* (Indonesian dry beef curry) slow cooked over charcoal. Other dishes include the *ayam belado hijau* (chicken in a secret green chilli marinade) and the crispy *tahu telur* (fried tofu mixed with blanched bean sprouts, peanuts, and a dark sweet soy sauce). **Known for:** its status as a Kampong Glam institution; traditional West Sumatra recipes; famous beef rendang cooked over charcoal. $ *Average main: S$8* ⊠ *18 & 18A Kandahar St., Kampong Glam* ☎ *6294–4805* ⊕ *www.minang.sg* ▤ *No credit cards* Ⓜ *Bugis.*

★ Zam Zam

$ | **ASIAN** | In business for more than a century, this hole-in-the-wall eatery serves what's arguably Singapore's best *murtabak*. Stuffed with mutton, chicken, or beef, it's a bit like a folded dough omelette with egg mixed in, *roti prata* (a fried flat bread), onions, and spices, all of it grilled together and served with a side of curry sauce. **Known for:** Singapore's best murtabak; casual and cheap local street food; late-night eatery. $ *Average main: S$5* ⊠ *697 North Bridge Rd., Kampong Glam* ☎ *6298–6320* ⊕ *www. zamzamsingapore.com* ▤ *No credit cards* Ⓜ *Jalan Besar.*

☕ Coffee and Quick Bites

★ All Things Delicious

$$ | **BAKERY** | You can count on this halal bakery and café (founded by food personality Dewi Imelda Wadhwa) to turn out some of the island's best pastries and desserts. The ATD To Go Dessert Box, an 8-piece taster of their most popular items, includes the bakery's signature gula Melaka scone and Paris brest. **Known for:** gula Melaka scone; Sticky Toffee Pudding; ATD To Go Dessert Box. $ *Average main: S$25* ⊠ *34 Arab St., Kampong Glam* ☎ *6291–4252* ⊕ *www.allthingsdelicious.sg* Ⓜ *Bugis.*

Konditori

$ | **CAFÉ** | This cute Swedish cafe's halal bakes are slightly pricey, but they're favored by local café aficionados. Stick to signature items like the strawberry cream cheese Danish and traditional semla bun, available year round. **Known for:** creative baked goods; traditional semla bun; halal-certified pastries and breads. $ *Average main: S$5* ⊠ *33 Bussorah St., Kampong Glam* ☎ *6209–8580* ⊕ *www.konditori.sg* Ⓜ *Bugis.*

Hotels

Hotel G Singapore

$ | HOTEL | Although it has somewhat small rooms, this urban hotel with slick decor and tech-outfitted rooms fits right in with its buzzy location minutes away from Bugis Village and Kampong Glam. **Pros:** burger bar and fitness center on-site; good location; eco- and tech-friendly. **Cons:** no pool; if you're traveling with infants, rooms can't accommodate a crib; rooms are small. Ⓢ *Rooms from: S$150* ✉ *200 Middle Rd., Kampong Glam* ☎ *6809–7988* ⊕ *www.hotels-g.com* ↩ *308 rooms* ❍ *No Meals* Ⓜ *Bugis.*

The Sultan

$ | HOTEL | Just a five-minute walk from Sultan Mosque, this small boutique hotel spread across 10 heritage shophouses is an affordable option for short stays, though the standard rooms can feel small. **Pros:** convenient location; charming design details; on-site restaurant. **Cons:** thin walls; street noise; some rooms do not have windows. Ⓢ *Rooms from: S$150* ✉ *101 Jalan Sultan, #01–01 The Sultan, Kampong Glam* ☎ *6723–7101* ⊕ *www.thesultan.com.sg* ↩ *64 rooms* ❍ *No Meals* Ⓜ *Bugis.*

🍸 Nightlife

★ Atlas

BARS | Truly one of a kind, this grandiose bar with a high, ornate ceiling is mesmerizing—and one of the most buzzed-about lounges in Singapore. It holds more than 1,000 gins and 250 Champagnes, including a rare bubbly that was served on the *Titanic* (yes, the actual *Titanic*). The revolving, themed menus are inspired by the 1930s with a strong focus on (you guessed it) gin and Champagne. For a splurge, any cocktail can be made with your Champagne of choice, and there's also a dining and high tea menu. ✉ *Parkview Square, 600 North Bridge Rd., Kampong Glam* ☎ *6396–4466* ⊕ *www.atlasbar.sg* Ⓜ *Bugis.*

BluJaz Cafe

LIVE MUSIC | An institution of the Kampong Glam area and Singapore's live music scene, this lounge-bar fills three floors and has a spacious outdoor seating area. Known as a hub for stand-up comedy acts, live music (especially jazz), and international DJs, it always has a lively vibe. The bar menu is a mix of Eastern and Western dishes. The owners also own the nearby Mexican restaurant Piedra Niegra, on the corner of Beach Road and Haji Lane, and have a second outpost on Pekin Street. ✉ *11 Bali La., Kampong Glam* ☎ *9710–6156* ⊕ *www.blujazcafe.net* Ⓜ *Bugis.*

Ginett Singapore

WINE BARS | Drinking isn't a cheap affair in Singapore unless you plan to guzzle beers at a hawker center, and sometimes not even then. That's exactly why Ginett deserves special mention for its extensive wine menu with affordable pours for both glasses and full bottles. There's also a full (mainly French) food menu—items from the charcoal grill are recommended. ⊠ *Hotel G Singapore, 200 Middle Rd., Kampong Glam* ☎ *6809–7989* ⊕ *www.randblab. com/ginett-sg* Ⓜ *Bugis.*

★ **Good Luck**

PUBS | If the only Singapore beer you're acquainted with is Tiger, you're in luck—quite literally—at this bar offering nine different local brews on tap. The offerings range from pilsners to IPAs and even a stout; ask the bar staff to decode each to match your preferred beer profile. Their menu of local bites like XO Carrot Cake and a ramly burger with all the trimmings does a good job of lining your stomach so you can drink well into the night. ⊠ *9 Haji Lane, Kampong Glam* ☎ *8028–4804* ⊕ *www.goodluckgoodluck.sg* Ⓜ *Bugis.*

🎟 Performing Arts

FILM
★ The Projector

FILM | What was once Singapore's historic Golden Theatre has been transformed into an indie theater space and hangout spot for Singapore's creative talents. There's always something going on, thanks to an eclectic rotation of films (schedules are released every Tuesday), documentaries, festivals, and themed screenings. The Intermission Bar bar enables you to enjoy a glass of wine or a cold beer during a show. There are also pop-up Projector locations at The Picturehouse. ⊠ *Golden Mile Tower, 6001 Beach Rd., Level 5, Kampong Glam* ⊕ *www.theprojector.sg* Ⓜ *Bugis.*

🛍 Shopping

CLOTHING AND ACCESSORIES
★ AS'FALL

WOMEN'S CLOTHING | Haji Lane is known for turning up some of the island's more unusual fashion finds so it's no surprise that founder Astou Montfort decided to set up shop there. In particular, AS'FALL's seasonal collection of made-in-Singapore clothing sports intricate embroidery specially crafted by Senegalese artisans for the brand. With limited runs and monthly rotating cultural patterns and motifs, each season sees different ethnic fabrics (batik, wax African fabric) being used, turning out truly unique luxe-yet-ethical clothing. ✉ *28 Haji La., Kampong Glam* ☎ *9177–2872* ⊕ *www.asfall.com* Ⓜ *Bugis.*

Crafune

LEATHER GOODS | Rather than buy a ready-made memento, why not spend a few hours learning the art of leathercraft and personalizing your own souvenir? At local leather brand Crafune, the 3 Small Accessories workshop ($65) teaches one how to craft and personalize a key holder, coin pouch, and card sleeve. If you're short on time, the retail store has a variety of leather goods to choose from. ✉ *38 Haji La., #02-01, Kampong Glam* ☎ *9107–5168* ⊕ *www.crafune.com* Ⓜ *Bugis.*

NEIGHBORHOODS

★ Haji Lane

NEIGHBORHOODS | Need a break from Singapore's fun but sometimes suffocating mall culture? Head to the open air and this strip of restored shophouses, which stretches from Beach Road to North Bridge Road in Kampong Glam. Among the numerous indie fashion and lifestyle shops like Flame Vintage Store (genuine branded vintage finds), Crafune (DIY leather goods), Hygge (imported bags, handcrafted accessories), and The Nail Social (which uses nontoxic, eco-friendly, fair-trade, and cruelty-free nail products). The best way to tackle Haji Lane is to simply give yourself a few hours to wander and window-shop at random. ✉ *Between Beach Rd. and North Bridge Rd., Kampong Glam* Ⓜ *Bugis.*

PERFUME

★ Jamal Kazura Aromatics

PERFUME | Locals flock to Jamal Kazura Aromatics for high-quality perfumes and essential oils. Allow about 30 minutes for a consultation with one of the shop's staff members, who'll ask you a few questions about your lifestyle and favorite smells before concocting your personalized take-home fragrance. Call ahead to make an appointment. There are two other nearby outlets: one at 21 Bussorah Street and another at 39 Bussorah Street. ✉ *728 North Bridge Rd., Kampong Glam* ☎ *6293–2350* ⊕ *www.jamal-kazura-aromatics.myshopify.com/* Ⓜ *Jalan Besar, Bugis.*

Sifr Aromatics

PERFUME | The hip offshoot of local perfumer Jamal Kazura Aromatics offers a more bespoke experience than its parent store. Drop in to custom blend a scent (reservations required; put aside at least 90 minutes) at the elaborate perfume organ. Aside from the sweet, woody base note of oud, unusual ingredients like ambergris, agarwood chips, and white amber can be incorporated. There are also pre-made scents, soy-based candles, and vials of essential oil for sale, as well as perfume workshops for enthusiasts. ✉ *42 Arab St., Kampong Glam* ☎ *6392–1966* ⊕ *www.sifr.sg* Ⓜ *Bugis.*

TEXTILES

Toko Aljunied

FABRICS | Since 1940, this heritage business has sold authentic batik (traditional hand-dyed textiles originating from Java, Indonesia) either by the meter or as pre-made pieces to bring home. They also sell small gifts, tablecloths, and napkins. Store assistants can help with sizing and pairing matching accessories. ✉ *91 Arab St., Kampong Glam* ☎ *6294–6897* Ⓜ *Bugis.*

 Activities

SPAS

Green Apple Spa

SPAS | When you're fatigued from exploring the city, head to this trusted spa for a foot massage that takes place in a mini-movie theater setting, complete with comfortable recliner chairs. It's open until 4 am, and the treatment menu includes other services like tui'na and deep-tissue massages. There's always a special promotion going on, so you might just stay longer than intended. ✉ *765 North Bridge Rd., Kampong Glam* ☎ *6299–1555* ⊕ *www. facebook.com/greenapplespa/* 🖼 *Foot massage from $30; body massage from $63* Ⓜ *Bugis.*

Bugis

A great base from which to explore the historic Kampong Glam area, which is within walking distance, Bugis buzzes with a youthful energy that gives it the vibe of a university town. It's also a shopping hub known for its youth-friendly stores, where you can find everything from cosplay outfits to game arcades. The area has come a long way: it was Singapore's red light district until the 1980s, when the government transformed into the flourishing retail precinct it is today.

◉ Sights

Kwan Im Thong Hood Cho Temple

TEMPLE | The dusty, incense-filled interior of this popular temple has altars heaped with hundreds of small statues of gods from the Chinese pantheon. Of the hundreds of deities, Kwan Im, more often known as Kuan Yin, is perhaps most dear to the hearts of

Buddhist Singaporeans. Legend has it that just as she was about to enter Nirvana, she heard a plaintive cry from Earth. Filled with compassion, she gave up her place in paradise to devote herself to alleviating the pain of those on Earth. Her name means "to see and hear all." People in search of advice come to the Kwan Im temple, shake *cham si* (bamboo fortune sticks), and wait for an answer. The gods are most receptive on days of a new or full moon. ✉ *178 Waterloo St., Bugis* ⊕ *www.facebook.com/kwanimthonghoodchotemple* Ⓜ *Bugis.*

🛏 Hotels

Andaz Singapore

$$ | HOTEL | This energetic five-star hotel by the Hyatt group features locally inspired decor, communal spaces with all-day refreshments, an infinity pool, and a popular rooftop bar (Mr Stork) with 360-degree skyline views (and tepees for you to stargaze from). **Pros:** warm, inviting rooms; floor-to-ceiling windows; complimentary minibar and all-day refreshments in the Sunroom lounge. **Cons:** reception is on the 25th floor; no porters; hotel is located within an office building. ⑤ *Rooms from: S$250* ✉ *DUO Tower, 5 Fraser St., Level 25, Bugis* ☎ *6408–1234* ⊕ *www.hyatt.com* 🛏 *347 rooms* ⑽ *No Meals* Ⓜ *Bugis.*

InterContinental Singapore

$$$ | HOTEL | FAMILY | With its gorgeous Peranakan-style furnishings, silk wall coverings, elegant chandeliers, and rooms styled after 1920s heritage shophouses, this pet-friendly Bugis Junction hotel is luxuriously local. **Pros:** connected to the Bugis MRT station; pet- and family-friendly; 24-hour fitness center. **Cons:** neighborhood gets busy on weekends; a distance from the main business and shopping areas; rooms feel slightly closed in. ⑤ *Rooms from: S$390* ✉ *80 Middle Rd., Bugis* ☎ *6338–7600* ⊕ *www.singapore.intercontinental.com* 🛏 *403 rooms* ⑽ *No Meals* Ⓜ *Bugis.*

🎭 Performing Arts

BALLET

Singapore Ballet Ltd

MODERN DANCE | FAMILY | Founded in 1988, this dance company (previously known as The Singapore Dance Company) has a repertoire that ranges from classical to contemporary ballet. Periodic performances are held at the Esplanade Theatre, as well as on outdoor stages in Fort Canning Park. It also offers various dance classes catering to different skill levels. ✉ *Bugis +, 201 Victoria St., #07–02/03, Bugis* ☎ *6338–0611* ⊕ *www.singaporeballet.org.*

Chapter 7

ORCHARD

Updated by
Olivia Lee

⊙ Sights   🍴 Restaurants   🛏 Hotels   ⬤ Shopping   🍸 Nightlife

★★★★☆   ★★★★★   ★★★★★   ★★★★★   ★★★★★

NEIGHBORHOOD SNAPSHOT

TOP EXPERIENCES

■ **Shop 'til you drop:** Orchard Road is right up there with New York's Madison Avenue or London's Oxford Street.

■ **The Botanic Gardens:** You could spend days walking around these world-class tropical gardens.

■ **Emerald Hill:** This pretty street, full of colorful Peranakan-style houses that have been turned into bars.

■ **Sky-high views:** Immerse yourself in 360-degree views of the city from the 56th floor of a mall.

■ **The city's largest bookstore:** Books Kinokuniya, in Ngee Ann City Mall, is home to a sprawling maze of tomes.

■ **Local hidden gems:** Almost every mall on Orchard Road has a food court in the basement.

GETTING HERE

Orchard Road stretches for just over 2 km (1.25 miles), served by the Orchard, Somerset, and Dhoby Ghaut MRT stations, all of which are on the North South Line (red). Bus stops line Orchard and Scotts roads, but the one-way system can be a little confusing. To go east, you can use any of the Orchard Road stops, but you have to cross behind the street to Orchard Boulevard for buses heading towards the west.

PLANNING YOUR TIME

Set aside a few hours to peruse the malls and watch the flood of pedestrians strolling down the wide sidewalks, then return at night for dinner and drinks.

VIEWFINDER

■ Surround yourself in 360-degree views at ION Sky—56 floors above Orchard Road. It's a unique opportunity to see the otherwise towering malls and office blocks of Orchard from above, and on a clear day you can see right across the island.

PAUSE HERE

■ Orchard Road is one of the busiest streets in Singapore, so there aren't many places to find peace. Fortunately, you have the wonderful Botanic Gardens near the top, and **Istana Park** near the bottom, the latter a small oasis between busy roads, with a floral display that changes according to the celebratory events of the year.

Orchard Road, Singapore's bustling shopping drag, is a three-lane-wide, one-way street flanked by tree-lined walkways. The road was named for the fruit plantations found here in the 19th century. The first malls made their debut back in the 1970s, and it's been under nonstop development ever since.

The road is a true shopper's paradise. Instead of being lined with traditional shops, it's lined with enormous malls, each one housing countless fashion, retail, and food outlets, and each one providing a cooling escape from Singapore's sweat-inducing outside world. In fact, wide underground tunnels connect the various shopping centers, so you never really have to leave the air-conditioning.

Orchard Road's ION and Somerset 313 malls are among the two most popular, packed with top fashion labels across multiple floors. The Shaw Centre is another good choice, loved for its IMAX cinema and excellent basement food court. Because of Orchard's convenient location—a central point between the east, west, and downtown districts—you can find a number of the city's best hotels here. It's also a foodie paradise, with restaurants of all kinds crammed into every mall on every street.

In the evening, the street transforms from a shopping domain to a place for wining and dining. Especially popular is colorful Emerald Hill, a lane filled with restored, traditional, bright red and green shophouses, where you can get a drink at one of the laid-back bars. And just one stop on the MRT brings you to Newton Circus (of *Crazy Rich Asians* fame)—a hawker center that is always packed at night thanks to its great (albeit a little overpriced) seafood and local treats.

Orchard

◉ Sights

Orchard Road isn't especially known for its sights; people mainly come here to eat and shop. Still, there are several places of interest worth checking out—provided your hands aren't too full of shopping bags. Of note are the nearby Botanic Gardens, as well as a number of independent galleries and theaters that showcase work from local and international artists.

Goodwood Park Hotel

HOTEL | Though it's 30 years younger than the more widely known Raffles, this hotel is just as much a landmark. Built in 1900, it was previously used as a German club and, during World War II, as a Japanese army headquarters. In 1989, the Tower Wing, with its pointy terracotta-colored roof, was named a national monument. Today, the interior is modeled on European designs, and, in true British fashion, you can enjoy an elegant afternoon tea near the lobby at L'Espresso—the perfect break from all that shopping. ⊠ *22 Scotts Rd., Orchard* ☎ *6737–7411* ⊕ *www.goodwoodparkhotel.com* Ⓜ *Orchard.*

ION Art Gallery

ART GALLERY | ION Art showcases modern and contemporary art and design, including multimedia and digital works. Part of the ION Mall, this free gallery focuses on Asian artists—both emerging and established—with a spectrum of art-based events and exhibitions held throughout the year. ⊠ *ION Orchard, 2 Orchard Turn, #4, Orchard* ☎ *6238–8228* ⊕ *www.ionorchard.com/ion-art* Ⓜ *Orchard.*

★ ION Sky

VIEWPOINT | ION Sky offers panoramic views of Singapore from the 56th floor of ION Mall, 718 feet above the ground. It's free to enter, but only after spending S$50 in ION Mall (you need to download the ION Orchard app, then scan your receipt to receive your QR ticket). Your admission includes a complimentary welcome drink at 1-Atico Lounge. Alongside the great views are a number of interactive exhibits, including films screened on the glass walls and historic portrayals of how Singapore once looked. ⊠ *ION Orchard, 2 Orchard Turn, Level 56, Orchard* ☎ *6238–8228* ⊕ *www.ionorchard.com/ion-sky* 🖾 *Free (with S$50 purchase at Ion Mall)* ⊙ *Closed Sun. and Mon.* Ⓜ *Orchard.*

The Istana

GOVERNMENT BUILDING | Built in 1869, this elegant neo-Palladian style building set in extensive tropical gardens once served as the British colonial governor's residence. Today, it is the official residence of the president of Singapore (Istana means "palace" in Malay). The building and grounds are open to the public only on the holidays listed on its website. On the first Sunday of each month, a changing-of-the-guard ceremony at the main gates on Orchard Road is held at 5:45 pm. ⊠ *35 Orchard Rd., Orchard*

☎ 8720–6021 ⊕ www.istana.gov.sg ✉ S$2 entry for foreign tourists, self-guided tour S$4, guided tour S$10 Ⓜ Dhoby Ghaut.

Library@Orchard

LIBRARY | If you like books and appreciate beautiful design, you will enjoy an hour spent within the walls of Library@Orchard. There are more than 100,000 books housed in the swirling, spiraling bookcases, making it popular among social media users who like to snap and share the intricate designs. It's also a lovely spot to escape Singapore's scorching heat. ✉ 277 Orchard Rd., #03–12 / #04–11, Orchard ⊕ www.nlb.gov.sg Ⓜ Somerset.

★ Newton Food Centre

MARKET | Also known as Newton Circus, this is one of the best-known hawker centers in town. (The "circus" refers to a roundabout, as in Piccadilly Circus.) It's a great place to visit at night, when the atmosphere is buzzing, and it's usually very busy no matter which evening you go. Food vendors here often get pushy with their menus, so walk with confidence if you don't want to be accosted. Note that you can sit anywhere: it can feel strange buying food at one stall, then sitting down in front of another, but that's the practice. In fact, it can sometimes be hard to find a table, so grab whatever you can get. The barbecue seafood stalls are famous here, though things like tiger prawns and chilli crab are priced by weight, so have the bill tallied up ahead of time to avoid expensive surprises. ✉ 500 Clemenceau Ave. N, Orchard Ⓜ Newton.

Opera Gallery

ART GALLERY | This cool, contemporary space is one of Singapore's most well-known galleries, with works of art from some of the greatest painters in the world, including Salvador Dalí and Andy Warhol. The gallery, which also has outlets from Paris to New York, hosts a number of specialist exhibitions throughout the year in the Singapore branch. Many of the paintings and sculptures are also available to buy, though expect a hefty price tag. ✉ ION Orchard, 2 Orchard Turn, #02–16, Orchard ☎ 6735–2618 ⊕ www.operagallery. com Ⓜ Orchard.

Peranakan Place

PLAZA/SQUARE | The building on the corner of Orchard and Emerald Hill roads is a masterpiece—albeit a somewhat diluted one—of Peranakan architecture. This style, a blend of Chinese and Malay aesthetics, emerged in the 19th century, when Chinese people born in what was then called the Straits Settlements (including Singapore) adopted, and often adapted, Malay fashion, cuisine, and design. The surrounding area is now a mix of upscale residences, with renovated shophouses doubling as bars and

KEY

1 *Sights*
1 *Restaurants*
1 *Quick Bites*
1 *Hotels*

0 ⊢——————⊣ 1,000ft
0 ⊢——————⊣ 200m

Orchard

Sights

Goodwood Park
Hotel, **5**

ION Art Gallery, **2**

ION Sky, **3**

The Istana, **8**

Library@Orchard, **6**

Newton
Food Centre, **9**

Opera Gallery, **4**

Peranakan Place, **7**

Singapore Botanic
Gardens, **1**

Restaurants

Akashi, **2**

Blue Label Pizza
& Wine, **12**

Corner House, **1**

Food Opera
@ ION Orchard, **5**

Food Republic @
Shaw House, **7**

Hai Di Lao, **13**

Hainanese
Delicacy, **10**

Jinjo, **8**

Les Amis, **9**

Nam Nam
Noodle Bar, **6**

Soup
Restaurant, **11**

Sushi Kimura, **4**

Thai Tantric, **3**

Quick Bites

Bacha Coffee, **1**

Glyph Supply Co, **3**

Signature KOI
@ ION Orchard, **2**

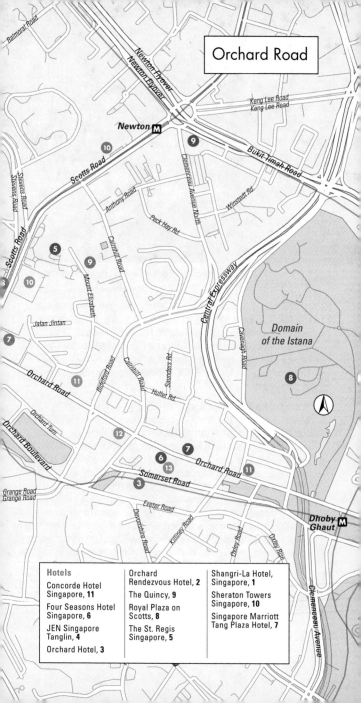

Orchard Road

Hotels

Concorde Hotel Singapore, **11**

Four Seasons Hotel Singapore, **6**

JEN Singapore Tanglin, **4**

Orchard Hotel, **3**

Orchard Rendezvous Hotel, **2**

The Quincy, **9**

Royal Plaza on Scotts, **8**

The St. Regis Singapore, **5**

Shangri-La Hotel, Singapore, **1**

Sheraton Towers Singapore, **10**

Singapore Marriott Tang Plaza Hotel, **7**

A "Curtain of Roots" at the Singapore Botanic Gardens leads to many stunning green spaces.

restaurants. Parts of Emerald Hill, from Orchard Road through the Ice Cold Beer bar, are for pedestrians only; there are several outdoor cafés and restaurants along the stretch. Stroll the arcaded street, and check out fretted woodwork, pastel washes, ornate wall tiles, and other typical Peranakan touches. ✉ *180 Orchard Rd., Orchard* ☎ *6732–6966* ⊕ *www.peranakanplace.com* Ⓜ *Somerset.*

★ Singapore Botanic Gardens
GARDEN | FAMILY | The first site in Singapore to gain UNESCO Heritage status is also the first and only tropical botanic gardens in the world to make the list. Once you start to explore the winding trails of the enormous park, which sprawls across more than 128 acres of lush greenery, you'll understand why. It is neatly segmented into different gardens featuring all the hallmarks of Victorian design—gazebos, pavilions, and ornate bandstands included. Highlights are the National Orchid Garden, showcasing over 1,000 species of brightly colored blooms, and the Ginger Garden, where several hundred varieties of ginger grow. Try to time your visit to coincide with the free guided tours that almost always take place around 9 am on Saturday (see the National Parks website for more details). ✉ *1 Cluny Rd., Botanic Gardens* ☎ *800/471–7300 Singapore Botanic Gardens, 6475–5060 Orchid Garden* ⊕ *www. nparks.gov.sg/sbg* ▦ *Free* Ⓜ *Botanic Gardens.*

 **Restaurants**

★ Akashi

$$ | **JAPANESE** | This intimate restaurant almost succeeds in transporting you to Japan, with its traditional tea-house decor, its kimono-clad servers, and its chefs who belt out *irrashimase* (welcome). Alongside a generous sushi menu, Akashi serves delicious, beautifully presented set meals featuring green tea noodles and crispy tempura or thick udon and fried tofu. **Known for:** beautiful sashimi plates; staff in pretty kimonos; authentic Japanese atmosphere. $ *Average main: S$24* ✉ *Orchard Rendezvous Hotel, 1 Tanglin Rd., #01–01A, Orchard* ☎ *6732–4438* ⊕ *akashi.com.sg* Ⓜ *Orchard.*

Blue Label Pizza & Wine

$$ | **PIZZA** | Dive into stone-fired pizza at this hip spot in Mandarin Gallery. The long-fermented pizza dough is crisp and generously topped with unique ingredients like sliced steak and French's mustard bechamel ("I Wish I Was A Baller"), or chorizo ragu with Hokkaido octopus ("Summer in San Sebastian"). **Known for:** thin-crust pizza; great wine list; 1970s and '80s rock music. $ *Average main: S$40* ✉ *Mandarin Gallery, 333A Orchard Rd., #03–02, Orchard* ☎ *9785–7799* ⊕ *bluelabelpizza.com* Ⓜ *Somerset.*

Food Opera @ ION Orchard

$ | **ASIAN** | Celebrating Singaporean heritage dishes across 27 different vendors, this basement food court's stalls sell everything from crispy fried carrot cake to spicy prawn noodles and rich chicken satay. The food court takes its design inspiration from the British colonial decor of the early 1890s, with a light blue, ivory, and copper-gold palette, and lush green plants. **Known for:** old-school design; Singaporean heritage dishes; friendly vendors. $ *Average main: S$4* ✉ *ION Orchard, 2 Orchard Turn, #B4–03/04, Orchard* ☎ *6509–9198* ⊕ *foodrepublic.com.sg/food-republic-outlets/food-opera-ion* Ⓜ *Orchard.*

★ Corner House

$$$$ | **ASIAN FUSION** | Nestled among the exotic flora of the Botanic Gardens and in a colonial house named after an important 20th-century botanist, Corner House is chef David Thien's "ode to Asia with French undertones." The setting is exceptionally romantic, matched only by the omakase experience and curated wine list. The menu uses French techniques to present Asian ingredients in innovative ways, and each dish comes with an accompanying note to expand on the chef's inspiration. **Known for:** historic location; menu-inspiration cards; French-Asian fusion fine dining. $ *Average main: S$228* ✉ *Singapore Botanic Gardens; 1 Cluny Rd, Botanic Gardens* ⊹ *Use the Nassim gate at junction of*

Breakfast of Champions: Kaya Toast 🍴

Singaporeans love kaya toast, a traditional breakfast dish consisting of two slices of charcoal-toasted bread, slabs of chilled butter, and a generous spreading of kaya jam, which is made from coconut milk, eggs, and sugar. This is usually served alongside two soft-boiled eggs—mixed with dark soy sauce—and a strong cup of local *kopi* (coffee) sweetened with condensed milk. The dish is said to have originated when Hainanese Chinese ship workers started adapting the food served in British shops to the local *kopi tiam* (coffee stall) culture of Singapore. Western jam was replaced with local coconut jams, and tea was replaced with local kopi.

One of the most popular outlets serving this sickly-sweet breakfast treat is **Ya Kun Kaya Toast**, a coffee shop established in 1944 that's now synonymous with the dish. There are seven outlets along Orchard Road alone, as well as in other countries. Another popular chain is **Killiney Kopitiam**, the oldest Hainanese coffee shop in Singapore, dating from 1919.

Ya Kun Kaya Toast has several varieties on its menu, including cheese toast with kaya and butter sugar toast. If you haven't tried it before, play it safe with the classic "kaya toast with butter set"—but be prepared for the inevitable sugar rush.

Cluny Rd. and Nassim Rd. ☎ *6469–1000* ⊕ *cornerhouse.com.sg* ⊙ *Closed Mon.* Ⓜ *Botanic Gardens.*

Food Republic @ Shaw House

$ | ASIAN | In the basement of Shaw House, this vibrant food court has more than 20 colorful stalls selling everything from Thai curries to duck wonton. It's always busy at lunch and dinner, so do as the locals do, and *chope* (reserve) a space by leaving a packet of tissues or a personal item at the table before you order. **Known for:** lots of local dishes; contemporary design; great juices. $ *Average main: S$4* ⊠ *350 Orchard Rd., #B1–02, Orchard* ☎ *6235–0995* ⊕ *shawcentre.sg* Ⓜ *Somerset.*

Hai Di Lao

$$ | CHINESE | FAMILY | There is always a very long line at this do-it-yourself Chinese hotpot restaurant, but in Hai Di Lao's case, that's not such a bad thing—while you wait, you can enjoy quirky (and free) services, treats, and swag like gel manicures, popcorn, ice cream, and iPhone screen-protector replacements. It can sometimes take several hours to reach the front of the line, but when you do, you'll realize what the wait was for: the dining

experience is highly theatrical. **Known for:** DIY hotpot (cooking meats and veg in broth); waiters who perform "noodle dances"; free dishes in exchange for completing challenges. $ *Average main: S$30* ✉ *313@Somerset, 313 Orchard Rd., #04–23/24, Orchard* ☎ *6835–7227* ⊕ *www.haidilao-inc.com/sg* Ⓜ *Somerset.*

★ Hainanese Delicacy

$ | **SINGAPOREAN** | Despite being hidden away on Level 5 of the Far East Plaza mall, Hainanese Delicacy always has a long line outside at lunchtime. It's renowned among locals as serving one of the best Hainanese chicken rice dishes on Orchard Road. **Known for:** the best chicken rice around; braised eggs as a side dish; local flavors at low prices. $ *Average main: S$5* ✉ *Far East Plaza, 14 Scotts Rd., #05–116, Orchard* ⊹ *Up the escalators to level five* ☎ *6734–0639* ⊙ *Closed Mon.* Ⓜ *Somerset.*

★ Jinjo

$$$ | **JAPANESE** | The decor at this chic sumiyaki restaurant celebrating Japanese charcoal-grilling is as authentic as the food. It's styled after traditional Japanese izakayas, with bar seating where you can watch the chefs delicately fan the meat and vegetables cooked over open coals. **Known for:** Izakaya decor; Jinjo-branded sake; small plates. $ *Average main: S$45* ✉ *Shaw Centre, 1 Scotts Rd., #02–19/20, Orchard* ☎ *6732–2165* ⊕ *www.jinjo.com. sg* Ⓜ *Somerset.*

★ Les Amis

$$$$ | **FRENCH** | Mingle with Singaporean tycoons and celebrities at the island's finest French restaurant, where you can admire the adjoining bar's grand chandelier and curtain-draped wine cabinets before adjourning to the intimate dining area. The breathtakingly expensive seasonal menu changes regularly, but expect such exquisite French classics as foie gras, roasted whole pigeon, and white asparagus. **Known for:** unmatched service; enormous wine collection; chandelier-lit dining. $ *Average main: S$415* ✉ *Shaw Centre, 1 Scotts Rd., #01–16, Orchard* ☎ *6733–2225* ⊕ *www. lesamis.com.sg* Ⓜ *Orchard.*

Nam Nam Noodle Bar

$ | **VIETNAMESE** | The enormous bowls of *pho* at this casual quick-serve noodle bar are excellent. At lunch time, you can get a bowl of chicken or beef *pho*, a green papaya salad, and a tea or coffee for under S$14. **Known for:** huge bowls of pho; great side dishes; beautiful tableware. $ *Average main: S$14* ✉ *Wheelock Place, 501 Orchard Rd., #B2–02, Orchard* ☎ *6735–1488* ⊕ *namnam.net* Ⓜ *Orchard.*

Soup Restaurant

$$ | CHINESE | Don't be fooled: soup is hardly the only thing on the menu at this popular Cantonese chain. It's an excellent spot to taste a variety of Chinese-style food, from double-boiled pork ribs and dried scallops to tofu prawns and chicken rice, perhaps the most popular dish in Singapore. **Known for:** signature Cantonese classics; Samsui ginger chicken; excellent homemade tofu. ⑤ *Average main: S$25* ⊠ *Paragon Mall, 290 Orchard Rd., #B1–07, Orchard* ☎ *6333–6228* ⊕ *www.souprestaurant.com.sg* Ⓜ *Orchard.*

★ Sushi Kimura

$$$$ | SUSHI | Experience Edomae-style delicacies at this 22-seater sushi restaurant in Palais Renaissance. All ingredients are delivered directly from Japan, including organic rice from a farm in Yamagata prefecture and spring water from Hokkaido. **Known for:** high-grade sushi; imported Japanese ingredients; traditional interior. ⑤ *Average main: S$180* ⊠ *Palais Renaissance, 390 Orchard Rd., #01–07, Orchard* ☎ *6734–3520* ⊕ *www.sushikimura.com.sg* ⊗ *Closed Sun. and Mon.* Ⓜ *Orchard.*

★ Thai Tantric

$$ | THAI | This windowless, no-frills, Thai restaurant might be tucked away on the third floor of the slightly sleazy Orchard Towers, but the locals still pile in for the delicious, authentic, and very affordable food. The menu packs all the classics, from massaman curry to traditional fishcakes, each served in generous portions. **Known for:** quick and cheap; authentic flavors and huge portions; great green curry. ⑤ *Average main: S$15* ⊠ *Orchard Tower, 400 Orchard Rd., #03–44, Orchard* ⊹ *Head into the Orchard Towers entrance by the 7/11 and take the elevator to Level 3.* ☎ *9625–7523* ⊕ *www.facebook.com/ThaiTantricSingapore* ⊗ *Closed Sun.* Ⓜ *Orchard.*

☕ Coffee and Quick Bites

★ Bacha Coffee

$ | CAFÉ | The historic Moroccan coffee brand has a beautiful café/dining room on ION Orchard's first floor. No visit is a quick one though: you may come for a coffee and pastry, but you'll soon find yourself whiling away the time exploring the vast array of 100% arabica coffee beans housed in large sunset orange tins. **Known for:** arabica coffee from around the world; traditional café interior; excellent pastries and cakes. ⑤ *Average main: S$12* ⊠ *ION Orchard, 2 Orchard Turn, #01–15/16, Orchard* ☎ *6363–1910* ⊕ *bachacoffee.com* Ⓜ *Orchard.*

Glyph Supply Co

$ | **CAFÉ** | For a serious cup of coffee near Somerset, drop by this pristine-white café that is usually full of coffee aficionados sipping on in-house roasted brews. You can also pick up fresh beans and coffee-making accoutrements to take home. **Known for:** well-roasted coffee; cool, modern space; coffee-making supplies. ⑤ *Average main: S$10* ⊠ *111 Somerset, 111 Somerset Rd., #01–06, Orchard* ⊕ *www.glyphsupply.co* Ⓜ *Somerset.*

Signature KOI @ ION Orchard

$ | **CAFÉ** | If tea is your thing, be sure to visit Signature Koi—pioneers of the bubble tea culture in Singapore. Try the Earl Grey milk tea with signature pearls (tapioca balls) for the original experience. **Known for:** bubble tea pioneers; flavored green teas; cozy seating space. ⑤ *Average main: S$8* ⊠ *ION Orchard, 2 Orchard Turn, #B3–15/16, Orchard* ☎ *6612–0385* ⊕ *www.koithe.com* Ⓜ *Orchard.*

🛏 Hotels

Concorde Hotel Singapore

$$ | **HOTEL** | Once appropriately called the Glass Hotel, the Concorde has a glass canopy that curves down from the ninth story over the entrance, facing southeast for good fortune. **Pros:** nice swimming pool; clean, spacious rooms; boutique style. **Cons:** no hotel smoking area; could do with a refresh; breakfast is average. ⑤ *Rooms from: S$270* ⊠ *100 Orchard Rd., Orchard* ☎ *6733–8855* ⊕ *singapore.concordehotelsresorts.com* ⇌ *407 rooms* ⦿ *No Meals* Ⓜ *Dhoby Ghaut.*

★ Four Seasons Hotel Singapore

$$$ | **HOTEL** | **FAMILY** | Rooms are spacious at this refined hotel with a design inspired by the nearby Singapore Botanic Gardens, including a natural color palette with Peranakan tiles and Asian art. **Pros:** family-friendly; great selection of dining options; 24-hour gym and outside pool on the 20th floor. **Cons:** on a busy road; surrounded by malls; interiors are a little dated. ⑤ *Rooms from: S$500* ⊠ *190 Orchard Blvd., Orchard* ☎ *6734–1110* ⊕ *www.fourseasons.com/singapore* ⇌ *279 rooms* ⦿ *No Meals* Ⓜ *Orchard.*

JEN Singapore Tanglin

$$ | **HOTEL** | Connected to the Tanglin Mall, this hotel (part of the Shangri-La group) has all the essentials—including a lovely outdoor pool surrounded by leafy greenery and comfortable rooms with plenty of light from their bay windows. **Pros:** 24-hour room service; great access to malls and nearby MRT; chilli crab at Ah Hoi's Kitchen. **Cons:** small rooms; breakfast is a little too busy; smokers have to leave the hotel for a smoking area around

the corner. $ Rooms from: S$200 ⊠ 1A Cuscaden Rd., Orchard ☎ 6738–2222, 0800/028–3337 for reservations in the U.K., 800/565–5050 for reservations in the U.S. ⊕ www.shangri-la.com ➷ 565 rooms ¹⊙¹ No Meals Ⓜ Orchard Boulevard.

Orchard Hotel

$$ | HOTEL | FAMILY | The stellar location at the top of Orchard Road has no doubt contributed to this hotel's popularity, not to mention its range of well-designed rooms and suites. **Pros:** premier lounge access; family-friendly rooms; beautiful Singaporean furnishings. **Cons:** lines for reception at busy times; busy street; limited amenities. $ Rooms from: S$280 ⊠ 442 Orchard Rd., Orchard ☎ 6734–7766 ⊕ www.millenniumhotels.com/en/singapore/orchard-hotel-singapore ➷ 656 rooms ¹⊙¹ No Meals Ⓜ Orchard.

Orchard Rendezvous Hotel

$$ | HOTEL | FAMILY | In this warm and colorful Mediterranean hotel, the botanical-inspired rooms are spacious, and family rooms have extra single beds and a dining area. **Pros:** family-friendly rooms; stylish Club Lounge; outdoor pool bar. **Cons:** surrounded by shopping malls; busy on the weekends; bathrooms are a little dated. $ Rooms from: S$315 ⊠ 1 Tanglin Rd., Orchard ☎ 6737–1133 ⊕ www.rendezvoushotels.com ➷ 385 rooms ¹⊙¹ No Meals Ⓜ Orchard.

★ The Quincy

$$$ | HOTEL | This boutique hotel bills itself as a refuge where you can savor life to the fullest in style, and every element of your stay here reflects that sentiment. **Pros:** infinity pool overlooking the city; quiet location; complimentary minibar. **Cons:** food is not as great as outside the hotel; smaller pool, limited seating; busy breakfast. $ Rooms from: S$360 ⊠ 22 Mt. Elizabeth, Orchard ☎ 6738–5888 ⊕ www.quincy.com.sg ➷ 108 rooms ¹⊙¹ Free Breakfast Ⓜ Orchard.

Royal Plaza on Scotts

$$ | HOTEL | The lobby here makes a bold statement, with Italian marble floors, two grand staircases, Burmese teak paneling, stained-glass skylights, and tapestries. **Pros:** comfy beds; biodegradable amenities; great buffet restaurant. **Cons:** some rooms are still a little dated; some rooms have street noise; room service is not 24 hours. $ Rooms from: S$350 ⊠ T Galleria By DFS, 25 Scotts Rd., Orchard ☎ 6737–7966 ⊕ www.royalplaza.com.sg ➷ 511 rooms ¹⊙¹ No Meals Ⓜ Orchard.

★ Shangri-La Hotel, Singapore

$$$ | HOTEL | FAMILY | Often referred to as "Singapore's other botanical garden" (due to its 15 acres of tropical landscaped gardens), this oasis has been one of Singapore's top hotels for more than three decades. **Pros:** 15 acres of flowers and plants; beautiful spa and pool; indoor and outdoor family facilities. **Cons:** a short hike to Orchard Road and MRT; dated exterior; breakfast area can be a little too busy. $ Rooms from: S$380 ⊠ 22 Orange Grove Rd., Orchard ☎ 6737–3644, 800/028–3337 for reservations in the UK, 866/565–5050 for reservations in the U.S. ⊕ www.shangri-la.com/singapore/shangrila ⮑ 972 rooms ◉ No Meals Ⓜ Stevens.

Sheraton Towers Singapore

$$ | HOTEL | Just a quick walk from Orchard Road, this relaxed hotel is also within walking distance of the hawker stalls at Newton Circus. **Pros:** good breakfast buffet; comfortable rooms; near Newton Circus. **Cons:** aging property; street noise on lower floors; some rooms could do with a refresh. $ Rooms from: S$310 ⊠ 39 Scotts Rd., Orchard ☎ 6737–6888 ⊕ www.marriott.com ⮑ 421 rooms ◉ No Meals Ⓜ Newton.

★ Singapore Marriott Tang Plaza Hotel

$$$ | HOTEL | This striking, 30-story, pagoda-inspired property stands at the intersection of Orchard and Scotts roads in the heart of Singapore's shopping district. **Pros:** excellent location; unique architecture and design; exlcusive access to M Club lounge. **Cons:** busy street outside; street-facing rooms are noisy; slow elevators. $ Rooms from: S$430 ⊠ 320 Orchard Rd., Orchard ☎ 6735–5800 ⊕ www.marriott.com ⮑ 403 rooms ◉ No Meals Ⓜ Orchard.

The St. Regis Singapore

$$$ | HOTEL | The high rates at this luxury hotel on Tanglin Road come with high-quality service, including the brand's signature butler service, available 24 hours a day. **Pros:** decadent Sunday Champagne brunch; first-rate spa; personal butler service. **Cons:** lines at breakfast; expensive; pool area is not quite as elegant as everywhere else. $ Rooms from: S$490 ⊠ 29 Tanglin Rd., Orchard ☎ 6506–6888 ⊕ www.marriott.com ⮑ 299 rooms ◉ No Meals Ⓜ Orchard.

🍸 Nightlife

Acid Bar

LIVE MUSIC | This bustling bar alongside Emerald Hill has been rocking for more than 15 years. It has a nice outside seating area—great for people-watching—and a cozy interior where live bands play every evening. The artists tend to be up-and-coming, so the music can sometimes be hit or miss, but it's a good place for a few drinks and dancing. It tends to be quite noisy, so don't come if you're looking for a quiet conversation. ✉ *180 Orchard Rd., Orchard* ☎ *8338–6966* ⊕ *www.acidbar.sg* Ⓜ *Somerset.*

Ice Cold Beer

PUBS | Set in a 1910 townhouse noted for its Straits-Chinese architecture, this bustling pub attracts expats and locals alike and serves some 60 beers on tap or in bottles (they're "ice cold" from being in vast ice tanks). At the back of the bar, you can play darts; upstairs, you can play pool and arcade games. If you get peckish, the range of international bar snacks includes hot dogs, chicken wings, and mini-burgers. ✉ *9 Emerald Hill Rd., Orchard* ☎ *6735–9929* ⊕ *www.ice-cold-beer.com* Ⓜ *Somerset.*

KPO

BARS | Once the Killiney Post Office, this Orchard Road landmark is now a spacious two-level indoor and outdoor bar with a great ambience in the evening. Balcony tables upstairs offer views of the traffic whizzing by, while inside the mix of raw concrete walls and steel architecture contrasts with the chill tunes that usually play, often mixed by a local DJ. Tuck into solid local dishes like Hokkien mee or nasi lemak with your beer. Happy hour promotions run every day until 8 pm. ✉ *1 Killiney Rd., Orchard* ☎ *6733–3648* ⊕ *www.imaginings.com.sg* Ⓜ *Somerset.*

★ Manhattan Bar

BARS | Recalling the golden age of New York, with a menu that takes you on a journey of cocktail history, this dark and sultry cocktail bar in the Conrad Singapore Orchard offers more than 220 whiskeys. It's also the first in the world to craft negronis with ingredients that have been solera-aged—and right in the hotel's own 100-barrel rickhouse. No wonder it often ranks in the World's 50 Best Bars. ✉ *Conrad Singapore Orchard, 1 Cuscaden Rd., Level 2, Orchard* ☎ *6725–3377* ⊕ *www.hilton.com* Ⓜ *Orchard Boulevard.*

★ Muddy Murphy's

PUBS | Inside Claymore Connect is this Irish pub famed for being the raucous post-match meeting place for many of Singapore's sporting teams; renowned Sunday Roast lunches; live Irish-Celtic bands; and beverage selection that includes whiskeys, draft Kilkenny Ale, and Guinness Stout. The bar was actually built in Dublin in 1996 before being reassembled in Singapore. It's one of the most popular spots on Orchard Road to catch live sports, with huge TVs showing rugby, football, boxing, tennis, and more. Alongside the well-stocked bar is a full menu featuring Irish pub classics. ✉ *Claymore Connect, 442 Orchard Rd., #01–02 to 05, Orchard* ☎ *9396–6134* ⊕ *muddymurphys.com* Ⓜ *Orchard.*

★ No. 5 Emerald Hill Cocktail Bar

COCKTAIL LOUNGES | Pretty red lanterns hang above you at this chic cocktail bar inside a restored two-story Paranakan terraced house, reflecting the design style of the early-20th-century Straits-Chinese shophouses. There are a variety of enticing cocktails on offer (sampling the signature chilli-infused vodka is a must) plus an impressive selection of spirits, shooters, beers, and mocktails. You can enjoy regular live music and performances; sample the bar snacks, which include pizza and chicken wings; or just sit back and enjoy the ambiance. ⊠ *5 Emerald Hill Rd., Orchard* ☎ *6732–0818* ⊕ *www.emerald-hill.com* Ⓜ *Somerset.*

★ The Other Room

COCKTAIL LOUNGES | Recognized as one of Asia's 50 best bars, The Other Room is a moodily-lit speakeasy where mixologists sling cocktails until the early hours. The allure is its location: hidden behind a largely unmarked black door inside the Marriott Hotel. It's small and snug inside, so it's better to reserve ahead if you want to secure a table, especially if you want to try their version of the classic Reuben sandwich. The cocktails are the real stars, though, made using the 100 different cask-finished spirits blended in-house. ⊠ *Singapore Marriott Tang Plaza Hotel, 320 Orchard Rd. #01–05, Orchard* ☎ *6100–7778* ⊕ *www.theotherroom.com.sg* Ⓜ *Orchard.*

🛍 Shopping

ANTIQUES

Antiques of the Orient

ANTIQUES & COLLECTIBLES | Head to this long-established store inside the Tanglin Shopping Centre for an interesting selection of vintage Southeast Asian artifacts and collectibles, including original books, photos, maps, and prints. ⊠ *Tanglin Shopping Centre, 19 Tanglin Rd., #02–40, Orchard* ☎ *6734–9351* ⊕ *www.aoto.com. sg* Ⓜ *Orchard Blvd.*

BOOKS

★ Books Kinokuniya

BOOKS | One of the largest bookstores in Southeast Asia—and *the* largest in Singapore—has separate fiction and nonfiction sections that will make bookworms want to empty their wallets and fill up their suitcases. It would be easy to spend an entire day browsing the maze of shelves with books on history, travel, poetry, adventure, politics, and so much more. ⊠ *Takashimaya Shopping Centre Ngee Ann City, 391 Orchard Rd., Orchard* ✛ *Level 4, use the escalators in the center of the mall* ☎ *6737–5021* ⊕ *kinokuniya. com.sg* Ⓜ *Orchard.*

CLOTHING

Club 21

MIXED CLOTHING | The trendy fashion retailer Club 21 offers sharp men's and women's clothing lines from such well-known designers as Marc Jacobs, Stella McCartney, and Alexander McQueen. Naturally, the price tags match the big-brand names. There are several other branches around Singapore. ⊠ *Four Seasons Hotel Shopping Arcade, 190 Orchard Blvd., #01–02, Orchard* ☎ *6304– 1385* ⊕ *club21.com* Ⓜ *Orchard Boulevard.*

Coloc Tailor

MEN'S CLOTHING | This well-respected Singaporean tailor has stood the test of time by creating quality suits and custom-made dresses using the finest fabrics from Europe and Japan. Book an appointment for bespoke tailoring, or check out their mail order service online. ⊠ *Mandarin Hotel Gallery, 333A Orchard Rd., #03–07, Orchard* ☎ *6338–9767* ⊕ *www.coloc.com.sg* Ⓜ *Orchard.*

DEPARTMENT STORES

Don Don Donki

DEPARTMENT STORE | This Japanese shopping wonderland overwhelms the senses with its huge and eclectic inventory in a mishmash of vibrant colors and the "Don Don Donki" jingle that it plays endlessy (it's guaranteed to stick in your head for the rest of the day). Expect everything from hand fans to Japanese bin bags, ceramic bowls to rubber chickens. At the Orchard Central store, there is also an excellent food section, with freshly prepared bento lunches available to buy and eat at the nearby Don Don Donki bar and seating area. ⊠ *Orchard Central, 181 Orchard Rd., B1 and B2, Orchard* ☎ *6834–4311* ⊕ *www.dondondonki.sg* Ⓜ *Somerset.*

TANGS

DEPARTMENT STORE | The much-loved department store sells all the major brands across home, beauty, travel, and tech. Its basement is particularly good for household items, from Le Creuset pans to the latest coffee machines—less practical for short-term visitors to Singapore but a great place to shop if you plan to stick around a little longer. The food hall is a good place to buy Asian speciality foods, tea, and confections to take back home. ⊠ *Tang Plaza, 310 Orchard Rd., Orchard* ☎ *6737–5500* ⊕ *www.tangs.com.sg* Ⓜ *Orchard.*

JEWELRY

The Hour Glass

JEWELRY & WATCHES | One of the many upscale boutique jewelers located in Takashimaya, The Hour Glass carries designer watches from more than 50 international luxury brands, including Hublot, Patek Philippe, and Rolex. ⊠ *Takashimaya S. C., Ngee Ann City,*

391 Orchard Rd., #01–02, Orchard ☎ *6734–2420* ⊕ *www.thehour-glass.com* Ⓜ *Orchard.*

SHOPPING CENTERS AND MALLS

★ Design Orchard

MARKET | With its array of internationally-known brands and boutiques, looking for authentic local gifts can be difficult on Orchard. That's where Design Orchard comes into its own, showcasing some of Singapore's best-loved brands and designers. The space regularly shifts to accommodate new stores, but expect to find the latest in fashion, jewelry, furniture, cosmetics and more on the first floor of this space. It's an excellent place to browse for locally-made items and there are regular opportunities to meet designers as part of the workshops and events on the second floor. ✉ *250 Orchard Rd., Orchard* ☎ *8642–3576* ⊕ *www.designorchard.sg* Ⓜ *Somerset.*

Far East Plaza

MALL | Not to be confused with the nearby mall Far East Shopping Centre, Far East Plaza is a five-story mall packed with stores selling everything from electronics to trendy street wear to bespoke tailoring, and much more. Although it's on the older side, it's still a popular Orchard-area hangout for local teens. Of course, it wouldn't be a Singapore mall if there weren't also dozens of restaurants, snack counters, and cafés. ✉ *14 Scotts Rd., Orchard* ☎ *6734–2325* ⊕ *www.fareastplaza.com.sg* Ⓜ *Orchard.*

★ ION Orchard

MALL | With a bold, sci-fi-inspired facade and a 56th-floor viewing deck replete with high-powered telescopes, this is not your everyday megamall, even by Singapore's lofty standards. In addition to local boutiques and more than 300 luxury shops, you'll find a cavernous food hall and a range of international restaurants. But that's still not all: the fourth floor has the 3,640-square-foot ION Art Gallery, which regularly exhibits works by local and international artists. ✉ *2 Orchard Turn, Orchard* ☎ *6238–8228* ⊕ *www. ionorchard.com* Ⓜ *Orchard.*

Lucky Plaza

MALL | An old Orchard Road mainstay that now seems somewhat out of a place among the area's more modern and fashionable megamalls, Lucky Plaza is packed with six floors and a basement full of trinkets, clothing, jewelry, luggage, fashion accessories, and electronics—some of questionable authenticity. On the weekend, it's packed with locals looking for a bargain. ✉ *304 Orchard Rd., Orchard* ☎ *6235–3294* ⊕ *www.luckyplaza.com.sg* Ⓜ *Orchard.*

★ Ngee Ann City

MALL | The Japanese department store Takashimaya dominates this gigantic shopping mall, but there are also more than 130 other shops and dining outlets packed into the first few floors of the Ngee Ann towers. The basement food center is fun for snacking on everything from Hokkaido-style ice cream to bubble tea, and there's also, of course, a large food court if you're craving something more substantial. Books Kinokuniya—a must-visit—is one of the biggest bookstores in Southeast Asia, and special sales on clothing, housewares, and other goods are regularly held in the basement-level square. ⊠ *391 Orchard Rd., Orchard* ☎ *6506–0460* ⊕ *www.ngeeanncity.com.sg* Ⓜ *Orchard.*

Paragon

MALL | The glossy Paragon is worth a stroll, whether you're just window shopping or on the hunt for high-end fashions, jewelry, and accessories at boutiques such as Gucci, Ermenegildo Zegna, Salvatore Ferragamo, or Prada. Marks & Spencer, Mothercare, and Muji all have outlets here, plus there are branches of popular chain restaurants like Din Tai Fung, Crystal Jade, and Ya Kun Kaya Toast. ⊠ *290 Orchard Rd., Orchard* ☎ *6738–5535* ⊕ *www.paragon. com.sg* Ⓜ *Orchard.*

Plaza Singapura

MALL | Need an air-conditioned escape from the afternoon heat? Daiso, Muji, Marks & Spencer and Uniqlo stores, a Golden Village movie theater, a supermarket, and more than 50 food outlets are just some of the tenants of this enormous nine-level building at the bottom of Orchard Road. ⊠ *68 Orchard Rd., Orchard* ☎ *6332–9248* ⊕ *www.capitaland.com* Ⓜ *Dhoby Ghaut.*

★ Tanglin Mall

MALL | **FAMILY** | Not to be confused with Tanglin Shopping Centre or Tangs, this four-level mall tends to get lost in the Orchard Road shuffle, given that it's tucked away at the top of Orchard Road. It nevertheless remains popular with locals and expats alike thanks to its many clothing and homeware boutiques and family stores, as well as the upscale Australian grocery stores like Little Farms and Scoop Wholefoods. There's also a good selection of bakeries, brunch options, and restaurants throughout the mall. ⊠ *163 Tanglin Rd., Orchard* ☎ *6736–4922* ⊕ *www.tanglinmall.com.sg* Ⓜ *Orchard Blvd.*

Tanglin Shopping Centre

MALL | This is a recommended first stop if you're in the market for Asian antiques or Persian carpets. Antiques of the Orient, which deals in vintage charts, maps, and other antiquities, provides a unique shopping experience, plus there are more than 10 tailors here specializing in custom-made suits and alterations. ⊠ *19 Tanglin Rd., Orchard* ☎ *6737–0849* ⊕ *www.tanglinmall.com.sg* Ⓜ *Orchard Boulevard.*

★ 313@Somerset

MALL | One of Orchard Road's best-loved megamalls contains eight levels of shopping and dining distractions. Key fashion tenants include UNIQLO, Zara, and Love, Bonito, though there are plenty of tech, jewelery, and homeware stores, too. Along the mall's open-air Discovery Walk is a clutch of buzzing bars and restaurants, including JiBiru Yakitori & Craft Beer, which deals in local and imported microbrews. Refuel with a caffeine hit at uber-cool spots % Arabica or Flash Coffee, or join the long lines for bubble tea at Gong Cha. ⊠ *313 Orchard Rd., Orchard* ☎ *6496–9313* ⊕ *www.313somerset.com.sg* Ⓜ *Somerset.*

Wisma Atria

MALL | The Japanese department store Isetan anchors five floors of dining and retail revelry that includes multiple International-al fashion and jewelry stores. There's also a fourth-floor Food Republic, which offers more than 20 hawker-style food stalls with kitschy, retro design highlighted by mosaic tile floors and vintage bric-a-brac along the walls and the dining area. ⊠ *435 Orchard Rd., Orchard* ☎ *6235–2103* ⊕ *www.wismaonline.com* Ⓜ *Orchard.*

COSMETICS

Escentials

COSMETICS | This shop sells rare and upscale fragrances and beauty products from more than 30 leading international brands, including Acqua Di Parma, Diptyque, and Hermès. Personal makeovers, beauty events, and fragrance profiling are available by appointment. There are additional outlets in the TANGS and ION Orchard malls along Orchard Road. ⊠ *Paragon, 290 Orchard Rd., #03–02/05, Orchard* ☎ *6737–2478* ⊕ *www.escentials.com.sg* Ⓜ *Orchard.*

🏃 Activities

BOWLING

★ K Bowling Club

BOWLING | "A new generation of bowling" is what this venue promises at its cosmic-themed alley. Neon lights twirl, music blares, the drinks keep flowing, and the balls keep rolling. If you're not in the mood for bowling, there are also darts machines, karaoke booths, arcade games, and more—enough to keep you entertained all evening. ⊠ *313@Somerset, 313 Orchard Rd., #03–27, Orchard* ☎ *6737–5313* ⊕ *kbowlingclub.com* 🖅 *From S$11 per person per game* Ⓜ *Somerset.*

SPAS

Remède Spa

SPAS | From its eucalyptus steam room to its customized massages, the decadent spa at the St. Regis Singapore has the revitalizing experiences every traveler needs after a long day of shopping on Orchard. Note that guests staying at the St. Regis Singapore can get a better rate for their treatments. ⊠ *The St. Regis Singapore, 29 Tanglin Rd., Orchard* ☎ *6506–6896* ⊕ *www. remedespasingapore.com* 🖅 *Facials from S$125, massages from S$108 (30 minutes)* Ⓜ *Orchard Blvd.*

SPECIALTY ACTIVITIES

VR Sandbox Virtual Reality

LOCAL SPORTS | **FAMILY** | Step into the future at Sandbox VR, where you can immerse yourself in some of the most realistic VR games in the world. Combining motion capture with VR technology, the 30-minute experiences genuinely feel like you've been transported into a new world, whether you're doing battle on an alien planet or taking part in a pirate raid. There are clear boundaries in the game to prevent you from running into any walls. Aside from that, you can explore freely, experiencing the complex layers of your new universe. Games can be played with two to six people. ⊠ *Orchard Central, 181 Orchard Rd., #05–31, Orchard* ☎ *9832–5988* ⊕ *sandboxvr.com/singapore* 🖅 *From S$35 per person / per experience* Ⓜ *Somerset.*

WALKING TOURS

★ Disappearing Trades Tour

CULTURAL TOURS | Discover the masters of Singapore's disappearing trades in this popular cultural tour that charts Singapore's rise to modernity from the 1950s. Visit one of Singapore's oldest traditional bakeries, talk to a master paper-house maker (related to the Chinese custom of offerings to their ancestors) and sample Singaporean coffee at a traditional *kopi* roasting factory. Tours are run on Tuesday and Friday and start at Newton Food Centre (taxi drop-off point). ⊠ *Newton Food Centre, 500 Clemenceau Ave. N., Orchard* ⊹ *Taxi drop off* ☎ *9660–0687* ⊕ *tribe-tours.com* 🖅 *From $103 per adult* Ⓜ *Newton.*

Chapter 8

EASTERN DISTRICTS

Updated by
Marco Ferrarese

⊙ Sights　🍴 Restaurants　🏨 Hotels　🛍 Shopping　🍸 Nightlife
★★★★☆　★★★★★　★★★☆☆　★★☆☆☆　★★☆☆☆

NEIGHBORHOOD SNAPSHOT

TOP EXPERIENCES

■ **Jewel Changi Airport:** The world's largest indoor waterfall, an indoor forest, and more than 280 shops and eateries are here.

■ **East Coast Road:** A stroll down this street in Katong, with its brightly colored shophouses, is an immersive introduction to Singapore's Peranakan culture.

■ **Seafood at sunset:** Dinner at East Coast Seafood Centre is a memorable affair, as is fishing for your dinner at Smith Marine.

■ **Beaches and parks:** Picnic in the sun at Pasir Ris Park; spot sea turtles at Changi Beach, or go biking at East Coast Park.

GETTING HERE

The airport and Joo Chiat are easily accessible via the MRT, and buses serve the rest of the area. Paya Lebar, on the Circle Line (yellow) and East West Line (green), and Eunos, on the East West Line (green), all stop along Sims Avenue in Geylang, about a mile north of Katong. Joo Chiat Road and East Coast Road, in the heart of Katong, are accessible via buses 10, 14, and 16. Come 2024, the area will be served by two stations, Katong Park and Tanjung Katong, on the new Thomson–East Coast MRT line.

PLANNING YOUR TIME

Plan a day in Eastern Singapore when you arrive or depart from nearby Changi International Airport, devoting a few hours to Katong for lunch. Weekends are busiest.

VIEWFINDER

■ Joo Chiat's two rows of brightly colored Peranakan Houses are an iconic background for splendid pictures. Walk along Dunman Road and past Crane on Joo Chiat's main junction, then continue along Koon Seng Road to find yourself amid a rainbow of colored shutters, pillars, and doors.

Eastern Singapore may be the smallest of Singapore's five regions, but it's the most densely populated. It's also home to the country's two airports, Changi International Airport (a destination in itself) and Paya Lebar Air Base, with economic activity driven by aviation and manufacturing.

While the region isn't typically on first-time tourist hit lists because there aren't any big monuments or headline attractions, there is perhaps no better place to immerse yourself in true Singaporean culture and authentic local cuisine.

The pretty Katong neighborhood, the beating heart of Singapore's Peranakan and Eurasian culture, has the largest cluster of preserved Peranakan shophouses from the 1800s. Nearby Joo Chiat Road has by now well grown into its own hip and artsy district, with cafés, bars, and boutiques lining up both sides of the road.

Changi, at the easternmost tip of the island, is home to both the state-of-the-art Changi International Airport (with its newly opened retail, dining, and entertainment extension, Jewel) as well as the country's most rustic throwbacks: Changi Village and the island of Pulau Ubin, an easy side trip. And a trip to Geylang Serai, the home of Singapore's Malay community, affords a living, breathing look into the rich Singaporean Malay culture.

For foodies in particular, Eastern Singapore is a must-visit: many of the best hawker, Peranakan, and Malay bites are here, though most places are scattered throughout the area and may require more than one trip. Three of Singapore's most popular beaches—East Coast Park, Pasir Ris Park, and Changi Beach—are also in Eastern Singapore and provide a breezy breather from the urban landscape.

Changi

The northeastern section of Singapore is seldom visited by out-of-towners, but it has some worthwhile temples, beaches, and the showstopping Changi International Airport, which has been called one of the best airports in the world. If you have a long layover or

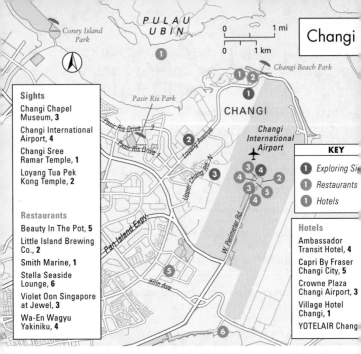

Changi

0	1 mi
0	1 km

PULAU UBIN

Coney Island Park

Changi Beach Park

Pasir Ris Park

CHANGI

Changi International Airport

Sights

Changi Chapel Museum, **3**

Changi International Airport, **4**

Changi Sree Ramar Temple, **1**

Loyang Tua Pek Kong Temple, **2**

Restaurants

Beauty In The Pot, **5**

Little Island Brewing Co., **2**

Smith Marine, **1**

Stella Seaside Lounge, **6**

Violet Oon Singapore at Jewel, **3**

Wa-En Wagyu Yakiniku, **4**

KEY

Exploring Si

Restaurants

Hotels

Hotels

Ambassador Transit Hotel, **4**

Capri By Fraser Changi City, **5**

Crowne Plaza Changi Airport, **3**

Village Hotel Changi, **1**

YOTELAIR Chang

Pasir Ris Drive 3

Pasir Ris Drive 1

Loyang Avenue

Upper Changi Rd. N

W. Perimeter Rd.

Pan-Island Expy.

Xilin Ave.

are staying in the area to catch a flight, there are certainly a few good options to fill your time. The area is also a jumping off point for trips to the island Pulau Ubin.

◉ Sights

Changi Chapel Museum

MILITARY SIGHT | Sprawling, squat, sinister-looking Changi Prison was built in the 1930s by the British and was used by the Japanese in World War II to intern some 70,000 POWs, who endured terrible hardships here. The museum, a replica of one of 14 chapels where 85,000 Allied POWs and civilians gained the faith and courage to overcome the degradation and deprivation inflicted upon them by the Japanese, reopened in 2021 displaying drawings, sketches, and photographs by POWs depicting their wartime experiences. Organized tours take you through the old British barracks areas to the former RAF camp, still part of an active military installation. Here, in **Block 151**—a prisoners' hospital during the war—you'll see the simple but striking murals painted by a British POW, bombardier Stanley Warren. The last admission is at 4:30 pm, and with little public parking, it's recommended that you take public transportation. ⊠ *1000 Upper Changi Rd. N,*

Changi ☎ 6242–6033 ⊕ *www.nhb.gov.sg/changichapelmuseum*
✉ *S$8* ☉ *Closed Mon.* Ⓜ *Tanah Merah.*

★ Changi International Airport

STORE/MALL | FAMILY | Singapore's slick airport hasn't just won multiple awards for World's Best Airport—it's also been named one of the world's most outstanding retail real-estate projects. And it's no wonder: The sprawling four-terminal complex houses hundreds of stores and restaurants, many of which can't be found elsewhere. If shopping and eating—the country's most popular pastimes—aren't your thing, there are plenty of other draws, like the **Butterfly Garden**, a **Canopy Park** (where you can walk across bouncy nets suspended across the top floor), and the **Rain Vortex**, a seven-story (and the world's tallest) indoor waterfall. ✉ *Changi International Airport, 70 Airport Blvd., Changi* ☎ 6595–6868 ⊕ *www.changiairport.com* Ⓜ *Changi Airport.*

Changi Sree Ramar Temple

TEMPLE | This breezy, tranquil Hindu temple by the sea is the only one of its kind in Southeast Asia devoted to the Hindu god Rama. Interestingly, it also serves as the spiritual center for many non-Hindus living in Eastern Singapore, because it houses Buddha and Goddess of Mercy idols. ✉ *51 Changi Village Rd., Changi* ☎ 6543–1463 ⊕ *www.sreeramartemple.org.sg* ✉ *Free.*

Loyang Tua Pek Kong Temple

TEMPLE | Tens of thousands of devotees visit this sprawling multi-religious temple every month to pay their respects to the Buddhist, Taoist, and Hindu deities and worship in the Muslim shrine here. Elaborately carved patterns on the ceilings demarcate the different areas in the temple, which is especially popular with those seeking wealth and good fortune. During the Nine Emperor Gods Festival in the ninth lunar month (from late October to early November), the temple takes on a carnival atmosphere as some 100,000 Taoist pilgrims descend on it, bringing exotic foods, flowers, joss sticks, and candles as offerings for their prayers. ✉ *Loyang Tua Pek Kong Temple, 20 Loyang Way, Changi* ⊕ *www.lytpk.org.sg.*

🌊 Beaches

Changi Beach Park

BEACH | One of Singapore's oldest and quietest coastal parks, Changi Beach is a two-mile stretch of sand dotted with coconut trees and public barbecue pits. Although its tranquility belies its dark history—this was one of the main sites of the Sook Ching massacre during the Japanese Occupation—today the area is a popular spot for couples as well as fishing and photography enthusiasts. **Amenities:** food and drink; toilets. **Best for:** solitude; swimming; walking. ⊠ *Nicoll Dr., Changi* ⊹ *Near Changi Village* ☎ *6471–7300* ⊕ *www.nparks.gov.sg.*

★ **Coney Island Park**

BEACH | FAMILY | A lesser-visited gem of a park in the northeast of Singapore, uninhabited Coney Island (aka Pulau Serangoon) boasts hidden white-sand beaches and plenty of mangrove-draped trails through coastal forests, casuarina woodlands, and grasslands filled with flora and fauna. Start at Punggol Point Park, where boats and a bridge go to Coney Island Park. There are five main beach areas, and the 2.5-km-long Coney Island Park Connector to explore by bicycle or walking. GoCycling at Punggol Jetty rents bikes for S$10 an hour. On selected Saturday mornings in the months of June, November, and December, National Parks volunteers conduct two-hour guided walks. **Amenities:** toilets. **Best for:** solitude; swimming; walking; cycling. ⊠ *Pulau Serangoon, Changi* ⊹ *Beside Punggol Promenade Nature Walk* ⊕ *www. nparks.gov.sg* ⊠ *Free* Ⓜ *Punggol.*

Pasir Ris Park

BEACH | FAMILY | This green lung within the Pasir Ris residential area is a popular picnic spot with families, thanks to its kid-friendly facilities that include one of Singapore's biggest (and free) outdoor playgrounds. The park is also home to a 15-acre mangrove forest, which you can explore via several walking trails, a wheelchair-accessible boardwalk, and a three-story birdwatching tower. **Amenities:** food and drink; parking; toilets. **Best for:** solitude; swimming; walking. ⊠ *Pasir Ris Central, Changi* ☎ *6471–7300* ⊕ *www.nparks. gov.sg* Ⓜ *Pasir Ris.*

🍴 Restaurants

Beauty In The Pot

$$$ | CHINESE | FAMILY | Hotpot meals are a big part of modern local culture, as the communal dining experience is considered a convenient way to celebrate special occasions with family and friends. Homegrown chain Beauty In The Pot is one of the country's most popular, serving up tasty collagen-infused broth into which you can dip gourmet cuts of meat, handmade noodles, and other ingredients. **Known for:** collagen broth with beauty benefits; top hotpot meals; excellent service. Ⓢ *Average main: S$50* ⊠ *Jewel Changi Airport, 78 Airport Blvd, #B2–224, Changi* ☎ *6242–5131* ⊕ *www.paradisegp.com/brand-beauty-in-the-pot* Ⓜ *Changi Airport.*

Little Island Brewing Co.

$$ | INTERNATIONAL | FAMILY | This laid-back, open-air microbrewery is a rare gem in the quiet Changi Village area, serving house brews with whimsical, psychedelic labels alongside hearty roasts and weekend brunches. Pour yourself a glass from the DIY draft counter and sit at a table under the fairy lights—it's the perfect place to while an evening away. **Known for:** tasty craft beers; laid-back vibe; good location. $ *Average main: S$20* ⊠ *6 Changi Village Rd., #01–01/02, Changi* ☎ *6543–9100* ⊕ *libc.co.*

★ Smith Marine

$$ | CHINESE | FAMILY | Located off the coast of Changi, this modern spin on the traditional *kelong* (floating fish farm) doles out meals to remember. You travel to it on an old-fashioned bumboat from Changi Ferry Terminal, then catch your own lunch or dinner in "sure-catch" ponds from the ship-like structure in the middle of the sea. **Known for:** novel dining experience; fresh seafood; catch-your-own meals. $ *Average main: S$30* ⊠ *Pulau Ubin Coastal Area, Changi* ⊹ *About 3.6 miles from Changi Ferry Terminal* ☎ *9792–7609* ⊕ *www.smithmarine.com.sg.*

★ Stella Seaside Lounge

$$ | BARBECUE | FAMILY | Mixing alfresco restaurant and seaside swimming pool, Stella is the first beachfront lounge along Tanah Merah Beach in the southeast of Changi, just a 10-minute drive from the airport. The brunch menu is big on sandwiches and toasts, grilled pork chops, and healthy breakfasts, while dinner is best for live seafood, charcoal grilled meats, and seafood-based pastas. **Known for:** frequent parties and events; swimming pool; beachfront location. $ *Average main: S$25* ⊠ *11 Changi Coast Walk, Changi* ☎ *6214–9168* ⊕ *www.stella.com.sg* ☉ *No lunch weekdays* Ⓜ *Tanah Merah.*

★ Violet Oon Singapore at Jewel

$$ | ASIAN FUSION | FAMILY | Violet Oon is one of Singapore's most celebrated Peranakan chefs, and her eponymous restaurant inside Changi International Airport is the only one with a terrace that offers a direct view of the airport's Rain Vortex, the world's tallest indoor waterfall. In addition to treats like her signature (and delightfully tangy) dry laksa, the restaurant has an open grill, a long bar, and a retail area where you can stock up on Oon's beautifully packaged pineapple tarts and Peranakan cookies. **Known for:** local celebrity chef; dry laksa; food souvenirs. $ *Average main: S$25* ⊠ *Jewel Changi Airport, 78 Airport Blvd., #01–205/206, Changi* ☎ *9834–9935* ⊕ *violetoon.com/violet-oon-singapore-at-jewel-changi-airport/* Ⓜ *Changi Airport.*

Wa-En Wagyu Yakiniku

$$ | JAPANESE | The latest import at Jewel Changi Airport, this Hong Kong *yakiniku* restaurant finally opened a Singapore branch in late 2022. It's largely known for its premium A4/A5 wagyu beef sourced from Japan's Miyazaki province. **Known for:** creative cocktails; reputed international brand; quality beef. $ *Average main: S$30* ✉ *Jewel Changi Airport, 78 Airport Blvd., #01–224, Changi* ☎ *6246–7488* ⊕ *wa-en.com.sg* Ⓜ *Changi Airport.*

🛏 Hotels

Ambassador Transit Hotel

$ | HOTEL | Rooms at this airport hotel are clean, fresh, and basic, and include use of the swimming pool, sauna, and fitness center. **Pros:** includes use of swimming pool and gym; good for early flights and layovers; bargain prices. **Cons:** basic rooms; far from the city; little atmosphere. $ *Rooms from: S$141* ✉ *Changi International Airport, Airport Blvd., Changi* ☎ *6507–9788* ⊕ *www.harilelahospitality.com* 🛏 *171 rooms* 🍽 *No Meals* Ⓜ *Changi Airport.*

Capri By Fraser Changi City

$$ | HOTEL | Located within Changi Business Park and walking distance to the Singapore Expo Convention & Exhibition Centre is this modern apartment-hotel. **Pros:** convenient location for business travelers working in the East; free high-speed Internet; rooms have kitchenettes for cooking. **Cons:** not centrally located; area has little personality; limited dining options nearby that aren't in a mall. $ *Rooms from: S$213* ✉ *Changi City Point, 3 Changi Business Park Central 1, Changi* ☎ *6933–9833* ⊕ *singapore.capribyfraser.com* 🛏 *313 rooms* 🍽 *No Meals* Ⓜ *Expo.*

Crowne Plaza Changi Airport

$$ | HOTEL | FAMILY | What may be the world's best airport hotel has many (soundproof) rooms that face the runway, as well as more tranquil terrace rooms that lead directly to the lushly landscaped pool. **Pros:** connected to the airport and MRT station; comfortable rooms; unique views of the runway. **Cons:** not centrally located; area isn't interesting; no free in-room Wi-Fi. $ *Rooms from: S$315* ✉ *Changi International Airport, 75 Airport Blvd., #01–01, Changi* ☎ *6823–5300* ⊕ *changiairport.crowneplaza.com* 🛏 *320 rooms* 🍽 *No Meals* Ⓜ *Changi Airport.*

Village Hotel Changi

$ | HOTEL | It's only 10 minutes from the airport and near many attractions, including a beach, boat rides to other islands, cafés, pubs, shops, golf facilities, and a museum; free shuttle buses are available to the airport and downtown. **Pros:** near the airport;

infinity pool; a quiet hideaway. **Cons:** far from the city; limited dining and retail options nearby; inaccessible via public transport. ⑤ *Rooms from: S$156* ✉ *1 Netheravon Rd., Changi* ☎ *6379–7111* ⊕ *www.villagehotels.asia/en* ⇨ *380 rooms* ⦿ *No Meals.*

YOTELAIR Changi

$ | HOTEL | Opened in 2019, this airport hotel offers modern, windowless cabins by the hour as well as day and overnight rates. **Pros:** close to the airport and shops in Jewel Changi Airport; brand new; free Wi-Fi and use of gym. **Cons:** windowless cabins; small rooms; a tad pricey. ⑤ *Rooms from: S$175* ✉ *Jewel Changi Airport, 78 Airport Blvd., #04–280, Changi* ☎ *6407–7888* ⊕ *www. yotel.com* ⇨ *130 rooms* ⦿ *No Meals* Ⓜ *Changi Airport.*

🌙 Nightlife

Tipsy Penguin Tampines

LIVE MUSIC | One in a group of affiliated bars and cafés that cater to young and debonair Singaporeans, Tipsy Penguin is a hotspot in the student-dominated eastern district of Tampines. Good vibes, a better-than-average choice of bar food, and live music make it a brilliant choice for a fun night out. It's popular for its Hyogo Japanese oyster platters, tenderloin steak fries, and Italian pastas. The menu also includes an eclectic choice of international tapas (from wagyu cubes to smoked chicken nachos). Patrons can rent popular board games while trying the literally mind-numbing selection of well-priced wines, beers, and shots. ✉ *NTUC Income@Tampines Junction, 300 Tampines Ave 5, #01–02A, Changi* ☎ *8223–2983* ⊕ *tipsycollective.com* Ⓜ *Tampines West.*

🛍 Shopping

SHOPPING CENTERS AND MALLS

★ Jewel Changi Airport

MALL | FAMILY | This sprawling 280-store complex is a one-stop shop for top Singapore labels, local gourmet snacks, and more than a handful of first-in-Southeast Asia brands. Highlights include In Good Company for sleek, minimalist womenswear; Pazzion for chic, cheerful shoes (this flagship boutique also houses the first-of-its-kind Pazzion Cafe); and the wildly popular Irvins Salted Egg snacks. If you're on your way in or out of Singapore, leave ample time for browsing. ✉ *Changi International Airport, 78 Airport Blvd., Changi* ⊹ *Connected to Terminal 1* ☎ *6956–9898* ⊕ *www.jewel-changiairport.com* Ⓜ *Changi Airport.*

🏃 Activities

BIKING

Changi Boardwalk

BIKING | FAMILY | Also known as Changi Point Coastal Walk, this popular wooden walkway along the water faces Pulau Ubin and attracts visitors thanks to its shade trees, coastal scenery, and night lighting. The 2.2-km (1.4-mile) path has six distinct sections and starts with **Creek Walk**, which affords views of boats sailing to Singapore's offshore islands. **Beach Walk** offers a perspective of Changi Beach, while **Sailing Point Walk** goes past moored yachts. The shortest 180-meter-long **Cliff Walk** has the most tree coverage and is followed by the **Kelong Walk,** an over-water path on stilts. The last stretch, aptly named **Sunset Walk,** is best visited when the sun sinks into the sea. ✉ *7A Gosport, Changi* Ⓜ *Tanah Merah, exit B and Bus 2 to Block 5.*

Changi Bay Point

BIKING | FAMILY | A 2022 addition to the Round-Island-Route, Changi Bay Point stretches for 3.6 km (2.2 miles) along Singapore's north-easternmost coastline facing unspoiled Tekong Island. It's another excellent coastal area to unwind on a sea-facing bench, cycle, or jog. The Changi Bay Point itself is an elevated lookout by the sea, from where stunning sunrises flare over the undeveloped surrounding coast—a rarity in Singapore. The park is open 24/7 and well-lit after 7 pm. There are no restaurants here, just one solitary vending machine, so bring snacks from the nearby Changi Village Hawker Center. If you need a longer jog, an additional 7-km (4.3-mile) Coastal Track connects Changi Bay Point to Changi Beach Park. ✉ *Aviation Park Rd., Changi* Ⓜ *Tampines East and then bus to Changi Village Bus Terminal.*

FISHING

Prawning at Ah Hua

FISHING | FAMILY | Prawning, or prawn-fishing, is a fun Singaporean pastime in which families or groups of friends gather around purpose-made ponds to fish for their lunch. Using rods or poles, you can catch prawns to grill up at the site's barbecue pit. You pay by the hour, not by the number of prawns you catch, so you might want to brush up on your fishing skills. The rate is inclusive of rods, bait, and all the prawns that you catch. ✉ *125 Pasir Ris Rd., Pasir Ris* ☎ *9487–7248* ⊕ *www.facebook.com/ahhuafishing* 💲 *From S$20 per hour (inclusive of rods, bait, and all the seafood you catch)* Ⓜ *Pasir Ris.*

HIKING

Jurassic Mile

HIKING & WALKING | FAMILY | More than 20 different life-sized dinosaur statues (the largest of which is 17 meters long) stretch for over one kilometer along a section of the Changi Airport Connector—a 3.5-km (2.2-mile) cycling and jogging path linking Changi International Airport to the East Coast Park and the Park Connector Network. It's Singapore's largest permanent outdoor display of prehistoric creatures, free to access and open 24/7. The path begins and ends at Hub & Spoke near Terminal 2, where you can rent bicycles, shower, or have a meal at the Hub & Spoke Cafe (⊕ www.hubnspokecafe.com). ✉ Changi International Airport Terminal 2, Changi ☎ 6595–6865 ⊕ www.changiairport.com/en/discover/changi-airport-connector/jurassic-mile.html ▧ Free Ⓜ Changi Airport.

Punggol Waterway Park

HIKING & WALKING | FAMILY | Built around a section of Punggol Waterway and located along Sentul Crescent, this park nestled on a river bend has benches to relax, waterfront views, bird-watching, and cycling paths. The dome-shaped Jewel and Sunrise bridges are scenic spots for pictures, while the Recreation Zone, equipped with a water play area, is what families with children need. Two raised planter boxes at the Therapeutic Garden even offer wheelchair users a chance to do plant maintenance and enjoy nature. ✉ Sentul Crescent, Changi ⊕ www.nparks.gov.sg ▧ Free Ⓜ Sam Kee.

WALKING TOURS

Free Singapore Tour

WALKING TOURS | If your layover at Changi International Airport is more than 5½ hours but less than 24 hours, check your bags at left luggage, and head to Terminal 2 or 3's Level 2 to sign up for a free English-language walking tour of the city (you can also pre-book on the airport's website). There are three 2½-hour options: the Jewel Tour, which takes you to the airport's jaw-dropping Jewel development, housing the Rain Vortex, Forest Valley, Canopy Park, and Singapore Coffee Museum; the Heritage Tour, which takes you into the city to see top neighborhoods including the Civic District and Merlion Park, Chinatown, Little India, and Kampong Glam; or the City Sights tour, covering Marina Bay Sands and Gardens by the Bay. To register, you'll need your passport, boarding passes, and valid entry visa. The tours are first-come, first-served, and note that you can only exit and enter the airport once during your layover. ✉ Changi International Airport, 75 Airport Blvd., T2 or T3, Level 2 Departure Transit Hall, Changi ⊕ www.changiairport.com/en ▧ Free Ⓜ Changi Airport.

Geylang Serai

Farther inland and closest to the city is Geylang Serai, which was once a red-light district but is now a thriving area with robust dining and shopping options. Whether you grab a bite at the market or stroll by the traditional shophouses, you'll surely catch a glimpse of traditional Singapore and its rich culture.

👁 Sights

Geylang Serai Market

OTHER SPECIALTY STORE | **FAMILY** | This double-story Minangkabau-style market and hawker center is the beating heart of Singapore's Malay community. Here, you can pick up a vast range of Malay groceries, fashion accessories, and some of the best—and most reasonably priced—Muslim food in town. The ground floor of the open-air structure contains a wet market that peddles everything from halal meat to the fabled *tongkat ali* drink (meant to help with male fertility). The second floor has a dry-goods bazaar and food center. ✉ *1 Geylang Serai, Geylang Serai* Ⓜ *Paya Lebar.*

Joo Chiat Complex

MALL | Take a trip back to Singapore in the 1980s at this retro two-complex shopping center filled with stores bursting at the seams with fabric, home furnishings and a hodgepodge of kitchenware. It's a chaotic riot of color and a lively change from the slick, polished malls of Orchard Road. ✉ *Joo Chiat Complex, 1 Joo Chiat Rd., Geylang Serai* ⊕ *www.joochiatcomplex.com* Ⓜ *Paya Lebar.*

🍴 Restaurants

Hjh Maimunah Restaurant

$ | **MALAYSIAN** | **FAMILY** | One of the most beloved Malay restaurants in Singapore offers more than 40 tasty dishes at any one time, which you can have with steaming white rice. It's easy to tailor a plate to your palate, since the range includes everything from more adventurous recipes like *sambal goreng pengantin* (stir-fried offal with prawns and spices) to tamer but no less tasty favorites like chicken curry. **Known for:** authentic Malay cooking; impressive variety; hard-to-find dishes. ⑤ *Average main: S$10* ✉ *20 Joo Chiat Rd., Geylang Serai* ☎ *6348–5457* ⊕ *hjmaimunah.com* Ⓜ *Paya Lebar.*

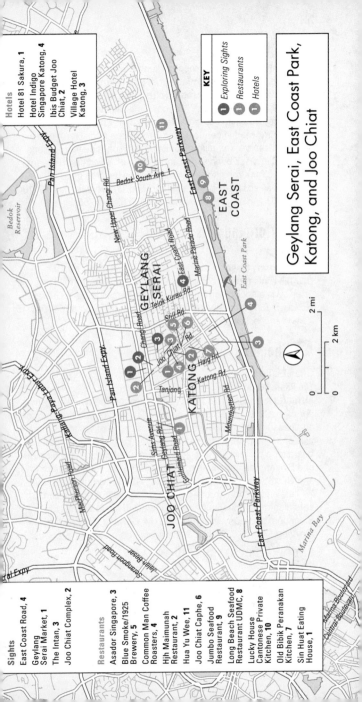

Geylang Serai, East Coast Park, Katong, and Joo Chiat

KEY
1 *Exploring Sights*
1 *Restaurants*
1 *Hotels*

Hotels
Hotel 81 Sakura, **1**
Hotel Indigo Singapore Katong, **4**
Ibis Budget Joo Chiat, **2**
Village Hotel Katong, **3**

Sights
East Coast Road, **4**
Geylang Serai Market, **1**
The Intan, **3**
Joo Chiat Complex, **2**

Restaurants
Asador Singapore, **3**
Blue Smoke/1925 Brewery, **5**
Common Man Coffee Roasters, **4**
Hjh Maimunah Restaurant, **2**
Hua Yu Wee, **11**
Joo Chiat Caphe, **6**
Jumbo Seafood Restaurant, **9**
Long Beach Seafood Restaurant UDMC, **8**
Lucky House Cantonese Private Kitchen, **10**
Old Bibik Peranakan Kitchen, **7**
Sin Huat Eating House, **1**

★ Sin Huat Eating House

$$$$ | **SEAFOOD** | It may be rough around the edges, it's in the red-light district of Geylang, and the cost of a full meal would make some fine-dining establishments blush, but there's good reason why the late food magnate Anthony Bourdain named Sin Huat one of the "10 places to eat before you die." Chef Danny's rich, gooey, briny, magnificent crab (or prawn) *bee hoon* (vermicelli-like rice noodles) is a stunning dish. Pair it with on-the-shell scallops slathered in black bean sauce and a plate of *kailan* (fresh greens) with garlic for a meal to remember. **Known for:** crab noodles; on-the-shell scallops; edgy neighborhood. ⑤ *Average main: S$100* ⊠ *659/661 Geylang Rd., Geylang Serai* ☎ *6744–9755.*

🎭 Performing Arts

THEATER

The Necessary Stage

THEATER | This theater company puts on original performances, often with a social, sometimes socialist message. ⊠ *Yi Guang Building, 180 Paya Lebar Rd., #10–06, Geylang Serai* ☎ *6440–8115* ⊕ *www.necessary.org.*

🛍 Shopping

COLLECTIBLES

The Panic Room

ANTIQUES & COLLECTIBLES | This quirky, alternative-style vintage barbershop (S$40 cut, S$25 ear cleaning) tucked on the first floor of an unassuming shophouse is a treasure trove of weird memorabilia and vintage stuff to watch and buy. Besides hair pomade and beard care products, there are clippers, used vinyl (rock, alt-punk, and Singaporean sounds), mint instant flex cameras, vintage toys, and all sort of pop culture collectibles—think Lemmy Kilmister, X-Files, and Freddy Krueger toys. Occasional live shows and DJ sets also make the Panic Room an ideal place to connect with Singapore's real underground. ⊠ *311A Geylang Rd., Geylang Serai, Geylang Serai* ☎ *8228–9063* ⊕ *thepanicroom.com.sg* Ⓜ *Eunos.*

SHOPPING CENTERS AND MALLS

City Plaza

MALL | Shop the latest Korean, Chinese, and Thai fashions at this retro, under-the-radar mall, where wholesalers plug their wares to local stores. You'll have to do some digging, but the thrill of finding a chic piece at a great price will likely make up for that. ⊠ *810 Geylang Rd., Geylang Serai* ⊕ *www.cityplaza.sg* Ⓜ *Paya Lebar.*

Colorful Peranakan houses line Joo Chiat's Koon Seng Road and East Coast Road.

East Coast Park, Katong, and Joo Chiat

The intersection of East Coast Road and Joo Chiat Road is the heart of Katong, a district steeped in the culture of the Perana-kans, the descendants of 17th-century Chinese immigrants who married local Malays. This part of town is where you will find the island's largest assortment of heritage shophouses, many painted in pretty pastel colors and featuring traditional Peranakan motifs.

This is a popular dining and entertainment enclave (avoid Mondays, when most businesses are closed) and the birthplace of one of Singapore's most famous local dishes, Katong laksa (rice vermicelli in a spicy coconut-based broth). The Betel Box hostel and bistro is known for organizing informative food tours of the neighborhood. Nearby, running along the southeastern coast, is East Coast Park, the biggest park in the country.

◉ Sights

★ East Coast Road

STREET | One of the earliest delineated thoroughfares in Singapore, East Coast Road is also one of the prettiest, with more than 800 heritage buildings from the early to mid 1900s, a time when the area served as a seaside retreat for the wealthy. Today, a stroll along this spirited enclave will give you a taste of the country's diverse culture—the stretch is dotted with colorful Peranakan shophouses, museums, and quaint stores, as well as eateries that serve up everything from traditional rice dumplings to Thai *mookata* and Greek-influenced wood-fired breads. ⊠ *East Coast Rd., East Coast Park.*

The Intan

OTHER MUSEUM | "Intan" refers to the rose-cut diamonds popularly used in Straits Chinese jewelry, and this privately owned, by-appointment-only Straits Chinese museum is a gem in its own right. Owner Alvin Yap amassed a vast collection of Peranakan paraphernalia in his quest to find out more about his culture, and then decided to open his home to the public so others could learn more about it, too. In this intimate space, you experience the Peranakan life as Yap takes you on a personally guided tour of the artifacts he's collected. ⊠ *69 Joo Chiat Terr., Joo Chiat* ☎ *6440–1148* ⊕ *www.the-intan.com* ☞ *By appointment only* Ⓜ *Eunos.*

🌊 Beaches

East Coast Park

BEACH | FAMILY | This breezy, 460-acre seaside park isn't just one of Singapore's largest beaches, it's also the most popular, with a plethora of dining and recreational activities. There's fun for the whole family here, whether you choose to cycle along the bike-dedicated paths, go waterskiing, have a seafood dinner, or even camp overnight, though if you do want to camp, remember to apply for an electronic camping permit first (⊕ *nparks.gov. sg*). A cable-ski park, **Wake Park** (⊕ *singaporewakepark.com*), is set up around a lagoon for wakeboarding enthusiasts. You can also go windsurfing, winging, sailing, or simply take a dip in the sea. **Aloha Sea Sports Center** (⊕ *www.alohaseasports.com*) offers rentals, storage, and courses, and also organizes occasional races. Further away along the wide, well-manicured park are public barbecue pits, 7.5 km (4.7 miles) of sandy beaches, and a hawker center. Before the upcoming Thomson–East Coast MRT Line connects the park with other parts of Singapore in 2024, a taxi or public bus is your best bet for getting here. **Amenities:** food and drink; parking; toilets; water sports. **Best for:** swimming; walking; windsurfing; winging. ⊠ *East Coast Park Service Rd., East Coast Park* ✣ *Along East Coast Pkwy. and East Coast Park Service Rd.* ⊕ *www.nparks.gov.sg.*

🍴 Restaurants

Asador Singapore

$$ | SPANISH | One of the city's best Spanish restaurants is all about good meat and excellent wines. Start with Pan Casero and Jamon Iberico, and then tear into a portion of Costillar de Ternera, the popular juicy short ribs of glazed Angus beef. **Known for:** authentic Spanish dining experience; attentive service; hand-made stone oven. *⑤ Average main: S$30 ⊠ 51 Joo Chiat Pl., Joo Chiat ☎ 9836–1792 ⊕ www.asadorsingapore.com ⊗ No lunch Mon.–Thurs.*

Blue Smoke/1925 Brewery

$$ | STEAKHOUSE | Part of the 1925 Brewery, this proud Asian smokehouse is decked out in dark, industrial-chic interiors. Western smoking techniques are tested on Asian meats to create such savory concoctions as wood-smoked stingray steak spiked with sambal belacan (shrimp paste), and Teochew-style braised kurobota pork (a Japanese variety). **Known for:** Asian-Western fusion BBQ; high-quality, slow-smoked meats; Asian-inspired artisan beer made on-site. *⑤ Average main: S$35 ⊠ 261 Joo Chiat Rd., Joo Chiat ☎ 8923–1425 ⊕ the1925.com.sg/bluesmoke/ ⊗ No lunch Tues.–Thurs.*

Common Man Coffee Roasters

$$ | ASIAN FUSION | The Joo Chiat outlet of this Singaporean ethical coffee franchise established in 2013 offers what they boast as the "best brunch in Asia"—a true statement, judging by the lines waiting by the door. The popular organic eggs Benedict (runny poached eggs served along with braised ox cheeks, chive hollandaise, and artisanal sourdough bread) is the explosion of tastes you need to power charge your day. **Known for:** popular brunch spot; organic coffee; zesty burgers. *⑤ Average main: S$20 ⊠ 185 Joo Chiat Rd., Joo Chiat ☎ 6877–4863 ⊕ commonmancoffeeroasters.com ⊗ No dinner.*

★ Hua Yu Wee

$$ | CHINESE | FAMILY | Time seems to stand still at this nostalgic, convivial Chinese restaurant that's the only survivor from an era when seafood restaurants used to line East Coast Road. Parked in a 1920s bungalow, the restaurant's menu, decor, and presentation touches—like the fresh purple orchids that top off delicious dishes—are old-school. **Known for:** unique local experience; reasonable prices; chilli crab. *⑤ Average main: S$15 ⊠ 462 Upper East Coast Rd., Bedok ☎ 6442–9313 ⊕ huayuwee5.wixsite.com/website-1 ⊗ No lunch.*

Joo Chiat Caphe

$$ | VIETNAMESE | Specializing in hearty, juicy Vietnamese banh mi sandwiches (come early as they sell out fast) and mackerel *otah* (with a mix of fish paste and flavorsome spices), this simple yet popular spot with tables spilling on the five-foot way is perfect for people-watching and a quick lunch fix. **Known for:** reasonable prices; Muslim-friendly; generous fillings. ⑤ *Average main: S$15* ⊠ *263 Joo Chiat Rd., Joo Chiat* ☎ *6988–1900* ⊕ *joochiatcaphe. com* ⊙ *Closed Mon. No dinner.*

★ Jumbo Seafood Restaurant

$$ | SEAFOOD | FAMILY | This atmospheric East Coast Seafood Centre staple is the perfect place to crack into a chilli or black pepper Sri Lankan crab, a glorious, delicious mess of a dish that's a true Singaporean specialty—be sure to order it with sides of fried buns to sop up the sauce. Prices are by the kilogram; some crabs are large enough to feed up to four people, but smaller ones for two are also available. **Known for:** chilli crabs; live seafood cooked to order; seaside location. ⑤ *Average main: S$34* ⊠ *East Coast Seafood Centre, Block 1206, East Coast Pkwy., #01–07/08, East Coast Park* ☎ *6342–3435* ⊕ *www.jumboseafood.com.sg* ⊙ *No lunch Mon.–Sat.*

Long Beach Seafood Restaurant UDMC

$$ | SEAFOOD | FAMILY | This seaside branch of one of Singapore's most long-standing seafood restaurant chains lets you pick your own fish, crab, lobsters, and more from tanks, then have it cooked the way you like. Whatever you choose, don't miss the black pepper crabs; Long Beach is the creator of the now-iconic Singaporean dish, and its version is still tops. **Known for:** live seafood; black pepper crab; seaside location. ⑤ *Average main: S$25* ⊠ *East Coast Seafood Centre, 1202 East Coast Pkwy., #01–04, East Coast Park* ⊕ *longbeachseafood.com.sg.*

★ Lucky House Cantonese Private Kitchen

$$$$ | CANTONESE | Slow-food champion Sam Wong runs this private dining experience from his vintage-furnished terrace house, at the back of which sits his wildly untamed fruit and vegetable garden. You'll have to book months ahead for a table, but the wait for his painstakingly made food—like a signature roast duck that undergoes three days of preparation and features homemade spices— is worth it. **Known for:** private dining; roast duck; locavore culture. ⑤ *Average main: S$80* ⊠ *Upper East Coast Rd., Siglap, Singapore* ☎ *9823–7268 For reservations; text only* ⊟ *No credit cards* ⊙ *By appointment only.*

Old Bibik Peranakan Kitchen

$$ | SINGAPOREAN | FAMILY | Enter a delectable world of Nonya tastes at this acclaimed Peranakan-style restaurant, housed in the ground floor of a traditional shophouse with tables spilling onto the street. The signature beef rendang, *ikan asam pedas* (spicy tamarind fish), *udang nenas masak* (prawn and pineapple coconut curry), grilled sambal barramundi, and *chinchalok* (fermented shrimp) omelet are all affordable, authentic and flavorsome dishes. **Known for:** homey dishes; old-school Peranakan atmosphere; attentive service. ⑤ *Average main: S$20* ⊠ *328 Joo Chiat Rd., #01–02, Joo Chiat* ☎ *8450–7996* ⊕ *oldbibik.com* Ⓜ *Dakota.*

🛏 Hotels

Hotel 81 Sakura

$ | HOTEL | Housed inside an azure Peranakan shophouse corner lot, this Japanese-themed budget hotel is in the very center of Joo Chiat. **Pros:** good value for money; close to transport and amenities; friendly housekeeping. **Cons:** few amenities in the room; rooms are a bit cramped; cleanliness can be hit or miss. ⑤ *Rooms from: S$88* ⊠ *181 Joo Chiat Rd., Joo Chiat* ☎ *6247–8181* ⊕ *www.wwhotels.com/hotel-81/sakura* 🛏 *75 rooms* ⦿ *No Meals* Ⓜ *Eunos.*

Hotel Indigo Singapore Katong

$$ | HOTEL | FAMILY | A stay here puts you in the heart of Singapore's bohemian Katong district and in one of the hotel's 131 colorful rooms decorated in vibrant, modern Peranakan style. **Pros:** plenty of food options nearby; rooftop infinity pool; interesting neighborhood. **Cons:** a distance from the city center; no free airport shuttle, as other hotels in the neighborhood have; no on-site bar. ⑤ *Rooms from: S$205* ⊠ *86 East Coast Rd., Katong* ☎ *6723–7001* ⊕ *www.hotelindigo.com* 🛏 *131 rooms* ⦿ *No Meals.*

Ibis Budget Joo Chiat

$ | MOTEL | This central, tall, mustard-colored building soars over the thick of Joo Chiat's bars and restaurants, offering clean, functional rooms with Peranakan-themed touches and a low price tag. **Pros:** clean; affordable; attentive staff. **Cons:** franchise-style feels less personalized; small bathrooms; nearby bars and nightlife can get noisy. ⑤ *Rooms from: S$85* ⊠ *219 Joo Chiat Rd., Joo Chiat* ☎ *6344–9888* ⊕ *www.all.accor.com* 🛏 *90 rooms* ⦿ *No Meals.*

Village Hotel Katong

$ | HOTEL | Located in a building that was formerly the Paramount Hotel, one of Katong's most iconic landmarks, this hotel sits at the top of East Coast Road. **Pros:** all rooms have balconies; walking distance to food, museums, and East Coast Park; free airport shuttle. **Cons:** no MRT station nearby (although there are bus stops); somewhat simple rooms; not centrally located. ⑤ *Rooms from: S$170* ✉ *25 Marine Parade Rd., Katong* ☎ *6344–2200* ⊕ *www.stayfareast.com* ⮌ *229 rooms* ⦿ *No Meals.*

🅨 Nightlife

★ Crane

GATHERING PLACES | What most people see of this beautiful 1920 corner lot shophouse is through the floor-to-ceiling windows of Japanese-inspired café Natsu, but like a hushed secret, what really happens at Crane is hidden both inside and on the charming rooftop. Part co-working space, part hipster café, and part community space (including a podcast recording studio) it's become a place to share urban experiences and transform them into real-life projects. On weekdays, people come for pizza nights on the terrace, interest groups' meet-ups, and private dining. On weekends, the East Comedy Club and a Farmer's Market bring the space's three delightfully retro floors to full-scale life. ✉ *285 Joo Chiat Rd., Joo Chiat* ⊕ *www.wearecrane.com.*

Lime House East Coast

PUBS | This Caribbean-inspired bar and bistro aims at bringing the laid-back rhythms and flavors of those far-away islands to Singapore's equally slow-paced Katong district. Rum and lime are the lifeblood of signature drinks such as Lime House Punch (spiked with sorrel, spices, honey, and fresh lime juice) and the tropical and refreshing Morris (with coconut water and cane sugar). A menu of Caribbean staples, from tapas to goat curry and sweet plantain lasagne, can be ordered for dinner or even brunch on weekends. ✉ *47–49 E Coast Rd., Katong* ☎ *6304–5328* ⊕ *www.limehouse.asia.*

Wine Mouth

WINE BARS | On the first floor of a shophouse, Singapore's first retail store and wine bar dedicated solely to natural wine—biodynamic farmed, organic, with minimal intervention in the wine-making process—is a spot to get a natural healthy hangover. You'll find reds, whites, oranges, rosé, sparkling, and spirits, though closing time is a fairly early 9 pm. ✉ *432A Joo Chiat Rd., Joo Chiat* ☎ *6974–7236* ⊕ *winemouthsg.com.*

🎭 Performing Arts

PERFORMANCE VENUES

Goodman Arts Centre

ARTS CENTERS | This arts hub holds multidisciplinary workshops ranging from dance to ceramic and visual arts on a weekly basis and for all ages. ⊠ *Goodman Arts Centre, 90 Goodman Rd., Katong* ☎ *6342–5790* ⊕ *artshouselimited.sg/gac.*

🛍️ Shopping

CRAFTS

La Tienda

CRAFTS | This female collective concept store housed in a Peranakan shophouse along Joo Chiat Road sells hip local and international products ranging from dresses and pumps to chalk paint, leather bags, and foulards, to outdoor candles and incense sticks. ⊠ *370 Joo Chiat Rd., Joo Chiat* ☎ *9774–0688.*

RECORDS

Retrocrates

MUSIC | Retrocrates specializes in jazz, blues, and world music, and it's a trusted spot to look for professional turntables, stereo amplifiers, speakers, and the like. They also grade and buy second-hand vinyl, the preferred format they stock and specialize in. ⊠ *450A Joo Chiat Rd., Joo Chiat* ☎ *8718–7370* ⊕ *www.retrocrates.com.*

SOUVENIRS

★ Kim Choo Kueh Chang

SOUVENIRS | **FAMILY** | Although this store is best-known for its traditional Peranakan rice dumplings and cakes, you can also pick up Peranakan porcelain pieces and other Peranakan-themed knick-knacks here. If you have more time, it also offers heritage tours and free sarong kebaya fitting sessions. ⊠ *111 East Coast Rd., Katong* ☎ *6741–2125* ⊕ *www.kimchoo.com* Ⓜ *Paya Lebar.*

★ Rumah Bebe

ANTIQUES & COLLECTIBLES | This lavishly decorated heritage shophouse peddles all manner of Peranakan goods, from traditional sarong kebaya clothing to snacks. It's owned by Peranakan beadwork specialist Bebe Seet, who also offers classes on beadwork and embroidery. ⊠ *113 East Coast Rd., Katong* ☎ *6247–8781* ⊕ *www.rumahbebe.com* Ⓜ *Paya Lebar.*

⚡ Activities

WALKING TOURS

★ Betel Box Food Tours

WALKING TOURS | Eastern Singapore is one of Singapore's best-known regions for food, so it's no surprise the area has numerous food tours. One of the most established and popular is the Joo Chiat/Katong Food Walk conducted by Betel Box, which takes participants on a 1.8-mile cultural and educational journey through the Joo Chiat and Katong neighborhoods and includes a sampling of more than 30 local specialities. Along the way, you'll learn about the history of the area, Singapore's housing system and architecture, the Peranakan culture, and much more. Wear comfortable walking shoes, be prepared for a brisk pace—and bring that appetite. ⊠ *Betel Box Hostel, 200 Joo Chiat Rd., Joo Chiat* ☎ *6247–7340* ⊕ *www.betelboxtours.com.*

WATER SPORTS

Singapore Wake Park

WATER SPORTS | FAMILY | At the city's only cable-ski park, you can wakeboard and kneeboard from day to night on the calm (and filtered) waters of East Coast Lagoon. The sprawling space caters to both beginners and experts, with three state-of-the-art cable systems that stretch over a total of 1,755 feet and have variable speeds and an obstacle course. Equipment, showers, lockers, and even free Wi-Fi—so you can upload photos of yourself riding the waves onto Instagram—are all provided. The on-site Coastal Rhythm Café is a tasty place to refuel and wakeboarder-watch when you need a break. ⊠ *1206A East Coast Pkwy., East Coast Park* ☎ *6636–4266* ⊕ *www.singaporewakepark.com* ⊠ *S$50 per hour (includes non-obstacle board, life vest, and helmet rental), S$20 per session for obstacle board rentals.*

Chapter 9

WESTERN DISTRICTS

Updated by
Olivia Lee

⊙ Sights   🍴 Restaurants   🛏 Hotels   ⬤ Shopping   🍸 Nightlife

★★★★★   ★★★★☆   ★★☆☆☆   ★★☆☆☆   ★★☆☆☆

NEIGHBORHOOD SNAPSHOT

TOP EXPERIENCES

■ **Wine and dine on Dempsey Hill:** Some of Singapore's chicest shops, restaurants, and bars are tucked into the lush greenery on the hill's peak.

■ **Go out in Holland Village:** Drink, eat, and be merry alongside the expats that call this international neighborhood home.

■ **Explore nature reserves:** From the rain forest of Bukit Timah to the tangle of trees at MacRitchie, there's plenty of wild green space to see.

■ **Day-trip to wildlife parks:** The Singapore Zoo, Night Safari, and Bird Paradise top the list of many travelers.

■ **Discover the magic of Haw Par Villa:** At this treasure trove of a park, you'll learn all about Chinese legends and mythology.

GETTING HERE

Western Singapore is made up of a number of sprawling neighborhoods. Fortunately, the entire area is well connected, with the Circle (orange) MRT Line serving Holland Village and the East–West (green) Line connecting the farther regions of Clementi and Jurong. On the East–West (green) line, Queenstown has a well-connected MRT station of the same name. Where the MRT lines don't go, there's usually a bus that does.

PLANNING YOUR TIME

Western Singapore is largely residential, so it can feel quiet during the week. This is a good time to visit the west's attractions, including the wildlife reserves or museums. Plan for a half day or full day for each major neighborhood.

VIEWFINDER

■ **Mount Faber** is Singapore's second highest hill, affording spectacular views of the coastline, city, and verdant foliage that surround the hilltop peak. Many people walk or cycle to the top, although you can also take a taxi or ride the cable car that leaves from VivoCity.

PAUSE HERE

■ **Pandan Reservoir** is the only elevated reservoir in Singapore—a huge pool of water with a 6-km walking trail around the rim. It's a beautiful place to stop and sit, taking in the reflections of the city or the otters that frequent its banks. Benches are occasionally dotted along the path, although there's little shade, so avoid the middle of the day.

Western Singapore is not so much a neighborhood as an entire corner of the country, sprawling from leafy Mount Faber park in the south to the industrial tip of Tuas in the far west. In between, you'll find malls, markets, museums, nature reserves, and residential pockets, where the local way of life thrives in a way you can't see in Singapore's glitzy center.

You could spend days visiting the many nature reserves, parks, museums, landmarks, and wetlands of the area and still not see them all. Visiting each will take some careful planning: the west is very spread out, and will likely require rides on both the MRT and buses (30 minutes to an hour or more) to reach the more remote attractions. It's worth the effort though—western Singapore is a welcome breath of fresh air after spending time in the more touristy neighborhoods down south.

There are four major neighborhood groupings that can be easily be paired together: Holland Village and Dempsey Hill for great restaurants and bars; Bukit Merah and Queenstown for the cool Henderson Waves and Mount Faber; Bukit Timah and its neighbors to the north (Kranji and the Central Water Catchment) for parks and the zoo; and Clementi and Jurong for an up-and-coming area with outlet malls. The best way to explore is just to pick a neighborhood and walk around, dipping into the many malls, markets, and hawker centers scattered about the region.

Dempsey Hill and Holland Village

Dempsey Hill first served as British Army barracks, then as a local military base. These days, it's a place to see and be seen—a refurbished enclave filled with tropical trees and some of the city's best restaurants, bars, and lifestyle shops, many of them in restored black-and-white, 19th-century colonial houses.

Nearby, you'll find Holland Village, one of Singapore's best-known expat districts, with many terraced homes remaining from the

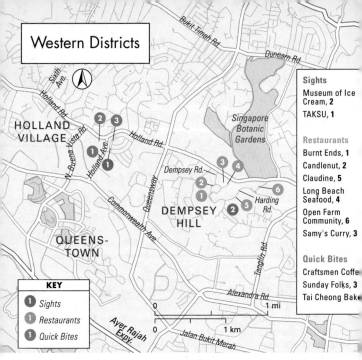

Western Districts

Sights
Museum of Ice Cream, **2**
TAKSU, **1**

Restaurants
Burnt Ends, **1**
Candlenut, **2**
Claudine, **5**
Long Beach Seafood, **4**
Open Farm Community, **6**
Samy's Curry, **3**

Quick Bites
Craftsmen Coffe
Sunday Folks, **3**
Tai Cheong Bak

KEY
1 Sights
1 Restaurants
1 Quick Bites

British Army before World War II. This small community, a village of sorts as it encompasses just a few streets, is filled with a buzzing selection of modern restaurants and bars that make it a fun place to explore in the evenings (particularly on weekends).

⊙ Sights

Museum of Ice Cream

OTHER ATTRACTION | FAMILY | Release your inner child at this fun, retro ode to everyone's favorite chilled treat. Housed in an old military building in Dempsey Hill, the "museum" comprises 14 interactive installations, including a giant pool of sprinkles and an old-school playground. Guided tours take between 60 and 90 minutes, with unlimited sweet treats as you make your way around. If you are still feeling peckish, you can have takeaway delivered directly to your hotel afterward. ⊠ *100 Loewen Rd., Dempsey Hill* ⊕ *museumoficecream.com* ⊠ *From S$36* ⊗ *Closed Tues.*

TAKSU

ART GALLERY | Nestled in the charming Chip Bee Gardens, Singapore's leading contemporary art gallery champions primarily Southeast Asian artists, and the exhibits tend to have a younger, more urban edge than is typically found on the island. The curated collection has over 2,000 works if you are interested in purchasing art during your stay. ⊠ *43 Jaln Merah Saga, #01–72, Holland Village* ☎ *6476–4788* ⊕ *www.taksu.com* 🖀 *Free* ⊗ *Closed Mon.* Ⓜ *Holland Village.*

🍴 Restaurants

Singapore is known for its food countrywide, but the culinary scene reaches its pinnacle in the residential west where locals want easy access to good food without having to travel into the center. Vibrant pockets of eateries and bars have sprung up in all of the west's most prominent neighborhoods, including Dempsey Hill and Holland Village—each one worthy of an evening of your time. It's a great way to see how the locals like to dine.

★ Burnt Ends

$$$ | BARBECUE | This internationally-renowned modern Australian barbecue restaurant, run by chef Dave Pynt, is always booked up, so plan your visit in advance. Classics like the Burnt End's Sanger (pulled pork sandwich) are a must-try. **Known for:** open-kitchen Aussie-style barbecue; filled donuts from the bakery; reservations essential. ⑤ *Average main: S$60* ⊠ *7 Dempsey Rd., #01–02, Dempsey Hill* ☎ *6224–3933* ⊕ *burntends.com.sg* ⊗ *Closed Sun. and Mon. No lunch Tues. and Wed.*

Candlenut

$$ | SINGAPOREAN | Candlenut was the world's first Michelin-starred Peranakan restaurant, serving a little-known traditional cuisine that blends Chinese ingredients with Malaysian and Indonesian spices and cooking methods. The restaurant's design reflects this style, with intricate tiles on the floor and straw lanterns hanging from the ceiling. **Known for:** Peranakan cuisine; "ah-ma-kase" set lunch and dinner menus; colorful dishes like blue swimmer crab curry. ⑤ *Average main: S$40* ⊠ *COMO Dempsey complex, Block 17A, Demsey Rd., Dempsey Hill* ☎ *6486–1051* ⊕ *www.comodempsey.sg.*

Claudine

$$$ | FRENCH | Honest, home-style French cooking set in a converted chapel needn't be this good, but chef Julien Royer and his team deliver with this "neo-brasserie" concept on Dempsey Hill. From the beef and onion soup to the apple tart with salted caramel, the dishes are refined versions of the classics. **Known for:** French brasserie cooking perfected; tableside theatrics; ex-army chapel dining space. ⑤ *Average main: S$70* ⊠ *39C Harding Rd., Dempsey Hill* ☎ *8031–9935* ⊕ *www.claudinerestaurant.com* ⊗ *Closed Mon. No lunch Tues.*

Dempsey Hill Through the Years ◉

On a small hill near the center of Singapore you will find one of the country's chicest lifestyle destinations, home to Michelin-star restaurants and fashion outlets—with price tags to match. But it hasn't always been this way.

Early Years
Dempsey Hill began its life as Mount Harriet, the site of an enormous nutmeg plantation that stretched from the hill to what is now the Singapore Botanic Gardens. A beetle blight devastated the plantation in the 1850s, and the land was sold to the British Forces, who cut down the trees and replaced them with the Tanglin Barracks.

WWII
The hill was named for General Sir Miles Christopher Dempsey, the commanding officer of the Second Army, the main British force involved in the 1944 D-Day landings. He served throughout World War II and the Japanese occupation. In 1945, the Japanese troops surrendered, and Singapore was returned to the British, who maintained the barracks until their withdrawal in 1971.

Today
The area gradually transformed into a retail enclave using the former soldier's barracks as shops and warehouses. Today, it is a place to see and be seen as you shop in the beautiful (if overpriced) produce stores, and wine and dine in the expensive but elegant restaurants, each housed in an original colonial building, with low-lying red-brick roofs and white-washed walls.

★ Long Beach Seafood

$$$ | SEAFOOD | Cracking into a black-pepper or chilli crab is one of those signature Singapore dining experiences, and there are few places that do it better than Long Beach. There are four restaurant locations across Singapore, including the main branch on the East Coast, near where it first opened in 1946, but this Dempsey Hill branch stands out for its convenience and outdoor seating deck (plus you can stop for a pre-dinner pint or two of tasty microbrews at the nearby RedDot Brewhouse). **Known for:** crab, crab, and more crab; Singapore's original seafood restaurant; open-air dining. $ *Average main: S$45* ✉ *Dempsey Rd., Blk. 25, Dempsey Hill* ☎ *6323–2222* ⊕ *www.longbeachseafood.com.sg.*

★ Open Farm Community

$$ | BISTRO | In the luscious greenery of Dempsey Hill, an urban farm takes the concept of farm-to-fork seriously in its self-named restaurant. If the adjacent farm doesn't grow it, produce is

sourced from smaller, independent farms around Singapore and Malaysia. **Known for:** local produced, most grown on-site; popular weekend brunch; independent, small domain-focused wine list. $ *Average main: S$40* ⌧ *130E Minden Rd., Dempsey Hill* ☎ *6471–0306* ⊕ *www.openfarmcommunity.com.*

★ Samy's Curry

$$ | INDIAN | Because of its airy, colonial edifice with wooden-louvered windows and overhead fans, Samy's Curry has a casual canteen feel that is distinct from the more upscale ambience typical of many Dempsey Hill eateries. Although the wait staff can be a little brisk, the restaurant remains a firm favorite among the locals thanks to the flavorful and filling north and south Indian dishes on offer at very affordable prices. **Known for:** delicious fish head curry; banana leaves in place of plates; classic Indian dishes including chicken tikka. $ *Average main: S$18* ⌧ *25 Dempsey Rd., Dempsey Hill* ☎ *6472–2080* ⊕ *www.samyscurry.com* ☾ *Closed Tues.*

😊 Coffee and Quick Bites

Craftsmen Coffee

$ | CAFÉ | At the edge of Holland Village, this independent speciality shop is a rare treat in a country where good coffee can be hard to come by. It sources single-origin beans from around the world, focusing on the aromas and tastes of each variety, and serves its coffee alongside simple snacks and meals, from fresh salads and pastas to sandwiches and croissants. **Known for:** coffee beans from around the world; cool brunch spot; sandwiches and pastries. $ *Average main: S$5* ⌧ *275 Holland Ave., Holland Village* ☎ *6463–1715* ⊕ *www.craftsmencoffee.com* Ⓜ *Holland Village.*

Sunday Folks

$$ | DESSERTS | The cool interior of this hip ice-cream and waffle house is a great place to escape the sun while exploring the boutiques at Chip Bee Gardens. The ice cream leans towards local flavors such as passionfruit and *gula melaka* (palm sugar), but the waffles are the real crowd-pleaser. **Known for:** handcrafted desserts; good coffee; hot waffles and soft serve. $ *Average main: S$15* ⌧ *Chip Bee Gardens, 44 Jln Merah Saga, #01–52, Holland Village* ☎ *6479–9166* ⊕ *sundayfolks.com* Ⓜ *Holland Village.*

Tai Cheong Bakery

$ | BAKERY | There's a reason why the line often snakes out the door of this Hong Kong bakery in Holland Village: Tai Cheong's egg tarts are renowned island-wide. These crumbly tart shells with gloriously wobbly egg custard filling are impeccable. **Known for:**

Hong Kong–style pastries; crumbly, rich egg tarts; classic Canton-ese dishes. $ *Average main: S$13* ✉ *31 Lor Liput, Holland Village* ☎ *9828–1954* ⊕ *www.taicheong.com.sg* Ⓜ *Holland Village.*

🍸 Nightlife

The nightlife in western Singapore seems elusive, but it's there if you know where to look. One place you'll have no difficulty finding it is Holland Village, with its many bars and eateries. Dempsey Hill, too, is a nice place to stroll at night, dipping into the various watering holes. Outside of these two expat enclaves, though, the nightlife options are more spread out. You won't be able to do much bar-crawling, but if you pick a spot and hunker down for the evening, you'll get a taste of how the locals like to drink.

Chimichanga

BARS | This hip Mexican joint is the perfect people-watching spot, positioned right in the center of Holland Village. The well-stocked bar has a range of ice-cold beers on tap, a solid selection of classic cocktails, and a pretty generous happy hour. There's also a substantial food menu of Mexican favorites, so grab a basket of tortilla chips and guacamole to munch on with your margaritas. ✉ *Holland Piazza, 3 Lor Liput, #01–02/03, Holland Village* ☎ *6974–7186* ⊕ *www.chimichanga.sg* Ⓜ *Holland Village.*

CM-PB

BARS | Set amid the tropical trees that fill Dempsey Hill, this rustic bungalow bar (the acronym used for its name stands for Contemporary Melting-Pot and Bar) is a great place to spend an evening with good food, great drinks, and plenty of live music. A selection of tapas inspired by the flavors of Asia counterbalances a wide array of beer, ciders, cocktails, and alcohol-free mocktails, and a comprehensive brunch menu is offered until late afternoon on the weekends. ✉ *Blk 7 Dempsey Rd., #01–05, Dempsey Hill* ☎ *6475–0105* ⊕ *www.cm-pb.net.*

Le Bon Funk

WINE BARS | This contemporary wine bar, which champions accessible organic and natural wines, is situated in a quiet corner of Holland Village. The European-style food menu changes daily, with a selection of small plates focused on seasonal produce. The outdoor terrace is a relaxing place to sip as the sun sets. ✉ *277 Holland Ave., Holland Village* ☎ *9833–9867* ⊕ *lebonfunk.com* Ⓜ *Holland Village.*

RedDot Brewhouse

BREWPUBS | Come for the excellent microbrews, stay for the location amid the lush greenery of Dempsey Hill. The food is satisfying—think pizzas, grilled meats, and tapas—but it's the range of delicious beers that take center stage, from IPAs to Czech pilsners. The most commonly served drink is RedDot's own Monster Green Lager, a tall glass of fluorescent beer that gets its hue from spirulina. It tastes better than it looks. ⊠ *Dempsey Rd., #01–01, Blk. 25A, Dempsey Hill* ☎ *6475–0500* ⊕ *www.reddotbrewhouse.com.sg.*

Wala Wala

PUBS | Holland Village has seen many bars open and close, but this wildly popular watering hole has stayed the same for decades, pairing its jugs of cocktails and other drinks with Western favorites like pizza and steak. Live music often plays upstairs, and there's a bustling bar downstairs that has a welcoming outdoor sitting area, which occasionally spills out onto the street on a Saturday night. ⊠ *31 Lorong Mambong, Holland Village* ☎ *6462–4288* ⊕ *www. walawala.sg* Ⓜ *Holland Village.*

🛍 Shopping

Shops in the west vary wildly depending on where you visit. Around Holland Village and Dempsey Hill, they tend to be high-end boutiques, catering to the affluent residents. Outside these wealthier pockets, you will find all manner of shops, from giant malls that keep local teenagers endlessly entertained to neighborhood stores that seem to sell everything from slippers to ironing boards. If you want to try some cheap local shopping, head to one of Singapore's many wet markets, where little stalls selling knick-knacks and trinkets pop up among the fruit and vegetable stands on weekend mornings.

ACCESSORIES

★ LINGWU

HANDBAGS | Browse sustainably made, super chic bags at local designer Ling Wu's boutique store. Ling's bags are known for sleek, modern designs that accentuate the elegance of the high-quality leather. And with her "Make Good" commitment, weaved designs use upcycled materials and fair trade principles to support communities in nearby Kalimantan and Sarawak. It's best to call or text ahead to book an appointment at the store. ⊠ *43 Jln Merah Saga, #02–78, Holland Village* ☎ *9696–3118* ⊕ *lingwuasia. com* Ⓜ *Holland Village.*

ART GALLERIES

REDSEA Gallery

ART GALLERIES | Contemporary works from more than 40 international artists are displayed in this gallery housed in a former army barracks. All pieces are handpicked by the gallery's owner, Chris Churcher, who meets with each artist before showcasing his or her work. ⊠ *Dempsey Hill, Block 9 Dempsey Rd., #01–10, Dempsey Hill* ☎ *6732–6711* ⊕ *www.redseagallery.com.*

CLOTHING
Kids 21

CHILDREN'S CLOTHING | FAMILY | Explore this large retail space and family club for designer kids' clothing, featuring collections from Stella McCartney Kids and Bobo Choses, and cute kid-friendly gifts and toys. ⊠ *16 Dempsey Rd., Dempsey Hill* ☎ *6304–1435* ⊕ *kids21.com.*

LEATHER GOODS
★ Bynd Artisan

LEATHER GOODS | Having a personalized notebook made for you by hand might be one of the greatest gifts in our digital age. In around 20 minutes, the artisans at Bynd can create a bespoke leather-bound notebook, complete with foil stamping on the cover forming your desired lettering. They can also personalize other gifts, including wallets and phone cases. ⊠ *44 Jln Merah Saga, #01–54, Holland Village* ☎ *6475–1680* ⊕ *www.byndartisan.com* Ⓜ *Holland Village.*

HOUSEWARES
★ Independent Market

HOUSEWARES | An excellent place to stock up on gifts with a distinctly Singaporean flavor, Independent Market sells everything from Peranakan-themed coasters and magnets to books on perfecting your Singlish. As the name suggests, the shop is a collection of independent Singaporean designers and publishers, so you can be sure your money spent here is supporting local artists. ⊠ *Holland Road Shopping Centre, 211 Holland Ave., #03-01, Holland Village* ☎ *9338–2663* ⊕ *www.independentmarket.sg* Ⓜ *Holland Village.*

★ Lim's Arts and Living

HOUSEWARES | Located in the Holland Road Shopping Centre, which is an expat landmark, Lim's Arts and Living carries an eclectic range of handcrafted furniture, silks, paper products, Asian-style housewares, and sundry knickknacks. Even if you don't buy anything, it's a fun shop to browse. This is just one of several of Lim's outlets across the city, having first opened in 1970. ⊠ *#02-01 Holland Road Shopping Centre, 211 Holland Ave., Singapore* ☎ *6466–3188* ⊕ *www.limslegacy.com* Ⓜ *Holland Village.*

★ Maywell Lifestyles

FURNITURE | The team here are experts in Burmese teak furniture, offering a treasure trove of pieces nestled in the leafy greenery of Dempsey Hill. While the larger signature pieces, which are hand-crafted by in-house "wood doctor" Kelvin, may be too large to fit in a suitcase, there's a huge selection of art, sculptures, and decorative pieces to marvel at throughout the shop. ⊠ *13 Dempsey Rd, #01–06, Dempsey Hill* ☎ *9693–2974* ⊕ *maywell.com.sg.*

SHOPPING CENTERS AND MALLS

Holland Road Shopping Centre

SHOPPING CENTER | Singapore's expats frequent this shopping complex, where they pick up lightweight clothes perfect for tropical weather, coral-encrusted handbags and flip flops from Bali, jewelry, and second-hand books. Lim's Arts and Crafts carries Southeast Asian houseware, furniture, and linen and rattan. ⊠ *211 Holland Ave., Holland Village* ☎ *6469–5334* Ⓜ *Holland Village.*

🏃 Activities

SPAS

Natureland Spa

SPAS | This island-wide spa favorite sits in a secluded spot in the heart of Holland Village. Take time out from perusing the shopping centers to grab one of the many massage and therapy options on offer. ⊠ *29/29a Lor Liput, Holland Village* ☎ *6467–6780* ⊕ *www. natureland.com.sg* 🍽 *Body therapy from S$72 (60 mins), foot reflexology from S$38 (30 mins)* Ⓜ *Holland Village.*

Bukit Merah and Queenstown

The southwest coast of Singapore stretches from Queenstown to Bukit Merah, encompassing the iconic Southern Ridges—a seamless span of green parks linked by a 10-km (6.2-mile) trail. Queenstown is home to the National University of Singapore, so you'll often find crowds of young people in the local bars. Bukit Merah, near Tiong Bahru and Chinatown, is a popular residential area thanks to its many green parks, including Mount Faber, and its close proximity to the city center. Holland Village is just a 10- to 15-minute walk away from Queenstown.

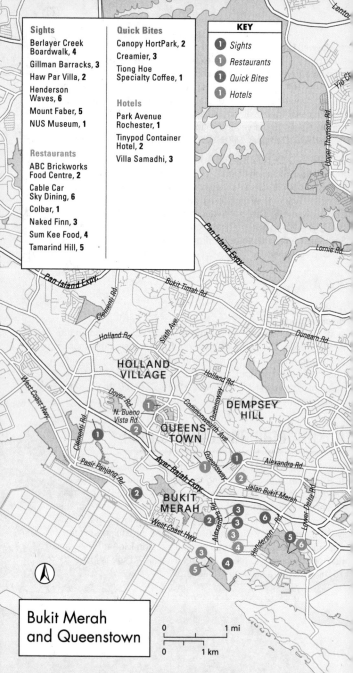

Sights

Berlayer Creek
Boardwalk, **4**

Gillman Barracks, **3**

Haw Par Villa, **2**

Henderson
Waves, **6**

Mount Faber, **5**

NUS Museum, **1**

Restaurants

ABC Brickworks
Food Centre, **2**

Cable Car
Sky Dining, **6**

Colbar, **1**

Naked Finn, **3**

Sum Kee Food, **4**

Tamarind Hill, **5**

Quick Bites

Canopy HortPark, **2**

Creamier, **3**

Tiong Hoe
Specialty Coffee, **1**

Hotels

Park Avenue
Rochester, **1**

Tinypod Container
Hotel, **2**

Villa Samadhi, **3**

KEY

1 Sights

1 Restaurants

1 Quick Bites

1 Hotels

Bukit Merah
and Queenstown

0   1 mi

0   1 km

HOLLAND
VILLAGE

DEMPSEY
HILL

QUEENS
TOWN

BUKIT
MERAH

Pan-Island Expy.

Bukit Timah Rd.

Holland Rd.

Sixth Ave.

Holland Rd.

Dunearn Rd.

Lornie Rd.

Pan-Island Expy.

Upper Thomson Rd.

Yio Cr.

Lentor

West Coast Hwy.

Clementi Rd.

Clementi Rd.

Pasir Panjang Rd.

Ayer Rajah Expy.

West Coast Hwy.

Dover Rd.

N. Bueno
Vista Rd.

Commonwealth Ave.

Queensway

Queensway

Alexandra Rd.

Jalan Bukit Merah

Alexandra Rd.

Henderson Rd.

Lower Delta Rd.

◉ Sights

Berlayer Creek Boardwalk

PROMENADE | The ½-mile Berlayer Creek Boardwalk near the neighborhood of Alexandra runs through one of the two remaining mangrove forests in southern Singapore. The boardwalk is raised, letting you peer over the sides at the swampy undergrowth, where 60 bird species, 19 fish species, and 14 mangrove plant species have been recorded. There are informative storyboards along the route, as well as look-out points where you can get closer to the area's unique biodiversity. Continue to the Alexandra Garen Trail and Bukit Cermin Boardwalk for the full Labrador Nature and Coastal Walk. ⊠ *Alexandra, Singapore* ⊹ *Join the trail from Labrador Park MRT* ⊕ *nparks.gov.sg* Ⓜ *Labrador Park.*

Gillman Barracks

ART GALLERY | This wonderful art space started out life in 1936 as a barracks for the British Army. Today, it champions Singaporean and Southeast Asian art in a number of galleries housed in the original army blocks. There are also regular events and workshops, including film weeks, rotating exhibitions, and evening talks. After you've browsed the galleries, kick back at one of the pretty on-site cafés or bars, each one surrounded by leafy foliage. ⊠ *9 Lock Rd., Bukit Merah* ⊕ *www.visitsingapore.com* ⊙ *Galleries closed on Mon.* Ⓜ *Labrador Park.*

Haw Par Villa

THEME PARK | **FAMILY** | Formerly known as Tiger Balm Gardens, Haw Par Villa is a charmingly bizarre park dedicated to Chinese legends and myths. Once part of an estate owned by the two eccentric brothers who created Tiger Balm ointment, the gardens were opened to the public after World War II and later transformed into this theme park. A highlight of the intriguing treasure trove of Chinese mythology, religion, and social mores is the walk-through "Ten Courts of Hell" display, which depicts a tale of life after death designed to teach traditional Chinese morality. Discover more about the display at the intriguing Hell's Museum, featuring specially curated displays that explore death and dying in belief systems around the world. ⊠ *262 Pasir Panjang Rd., Queenstown* ☎ *6773–0103* ⊕ *www.hawparvilla.sg* ⊠ *Park entrance free, Hell's Museum S$18* ⊙ *Hell's Museum closed Mon. and Tues.* Ⓜ *Haw Par Villa.*

★ Henderson Waves

BRIDGE | Singapore's highest pedestrian bridge is a fantastical, wave-like span suspended 118 feet above lush rain forest. It was built in 2008 to connect Mount Faber Park and Telok Blangah

Hill Park and quickly became a social media photo phenomenon thanks to its distinctive shapes and undulating design. It's just under 1,000 feet long, making it fairly quick to cross, but you'll want to allow extra time to capture the cool shapes on camera. Come early in the morning to avoid crowds. ⊠ *Henderson Rd., Bukit Merah* ⊕ *nparks.gov.sg* Ⓜ *Telok Blangah.*

Mount Faber

MOUNTAIN | The tall hill of Mount Faber Park is one of the oldest green spaces in Singapore, with excellent views across the city. While you can drive or walk to the top, taking the cable car from the Harbourfront station, the same cable car that continues on to Sentosa Island, is the most scenic way to reach the peak. The park has a number of dining and entertainment complexes at the top where you can grab a meal or a drink and look out over the park's vibrant lush rainforest, with the city in the distance beyond. ⊠ *Mount Faber Park, Telok Blangah Rd., Bukit Merah* ⊕ *www. nparks.gov.sg* Ⓜ *Telok Blangah.*

★ NUS Museum

ART MUSEUM | On the main campus of the National University of Singapore, the NUS Museum is the nation's oldest university museum. At any one time, it displays some 1,000 of its roughly 8,000 artifacts and artworks, which were first introduced by museum curator Michael Sullivan as a teaching collection in 1955. The works are split across four major exhibits, including the South and Southeast Asian Collection and the Straits Chinese Collection. Temporary exhibitions also pop up from time to time, alongside educational workshops. If you can't make the trip to the museum itself, you can also view more than 2,000 of the fascinating artifacts via the museum's online database. ⊠ *National University of Singapore, 50 Kent Ridge Crescent, Queenstown* ☎ *6516–8817* ⊕ *museum.nus.edu.sg* 🎫 *Free* ☉ *Closed Sun. and Mon.* Ⓜ *Kent Ridge.*

🍴 Restaurants

Being farther from the city center, you'll find the restaurants in the west frequented more by locals than tourists, which means you get a much more authentic experience.

★ ABC Brickworks Food Centre

$ | **SINGAPOREAN** | Tucked behind an imposing IKEA building, one of the island's oldest food centers is particularly popular with locals in the Alexandra area; expect lines on weekend mornings to snake across the hall. But the wait is worth it, as you'll find

Curving and twisting 118 feet above ground, Henderson Waves is Singapore's highest pedestrian bridge.

some of Singapore's best hawkers here. **Known for:** char siew BBQ pork buns; refreshing ice desserts; busy weekend lines. $ *Average main: S$6* ⊠ *6 Jalan Bukit Merah, Alexandra* ☎ *6225–5632* Ⓜ *Redhill.*

Cable Car Sky Dining

$$$$ | ASIAN | This dining-in-the-sky experience ticks a number of boxes: it's unique, the food is good, and it features an incredible view. As you travel up and down Mount Faber in a private cable-car cabin, you'll tuck into a four-course dinner (Deluxe) with welcome drinks at the Arbora Bistro at Mount Faber Peak, or a main and dessert (Private). **Known for:** unique dining experience; spectacular views; private setting. $ *Average main: S$98* ⊠ *Level 2 Faber Peak Singapore, 109 Mount Faber Rd., Bukit Merah* ☎ *6361–0088* ⊕ *www.mountfaberleisure.com/restaurant/cable-car-sky-dining* ⊗ *Closed Mon.–Wed. No lunch* ☞ *Boarding from 5:30 pm, last boarding at 6:30 pm.*

Colbar

$ | INTERNATIONAL | FAMILY | Built in 1953 as a canteen for the British army (and seemingly unchanged since), this gem of a café lies in a secluded spot near Queenstown. Although the building itself is a little rustic, the garden tables outside are perfect for lazy weekend afternoons, especially for those with young children. **Known for:** colonial decor; ales and fruit ciders; lovely outside seating area. $ *Average main: S$10* ⊠ *9A Whitchurch Rd, Queenstown* ☎ *6779–4859* ⊗ *Closed Mon.* Ⓜ *One North.*

Saturdays at Ghim Moh Market 🍴

In Queenstown, not far from Holland Village, lies the bustling Ghim Moh market. It's not well publicized to tourists, but it's the place to be on a Saturday morning for locals. The wet market overflows with produce fresh from the farms in Malaysia, offering some of the cheapest vegetables around. At the food center behind, people line up for breakfast from the many delicious stalls.

Naked Finn

$$$ | SEAFOOD | In a quiet, unpretentious building in Gillman Barracks, this seafood lover's delight focuses on simple preparations of fresh fish centered around the day's catch. The menu is ever-evolving, and though there are nods to local flavors (like spicy sambal sauces), the fish is always the star of the show. Japanese influences come through in some of the high-quality seafood and the well-curated wine and sake list. **Known for:** unpretentious seafood cooking; local flavors and ingredients; Japanese-imported ingredients. ⓢ *Average main: S$45* ✉ *39 Malan Rd., Alexandra, Bukit Merah* ☎ *6694–0807* ⊕ *www.nakedfinn.com* ☺ *Closed Sun. and Mon.* Ⓜ *Labrador Park.*

Sum Kee Food

$$ | CHINESE | Tucked away in an inconspicuous spot in Telok Blangah, this old-school Chinese eatery is loved for its hearty renditions of Cantonese classics. Signature dishes are a must, including ultraman chicken (fried chicken coated with salted egg) and pumpkin tofu (deep-fried minced pork, soft tofu, and creamy pumpkin sauce). **Known for:** old-school Cantonese classic dishes; salted egg chicken and pumpkin tofu; lively dining hall with outdoor space. ⓢ *Average main: S$30* ✉ *2 Telok Blangah St., #31, Bukit Merah* ☎ *6737–3233* Ⓜ *Labrador Park.*

★ Tamarind Hill

$$$ | THAI | This restaurant specializing in Thai and Shan (Burmese) cuisine is in a historic colonial building within the leafy surroundings of Labrador Park. The menu promises both modern and authentic dishes, with such recognizable classics like *tom yam soup* mixing with more innovative creations like duck with lychee. **Known for:** large Thai and Shan menu; romantic setting in a historic building; house-infused gins. ⓢ *Average main: S$45* ✉ *30 Labrador Villa Rd., Bukit Merah* ☎ *6929–2100* ⊕ *www.tamarindrestaurants.com* Ⓜ *Labrador Park.*

☕ Coffee and Quick Bites

Canopy HortPark

$$ | CAFÉ | This bright, airy café in HortPark has a large outdoor space, a pet-friendly area, and an abundance of greenery hanging from the ceilings. There's an all-day dining menu for larger bites, but the chilled, green space is a great place to grab a coffee and take a break from exploring the city. **Known for:** alfresco dining; all-day menu; pet-friendly garden. $ *Average main: S$25* ✉ *HortPark, 33 Hyderabad Rd., #01–01, Bukit Merah* ☎ *6556–1533* ⊕ *www. canopygardendining.com* Ⓜ *Labrador Park.*

Creamier

$ | ICE CREAM | Cool down from art gallery hopping in Gilman Barracks with a scoop of some of the Island's favorite handcrafted ice cream. Alongside classics like strawberry, chocolate, and pistachio, there are interesting local combinations, like blue pea (butterfly pea flower), Thai milk tea, or salted *gula melaka* (palm sugar). **Known for:** artisanal gelato; ice-cream-topped waffles; coffee. $ *Average main: S$7* ✉ *5A Lock Rd., Alexandra, Bukit Merah* ☎ *8772–3877* ⊕ *creamier.com.sg* Ⓜ *Labrador Park.*

★ Tiong Hoe Specialty Coffee

$ | CAFÉ | Tucked away in a quiet residential block in Queenstown, this small space is the gold standard of coffee roasting on the island. Initially started as a bean and machine wholesaler, the regular stream of coffee aficionados visiting for a drink soon convinced the owners to turn this space into a working café. **Known for:** cozy, residential coffee shop; high-quality brews; beans from around the world. $ *Average main: S$5* ✉ *170 Stirling Rd., #01–1133, Queenstown* ⊕ *Entrance inside the estate on the opposite side to the food center, next to the supermarket* ☎ *6474–5442* ⊕ *www.tionghoe.com* Ⓜ *Queenstown.*

🛏 Hotels

Hotels in the west are few and far between, mainly because visitors to Singapore prefer to stay a little closer to the center. Still, if you're planning a trip to one of the sights in the far west—or if you want to get closer to the local way of life—there are a few good options.

Park Avenue Rochester

$$ | HOTEL | This shiny hotel is located next to a number of great shopping malls, including Rochester Mall and The Star Vista, plus it's only a two-minute walk from Buona Vista MRT, connecting you directly to Tiong Bahru and Raffles Place. **Pros:** friendly, professional staff; great breakfast; good facilities, including a pool and gym. **Cons:** a little far from the center; expensive considering location; rooms and beds are small. Ⓢ *Rooms from: S$215* ✉ *31 Rochester Dr., Queenstown* ☎ *6808–8600* ⊕ *parkavenuegroup. com/property/rochester* ⤴ *351 rooms* ⦿ *No Meals* Ⓜ *Buona Vista.*

Tinypod Container Hotel

$$ | **APARTMENT** | A novel concept for Singapore is the city's first hotel made entirely from shipping containers, which is big on charm. **Pros:** pods can sleep up to four; Netflix in the rooms; different kind of experience. **Cons:** no physical front desk; no shared hotel facilities; breakfast not included. Ⓢ *Rooms from: S$250* ✉ *77 Ayer Rajah Crescent, Block 77 & 82, Queenstown* ☎ *6665–7500* ⊕ *www.tinypod.com* ⤴ *4 cabins* ⦿ *No Meals* Ⓜ *One North.*

★ Villa Samadhi

$$ | **HOTEL** | You might be tempted to forget you're in the heart of Singapore when you stay in this converted 1920 colonial garrison setting in the tropical secondary forest in Labrador Nature Reserve on the island's southwest coast. **Pros:** unique colonial-era design; quiet, tranquil location; excellent Thai restaurant. **Cons:** no kids under 16 allowed; expect insects and lizards; a bit tired in places. Ⓢ *Rooms from: S$330* ✉ *20 Labrador Villa Rd., Queenstown* ☎ *6929–2100* ⊕ *www.villasamadhi.com.sg* ⤴ *20 rooms* ⦿ *Free Breakfast* Ⓜ *Labrador Park.*

🍸 Nightlife

You might not call it "nightlife" in the traditional sense, but there are a lot of great spots in the west where you could spend an evening. Popular with locals who live nearby, these places are worth trying if you're in the neighborhood.

Handlebar

BEER GARDENS | Happily proclaimed as the first (and best) biker bar in Singapore, Handlebar is a cool beer garden slightly hidden down a hill in Gillman Barracks. Regular live music, house-brewed craft lagers, and a raucous clientele make this bar a fun place for evening and weekend drinks. There's a menu of beer-snacking classics, including hot wings, nachos, and burgers. ✉ *10 Lock Rd., Bukit Merah* ☎ *6268–5550* ⊕ *www.facebook.com/HandlebarSG-GillmanBarracks* Ⓜ *Labrador Park.*

Hooha! Café

LIVE MUSIC | Music industry insiders, club owners, and musicians congregate at this club in the small but busy Pasir Panjang Village entertainment hub. The Saturday night jamming and sing-along action may go into the early hours upstairs, with people leaving the bar to go directly to Mass in the morning. There's no band, but drum sets and guitars are available upstairs. Downstairs, there's a bar and restaurant, though the drinks are better than the food. ⊠ *Viva Vista Mall, 3 South Buona Vista Rd., #B01–06/11/50, Queenstown* ☎ *6250–6348* Ⓜ *Pasir Panjang.*

Hopscotch

BARS | This laid-back bar located in the art complex of Gillman Barracks has some serious cocktail credentials. Try Singaporean twists on classics, something a little more adventurous (like the Peranakan-inspired, tequila-soaked Tipsy Nonya), or even one of their bespoke creations. Food ranges from burgers and pizzas to large sharing plates straight from the grill, all good to soak up those boozy drinks. ⊠ *Gillman Barracks, 45 Malan Rd., Bukit Merah* ☎ *6339–0633* ⊕ *www.hopscotch.sg* Ⓜ *Labrador Park.*

★ Timbre+

GATHERING PLACES | This vibrant urban food park is a great place to while away an evening, with live music performances most nights of the week. You can watch the bands play on the big stage as you eat your way around food vans serving everything from charcoal-grilled kebabs to lip-tingling mala hotpot. There's also an excellent bar and bottle shop, where you can order craft beer on tap or choose from more than 120 beer and cider bottles. Timbre+ is located by One North MRT, one stop away from Holland Village on the Circle (orange) Line. ⊠ *JTC LaunchPad @ one-north, 73A Ayer Rajah Crescent, Queenstown* ☎ *9850–5769* ⊕ *timbreplus.sg* Ⓜ *One North.*

🛍 Shopping

FOOD

★ The Cheese Ark

FOOD | Tucked into one of the oldest residential areas in Singapore, this inconspicuous store hides a wealth of yellow gold. A collector of oft-forgotten, rare cheeses, founder Ai Ming Syu is incredibly passionate and knowledgeable about cheese from around the world; in fact, the shop will only sell you the right cheese when it is ripe and ready, so do go with an open mind. They also have crackers, chutneys, charcuterie, wine, and more. If you are looking for something to elevate your picnic, this is the perfect stop. ⊠ *49 Stirling Rd., #01–489, Queenstown* ☎ *9175–0090* ⊕ *www. thecheeseark.com* Ⓜ *Queenstown.*

JEWELRY

★ By Invite Only

JEWELRY & WATCHES | Founded by Trixie Kong initially to offer a range of skin-sensitive, non-toxic jewelry, the brand has grown into one of Singapore's best-loved jewelry brands. Focusing on producing elegant pieces ethically and sustainably, the range of gold and silver rings, necklaces, bracelets, and earrings are delicate and beautifully crafted. Try the pieces on at their flagship store in VivoCity. ⊠ *VivoCity, 1 Habourfront Walk, #01–K19, Bukit Merah* ☎ *9873–3729* ⊕ *www.byinviteonly.shop* Ⓜ *Harbourfront.*

SHOPPING CENTERS AND MALLS

Anchorpoint

MALL | Opposite IKEA, this mall is popular for its fashion and salon options. In the basement are a couple of interesting gift and lifestyle stores. You'll also find a great range of bakeries and coffee shops throughout. ⊠ *370 Alexandra Rd., Alexandra* ⊕ *www.anchorpoint.com.sg* Ⓜ *Redhill.*

Queensway Shopping Centre

MALL | Although its facade looks a little tired, Queensway is a well-respected mall when it comes to sportswear, equipment, and fashion. If you're looking for cheap running wear or swimwear for local trips, this mall is a safe bet. Among the rows of tennis racquets and cheap sneakers, there's a range of useful stores, including alteration shops, barbers, and printers. A branch of well-known 328 Katong Laksa is on the first floor and is worth a stop for a bowl of noodles. ⊠ *1 Queensway, Queenstown* ☎ *6479–8676* ⊕ *www.queenswayshoppingcentre.com.sg* Ⓜ *Queenstown.*

VivoCity

MALL | FAMILY | Step aside ION Orchard and Marina Square—this is the largest shopping mall in Singapore, at least for now. Located on the southwestern tip of the island—about 10 minutes by taxi from Orchard Road—and doubling as a de facto gateway to Sentosa, this monolithic complex has, as expected, hundreds of retailers and restaurants and a 15-screen movie theater. But it also has art installations, an outdoor playground for kids, and a rooftop amphitheater near huge pools of water in which you can splash about. Expect a full house during the weekend. ⊠ *1 Harbourfront Ave., Bukit Merah* ☎ *6377–6870* ⊕ *www.vivocity.com.sg* Ⓜ *HarbourFront.*

Clementi and Jurong

Clementi is the definition of up-and-coming. High-rise condos and malls are constantly sprouting up across the area as more people move out of Singapore's center and into the suburbs. Despite the modern transformation, Clementi still manages to maintain some of its traditional charm in its wet markets, hawker centers, and iconic landmarks that are scattered throughout the neighborhood.

To the west of Clementi lies Jurong, one of Singapore's westernmost regions. This is primarily a residential and industrial area separated into smaller neighborhoods, including Jurong East, Jurong West, and Boon Lay. It makes for a good day trip from the city center, with a number of Singapore's larger shopping malls found here, including the outlet mall IMM.

◉ Sights

Jurong Lake Gardens
NATIONAL PARK | FAMILY | Sprawled across 220 acres and encompassing the sites of Lakeside, as well as its Chinese and Japanese gardens, Jurong Lake Gardens is one of Singapore's largest green spaces. The popular escape for residents in the west offers a range of activities and wildlife-watching spots among its wetlands, eco ponds, freshwater swamps, and open fields. Other than appreciating the natural space, visitors can rent kayaks and pedal boats at **PAssion WaVe** on Jurong Lake, or swim in the only swimming pool in a national garden at **ActiveSG Park**. An iconic sculpture known as Lone Tree, surrounded by Chinese Fountain Grass, is a popular photo spot. ✉ *Yuan Ching Rd., Jurong East* ☎ *800/471–7300* ⊕ *www.nparks.gov.sg* ⊠ *Free* Ⓜ *Lakeside.*

Raffles Marina Lighthouse
LIGHTHOUSE | Also known as Johor Straits lighthouse, this picturesque lighthouse is free to visit and has a fantastic view across the straits to Malaysia. You'll need to travel to the end of the East–West (green) MRT line to visit, but the sunset over the water will make the journey worth it. The marina has a few eating and drinking options, but note you can't bring outside food or drink to the lighthouse. ✉ *10 Tuas West Dr., Tuas* ⊕ *www.rafflesmarina. com.sg* ⊠ *Free* Ⓜ *Tuas Link.*

★ Science Centre Singapore
COLLEGE | FAMILY | Aviation, nuclear science, robotics, astronomy, space technology, and Internet technology are entertainingly explored through audiovisual and interactive exhibits housed in the 14 galleries here. You can walk into a "human body" for a

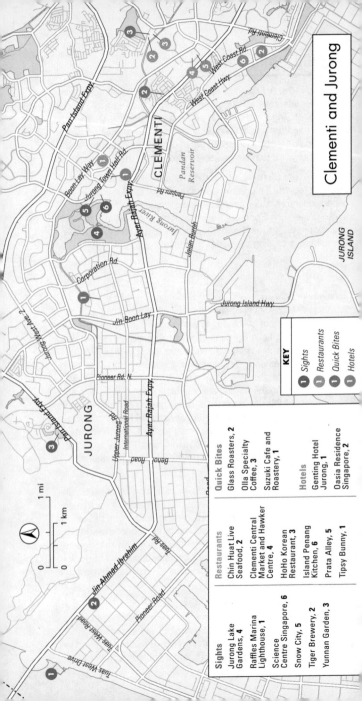

Clementi and Jurong

KEY

1 Sights
1 Restaurants
1 Quick Bites
1 Hotels

Sights

Jurong Lake
Gardens, 4

Raffles Marina
Lighthouse, 1

Science
Centre Singapore, 6

Snow City, 5

Tiger Brewery, 2

Yunnan Garden, 3

Restaurants

Chin Huat Live
Seafood, 2

Clementi Central
Market and Hawker
Centre, 4

HoHo Korean
Restaurant, 3

Island Penang
Kitchen, 6

Prata Alley, 5

Tipsy Bunny, 1

Quick Bites

Glass Roasters, 2

Olla Specialty
Coffee, 3

Suzuki Cafe and
Roastery, 1

Hotels

Genting Hotel
Jurong, 1

Oasia Residence
Singapore, 2

closer look at vital organs, test yourself via computer quiz games, or settle into the **Omni Theatre**, where movies and planetarium shows are screened. Other fascinating exhibitions include the Ecogarden, a living laboratory of flora and fauna in natural habitats, and "Climate Changed," which shows what life will be like if global warming continues—and what we can do to prevent it. ⊠ *15 Science Centre Rd., Jurong East* ☎ *6425–2500* ⊕ *www.science. edu.sg* 🎟 *S\$12* ⊗ *Closed Mon.* Ⓜ *Jurong East.*

Snow City

SPORTS VENUE | FAMILY | Snow is a novelty when you live in a country where it's tropical all year-round. Locals endure freezing temperatures for a rare chance to touch and play in real snow at the only permanent indoor snow center in Singapore. Although it's geared more toward locals, it's a fun way to spend some time if you're not used to experiencing freezing temperatures. Admission includes the use of winter jackets and boots. ⊠ *21 Jurong Town Hall Rd., Jurong East* ☎ *6560–2306* ⊕ *www.snowcity.com.sg* 🎟 *Two hours of Snow Play Time: S\$27* ⊗ *Closed Mon.* Ⓜ *Chinese Garden.*

Tiger Brewery

BREWERY | Tiger Beer is one of Singapore's most iconic exports and the beer of choice of many bars and hawker centers across the island. You'll probably drink it (or at least see it) more than once on your trip, so why not visit where it is made? At the official Tiger Brewery, on the far west end of the island, you can take a one-hour guided tour of the facilities every afternoon to see how the brewing process works. At the end of the tour, cool off during the two-hour "beer appreciation session" as you drink one (or more) icy-cold Tiger beers at the Tiger Tavern. Don't forget to bring your ID or passport. ⊠ *459 Jalan Ahmad Ibrahim, Tuas* ☎ *6860–3005* ⊕ *tigerbrewerytour.com.sg* 🎟 *S\$23 (weekday), S\$25 (weekend)* Ⓜ *Joo Koon to 182 Bus.*

★ Yunnan Garden

GARDEN | This heritage garden is on the grounds of the Nanyang Technological University; it's a little out of the way but certainly worth a visit. The grounds are well-maintained, and there are plenty of scenic photo spots, including a cascading waterfall, a small lake, and Chinese gates and pagodas. There are multiple trails to choose from, so you can wander across the boardwalks to explore the whole park. Try to visit in the early morning or late afternoon to avoid the heat. ⊠ *12 Nanyang Dr., Jurong West* ☎ *6791–1744* ⊕ *www.ntu.edu.sg* 🎟 *Free.*

🍴 Restaurants

Tourists rarely venture out to Clementi and Jurong, so you can almost guarantee most diners here are locals or expats. The food is great and as local as it gets, so enjoy trying something new.

★ Chin Huat Live Seafood

$$$ | SEAFOOD | Sunset Way is a residential area in Clementi and home to some of the West's best-kept secrets, including this restaurant popular with fans who travel across the island to bag a table at this pioneering seafood spot. Seafood prices are based on market price, and there's a huge à la carte menu of local classic dishes, such as seafood *hor fun* (thick rice noodles) and *kong bak pau* (braised pork buns). **Known for:** pick fresh seafood from a tank; crab in golden sauce; mantou (fried dumplings). ⑤ *Average main: S$55* ✉ *Sunset Way, 105 Clementi St. 12, #01–30, Clementi* ☎ *6775–7348* ⊕ *www.chinhuatliveseafood.com* ⊗ *Closed Tues.* Ⓜ *Clementi.*

Clementi Central Market and Hawker Centre

$ | CHINESE | This highly popular local hawker center is packed with stalls serving all kinds of delicious Singapore favorites, from roast duck noodles to succulent chicken and rice. As with almost all hawker centers in Singapore, it's hot and a little messy, but the food is always great—especially if you pick a stall with a long line. **Known for:** huge variety of hawker stalls; local flavors at low prices; covered, open-air setting. ⑤ *Average main: S$5* ✉ *448 Clementi Ave 3, Clementi* ▭ *No credit cards* Ⓜ *Clementi.*

★ HoHo Korean Restaurant

$$ | KOREAN | A small Korean restaurant with a loyal fanbase, this is yet another hidden gem found in residential Sunset Way. Popular dishes here include *haemul pajeon* (seafood and scallion pancake) and *tteokbokki* (soft rice cakes in a spicy sauce). **Known for:** bustling Korean favourite; authentic dishes; generous portions. ⑤ *Average main: S$25* ✉ *Sunset Way, 106 Clementi Street 12, #01–58/60, Clementi* ☎ *6250–3908* ⊗ *Closed Tues.* Ⓜ *Clementi.*

Island Penang Kitchen

$$ | MALAYSIAN | On the ground floor of a quiet residential corner on the west coast, this spot serves traditional Penang dishes in a lively café-style setting. Well-respected as one of Malaysia's best cuisines, food from Penang is similar to many of the local dishes you'll have seen in hawker centers around the island. **Known for:** popular neighborhood eatery; classic Penang-style dishes; low prices. ⑤ *Average main: S$20* ✉ *721 Clementi West Street 2, #01–126, Clementi* ☎ *8878–3323* ⊗ *Closed Tues.*

Jurong Bird Park is home to more than 5,000 birds from all over the world.

★ Prata Alley

$ | INDIAN | This south Indian restaurant is king of the *prata* (an Indian flatbread made by frying stretched dough flavored with ghee), and it is the centerpiece of their menu. The owners are especially proud of the "Big One," a Sicilian prata stuffed with pesto chicken, mozzarella cheese, shitake mushrooms, pineapples, and more. **Known for:** prata, especially the "Big One"; cozy bench seating; delicious dosas (savory pancakes). **⑤** *Average main: S$10* ✉ *321 Clementi Ave. 3, #01–12, Clementi* ☎ *6924–2037* ⊕ *www.prataalley.com* Ⓜ *Clementi.*

Tipsy Bunny

$$ | ASIAN FUSION | Part of the popular Tipsy Collective (you may see various "tipsy" animals across the island, from penguins to pandas), this lively bar and restaurant is a fun place to grab a bite. The food is mostly Asian fusion, with a range of wok and pasta dishes, although the signature pizzas are a crowd favorite. **Known for:** lively weekend atmosphere; international and Asian fusion dishes; beer sales support a sponsored penguin pair. **⑤** *Average main: S$30* ✉ *Jem, 50 Jurong Gateway Rd., #01–05, Jurong East* ☎ *8028–0093* ⊕ *www.tipsycollective.com* Ⓜ *Jurong East.*

☕ Coffee and Quick Bites

Glass Roasters

$ | CAFÉ | A hole-in-the-wall café and bean-roasting joint just off the Pandan River, this is a quiet spot to stop after a stroll around the

Pandan Reservoir. The coffee is excellent, and the outdoor seats are a peaceful spot in the heart of the residential West. **Known for:** minimalist interior; small coffee and tea menu; quiet neighborhood setting. Ⓢ *Average main: S$7* ⊠ *108 Faber Dr., Clementi* ⊕ *www.glassroasters.com* ⊘ *Closed Tues.* Ⓜ *Clementi.*

★ Olla Specialty Coffee

$$ | CAFÉ | Grab a caffeine fix at this premier coffee roastery in sleepy Sunset Way. Founded by a champion barista, Olla is a leading player in Singapore's burgeoning artisan roasting scene. **Known for:** buttermilk waffles; renowned coffee brews; breakfast burgers. Ⓢ *Average main: S$13* ⊠ *Sunset Way, 109 Clementi Street 11, #01–03, Clementi* ⊕ *www.ollacoffee.com* Ⓜ *Clementi.*

Suzuki Cafe and Roastery

$ | CAFÉ | Sitting, slightly incongruously, in a semi-industrial part of Jurong, this Japanese coffee roaster gives the distinct impression of being transported to the tea houses of Kyoto. Minimalist decor and a zen-like atmosphere make it a peaceful place to enjoy a cup of artisanal filter coffee or a matcha latte. **Known for:** beans roasted in-house; tranquil café setting; authentic Hokkaido sweet treats. Ⓢ *Average main: S$8* ⊠ *8 Chin Bee Ave., Jurong, Singapore* ☎ *9871–8315* ⊕ *www.suzukicoffee.com.sg* ⊘ *Closed Mon.* Ⓜ *Lakeside.*

🛏 Hotels

Genting Hotel Jurong

$$ | HOTEL | One of the only lodging options in the Clementi/Jurong area, this large, quiet hotel has a spacious lobby and clean, comfortable rooms near an MRT stop and offering a handy shuttle service to Resorts World Sentosa and its attractions. **Pros:** easy access to MRT and Jurong's malls; clean and well-maintained; spacious lobby and communal areas. **Cons:** some rooms are small, as are the hotel's facilities; not a central location; no dining options in the hotel. Ⓢ *Rooms from: S$270* ⊠ *2 Town Hall Link, Jurong East* ⊕ *www.rwsentosa.com* ⇦ *557 rooms* ○ *No Meals* Ⓜ *Jurong East.*

Oasia Residence Singapore

$$$ | HOTEL | Located near the ocean-facing West Coast Park in a residential part of Singapore, the serviced apartments of Oasia Residence feel like little homes away from home, including excellent on-site facilities. **Pros:** great for longer-stay guests; great facilities, including a pool and gym; free parking. **Cons:** far from the city and MRT; no breakfast on weekends; minimum six-night stay required. Ⓢ *Rooms from: S$400* ⊠ *123 W Coast Cres., Located* *within Seahill, Clementi* ☎ *6428–8600 Reservations, 6254–1746 Operator* ⊕ *www.oasiahotels.com* ⊐ *140 rooms* ❍❘ *Free Breakfast* ☞ *6-night min.* Ⓜ *Clementi to Bus 175.*

Nightlife

Bottoms Up

BARS | Expect to find a lively atmosphere on the deck of this neighborhood bar in Sunset Way, as patrons enjoy cheap beer and fried snacks. Quite unusually for Singapore, house drink prices are based on the clock: turn up at 2 pm and you can get a $2 beer. There are better food options around Sunset Way, so stick to the cheap drinks. ⊠ *Sunset Way, 106 Clementi Street 12, #01–46/50, Clementi* ☎ *6252–6588* ⊕ *bottomsupbar.sg* Ⓜ *Clementi.*

Fountain Microbrewery

BREWPUBS | House-crafted ales are the order of the day at this microbrewery in Jurong, which also serves a solid food menu of pub classics to live music. As it's located in Snow City, it's a great spot to indulge in some Singaporean "après-ski." ⊠ *Snow City, 21 Jurong Town Hall Rd., Level 2, Jurong East* ☎ *8121–5101* ⊕ *fountain.com.sg* Ⓜ *Jurong East.*

The Hidden Pipe

PUBS | This fun pub has international beers on tap, generous drink promotions, and large screens for sports fans. Situated in a strip mall in a quiet part of Clementi, The Hidden Pipe is frequented by locals, often for its generous bar menu. ⊠ *1 W Coast Dr., #01–88/90, Clementi* ☎ *6592–6829* ⊕ *www.thehiddenpipe.com* Ⓜ *Clementi.*

🛍 Shopping

SHOPPING CENTERS AND MALLS

Jem

MALL | A popular mall with a range of dining and shopping options also has a ten-screen cinema complex, rooftop gardens on level 7, and alfresco dining options on Jem Street. Jurong East MRT is connected to Jurong's mall complex, making all the malls here very accessible. ⊠ *50 Jurong Gateway Rd., Jurong East* ☎ *6225–5536* ⊕ *www.jem.sg* Ⓜ *Jurong East.*

Westgate

MALL | The heart of Jurong's cavernous malls, Westgate has a large range of international shops and some of Singapore's best-loved eateries. There's a popular version of Food Republic in the basement, which also houses a range of up-market hawker stalls.

Jurong's malls are connected by overhead walkways, so if you are looking for a particular brand or store, you may need to cross into another mall. ⊠ *3 Gateway Dr., Jurong East* ☎ *6908–3737* ⊕ *westgate.com.sg* Ⓜ *Jurong East.*

🏃 Activities

There's a lot to do in the west if you know where to look. Most of the activities aren't geared toward international visitors, but to the people that call the surrounding neighborhoods home. This means you can expect fair prices and fewer tourists, as well as a chance to mingle with locals.

ART INSTRUCTION

Thwo Kwang Pottery Jungle

OTHER ATTRACTION | FAMILY | Part workshop, part education center, this family-run operation is home to some of Singapore's most beautiful pottery, which you can admire, buy, or even try making for yourself. The regularly scheduled workshops will have you rolling up your sleeves and turning clay into mugs, vases, and bowls. The center uses one of the oldest surviving brick-built kilns in Singapore, the Dragon Kiln, to create its intricate works of art. ⊠ *No. 85 Lorong Tawas, Jurong West* ☎ *6268–6121* ⊕ *thowkwang.com. sg* 🎫 *From S$65 per 2.5-hr workshop* Ⓜ *Boon Lay to bus 172.*

BOWLING

Super Bowl Jurong

BOWLING | FAMILY | If you're looking to kill an hour or two, these bowling lanes, which also feature a small selection of arcade games, are a good way to pass the time. There is an additional charge of S$2 for shoe rental, and it's compulsory to wear socks. The adjoining Tipsy Cow bar is a popular choice for post-game drinks, and there are fast food options in the complex surrounds. ⊠ *1 Yuan Ching Rd., Jurong East* ☎ *6266–1000* ⊕ *www.superbowl.com.sg* 🎫 *From S$5.50 per game.*

Bukit Timah, Kranji, and the Central Water Catchment

The residential area of Bukit Timah lies close to the center of the island, sandwiched between the green lungs of the Botanic Gardens to the south and the Bukit Timah Nature Reserve to the north. The area is known for its great culinary scene, especially when it comes to brunching. In part, that's thanks to the number of locals and expats that call the sprawling neighborhood home.

To the north of Bukit Timah, heading all the way up to the border with Malaysia, you'll find the scenic sights of Kranji, a small suburb known for its countryside and artisanal farms. Between the two lies the enormous Central Water Catchment, a huge sprawl of parkland containing recreational sites like the Singapore Zoo and Night Safari.

 # Sights

Bird Paradise
ZOO | FAMILY | In the same area as Singapore Zoo and Night Safari, Bird Paradise is a 42-acre bird park home to 3,500 birds from over 400 avian species. Some of the world's most endangered species, including Philippine eagles and blue-throated macaws, can be seen here, as well as the socorro dove, which is now extinct in the wild. View birds from eight large, walk-through biomes representing different regions of the globe, including South American wetlands, African rainforests, Australian eucalypt forests, and more. Guests can take part in feeding sessions for an additional fee, and there are avian presentations from experienced birdkeepers that give a closer look at some of the park's most famous birds. ■TIP→ **To save a bit, you can buy a combo ticket for access to all four wildlife parks (Bird Paradise, Singapore Zoo, Night Safari, and River Wonders) or two of your choice, to be used within seven days of purchase.** ⊠ 20 Mandai Lake Rd., Mandai ☎ 6269–3411 ⊕ www.mandai.com/en/bird-paradise ☑ S$48 Ⓜ Khatib to Mandai Khatib Shuttle.

★ Bollywood Farms
FARM/RANCH | This lush sanctuary of a farm transports you far from the noise of the city and into the wild countryside of Kranji in the north. There's always something to do here, from touring the farm and getting your hands dirty in the paddy fields, to taking part in a cooking class or listening to a talk from the resident medicine woman about which plants and herbs can be used for medicinal purposes. There's also a great on-site bistro that celebrates farm-to-table dining in its most literal sense. ⊠ 100 Neo Tiew Rd., Lim Chu Kang ☎ 6898–5001 ⊕ bollywoodfarms.com ⊘ Closed Mon.–Wed.

Bukit Timah Nature Reserve
NATURE PRESERVE | Step away from Singapore's manicured urban parks and into 405 acres of wild rain forest at this sprawling nature reserve. The walking paths are well marked, but exploring here still gives you a sense of what the island was like when tigers still roamed the jungle. Towering trees, tangled vines, and prickly rattan palms line the footpaths, while long-tailed

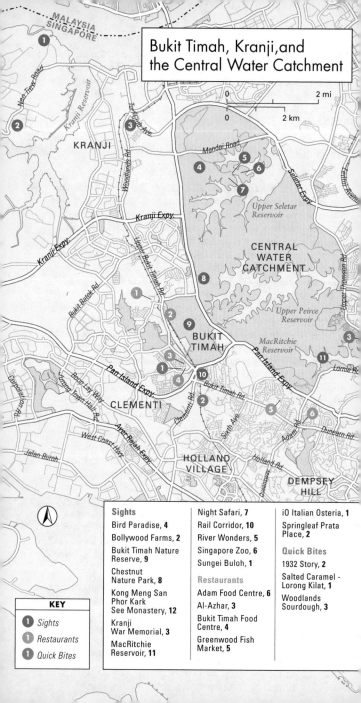

Bukit Timah, Kranji, and the Central Water Catchment

MALAYSIA
SINGAPORE

0 _____ 2 mi
0 _____ 2 km

KRANJI

Mandai Road

Upper Seletar Reservoir

CENTRAL WATER CATCHMENT

Upper Peirce Reservoir

BUKIT TIMAH

MacRitchie Reservoir

CLEMENTI

HOLLAND VILLAGE

DEMPSEY HILL

KEY
- **1** *Sights*
- **1** *Restaurants*
- **1** *Quick Bites*

Sights
Bird Paradise, **4**
Bollywood Farms, **2**
Bukit Timah Nature Reserve, **9**
Chestnut Nature Park, **8**
Kong Meng San Phor Kark See Monastery, **12**
Kranji War Memorial, **3**
MacRitchie Reservoir, **11**

Night Safari, **7**
Rail Corridor, **10**
River Wonders, **5**
Singapore Zoo, **6**
Sungei Buloh, **1**

Restaurants
Adam Food Centre, **6**
Al-Azhar, **3**
Bukit Timah Food Centre, **4**
Greenwood Fish Market, **5**

iO Italian Osteria, **1**
Springleaf Prata Place, **2**

Quick Bites
1932 Story, **2**
Salted Caramel - Lorong Kilat, **1**
Woodlands Sourdough, **3**

macaques, squirrels, and tree shrews scamper overhead. The trails circle Singapore's highest hill (535 feet), with some of the routes leading to the peak for spectacular views of the dense greenery. Wear good walking shoes—the trails are rocky and muddy after the rain—and make sure you bring water. You can buy maps from the visitor center. ✉ *Hindhede Dr., Bukit Timah* ☎ *1800/471–7300* ⊕ *www.nparks.gov.sg* 🖭 *Free* Ⓜ *Beauty World.*

Chestnut Nature Park

NATURE PRESERVE | Hikers and bikers can enjoy about 200 acres of greenery at Singapore's largest nature park, located just outside of the Central Catchment Nature Reserve. Its two hiking trails (a 2-mile route on the north side and a 1.3-mile route on the south side) and 5 miles of mountain biking trails offer adventurous escapes from the hustle and bustle of the city for a day. ✉ *Chestnut Ave., Bukit Panjang* ☎ *1800/471–7300* ⊕ *www.nparks.gov.sg* Ⓜ *Cashew.*

Kong Meng San Phor Kark See Monastery

RELIGIOUS BUILDING | The Bright Hill Temple, as it's commonly known due to its location on Bright Hill Road, is Singapore's largest Mahayana monastery. Built in the 1920s as one of the first traditional Chinese forest monasteries in Singapore, it's in a relatively modern complex made up of colorful buildings decorated with gilded carvings, as well as immaculate gardens and a large number of Buddha statues. Pick up a map of the temple at reception to help guide your wanderings, and don't miss the relaxing Zen Cafe to finish your visit. Ensure shoulders and knees are covered when visiting. ✉ *88 Bright Hill Rd., Ang Mo Kio* ☎ *6849–5300* ⊕ *www.kmspks.org* 🖭 *Free* Ⓜ *Bright Hill.*

Kranji War Memorial

MONUMENT | More than 4,400 white gravestones line the manicured hillside in neat rows at this World War II memorial site, honoring the men and women who died in the line of duty for Singapore. You'll also find a number of larger memorial stones, one of which bears the names of more than 24,000 Allied soldiers and airmen killed in Southeast Asia who have no known grave. Visiting is a poignant experience—a reminder of the greatness of the loss in this and all wars. ✉ *9 Woodlands Rd., Kranji* ⊕ *www.cwgc.org* 🖭 *Free* 🕙 *Closed Sat. and Sun.* Ⓜ *Kranji to Bus 170.*

★ MacRitchie Reservoir

TRAIL | **FAMILY** | This 30-acre park is a lush green wilderness, crisscrossed by a 10-km (6.2-mile) walking trail that loops around the reservoir. The trail is mostly flat and shaded, with only the warbling of birds and chatter of the park's many monkeys to break the peaceful reverie. Pick up the trail from MacRitchie Reservoir Park in the south, near the trail's main car park, where you can grab a drink from the cafés and kiosks before heading off. From here, you can follow signs towards the TreeTop Walk, which lies at around midway mark in the north of the park. This 820-foot-long suspension bridge soars above the trees, with spectacular views across the wild rain forest to the city skyscrapers in the distance. After completing the TreeTop Walk, continue following the trail towards Jelutong Tower—another spot with scenic views that lies in the west of the park—before looping back to the MacRitchie Reservoir Park along the picturesque waterside boardwalk. ⊠ *Lornie Rd., near Thomson Rd., Central Water Catchment, Singapore* ☎ *800/471–7300* ⊕ *www.nparks.gov.sg* ⊠ *Free* Ⓜ *Marymount.*

Night Safari

ZOO | FAMILY | Right next to the Singapore Zoo, the safari is the world's first wildlife park designed exclusively and especially for night viewing. More than 85 acres of secondary jungle provide a home to over 900 animals (from approximately 100 species) that are more active after the sun sets. Some 90% of tropical animals are, in fact, nocturnal, and to see them do something other than snooze gives their behavior a new dimension. From elephants, lions, and clouded leopards to flying foxes and rare pangolin, the Night Safari is an unusual way to spy animals after dark. Their habitats have been designed to come as close to their natural setting as possible, with just enough light for you to see what they're doing but not enough to limit the animals' normal activity. ■TIP➔ **To save a bit, you can buy a combo ticket for access to all four wildlife parks (Bird Paradise, Singapore Zoo, Night Safari, and River Wonders) or two of your choice, to be used within seven days of purchase.** ⊠ *80 Mandai Lake Rd., Mandai* ☎ *6269–3411* ⊕ *www. mandai.com/en/night-safari* ⊠ *S$55* Ⓜ *Khatib to Mandai Khatib Shuttle.*

★ Rail Corridor

TRAIL | FAMILY | The 24-kilometer-long former rail corridor is one of the best walking, running, and cycling routes in Singapore, shrouded in greenery and birdsong. Stretching from Tanjong Pagar up to Kranji in the north, it follows what was once a railway line that linked Singapore to Malaysia. While you could tackle the whole trail for a great workout, the most scenic parts are found around the non-operational Bukit Timah Railway station, first built in 1932. ⊠ *#1 Railway Station, Bukit Timah* ⊕ *railcorridor.nparks. gov.sg* ⊠ *Free* Ⓜ *King Albert Park.*

The Night Safari offers a unique chance to spot Singapore's wildlife after dark.

River Wonders

WILDLIFE REFUGE | FAMILY | Asia's first and only river-themed wildlife park is inspired by eight of the world's most iconic waterways. It's home to more than 11,000 aquatic and terrestrial animals, including Kai Kai, Jia Jia and Le Le—Singapore's resident pandas—plus the world's largest collection of freshwater vertebrates, as well as over 400 plant species and multiple river-themed zones. Most of the park is designed to be explored on foot, but the fun Amazon River Quest lets you enjoy its pretty nature from the water. ■**TIP→ To save a bit, you can buy a combo ticket for access to all four wildlife parks (Bird Paradise, Singapore Zoo, Night Safari, and River Wonders) or two of your choice, to be used within seven days of purchase.** ⊠ *80 Mandai Lake Rd., Mandai* ☎ *6269–3411* ⊕ *www. mandai.com/en/river-wonders* ⊠ *S$42* Ⓜ *Khatib to Mandai Khatib Shuttle.*

★ Singapore Zoo

ZOO | FAMILY | Sprawling over 65 acres of a 220-acre natural rain forest, this zoo has stunning views of nearby reservoir lakes. The zoo uses an open-concept design, with spacious enclosures using minimal glass and fencing to separate animals from zoo-goers: a 3-foot-deep moat, for instance, will keep humans and giraffes apart, since a giraffe's gait makes even a shallow trench impossible to negotiate. In total, there are about 4,200 animals from around 300 species here, spread across zones from Australasia to Wild Africa. The Asian elephant and Bornean orangutan enclosures are definitely worth a visit, but there's joy in stumbling across species less well-known as you wander through the park. The zoo is renowned for its conservation work, and up to 34% of the species living here are threatened in the wild. Make sure to ask for animal feeding times and keeper talks at the entrance. ■ TIP→ **To save a bit, you can buy a combo ticket for access to all four wildlife parks (Bird Paradise, Singapore Zoo, Night Safari, and River Wonders) or two of your choice, to be used within seven days of purchase.** ⊠ *80 Mandai Lake Rd., Mandai* ☎ *6269–3411* ⊕ *www.mandai.com/en/ singapore-zoo* ☞ *S$48* Ⓜ *Khatib to Mandai Khatib Shuttle.*

★ Sungei Buloh

NATURE PRESERVE | The Sungei Buloh wetlands are a true breath of fresh air in Singapore. They lie at one of the most north-westerly points of the island, a sprawling 500-acre ecological site of mangroves and mudflats. Migratory birds, crabs, and mud lobsters can be found in abundance, viewable from the trails or observation posts that dot the park. The site was designated as a nature park by the government in 1989, before being designated Singapore's first ASEAN Heritage Park in 2003. Stroll the raised boardwalks, watch a prawn-harvesting demonstration, or pick up a free guided tour from the visitor center. ⊠ *301 Neo Tiew Cres, Lim Chu Kang* ☎ *6794–1401 Visitor center* ⊕ *www.nparks.gov.sg* ☞ *Free.*

🍽 Restaurants

It might not be worth going out of your way to these restaurants, but if you're in the area after a day trip to the west, they're all great options for a bite to eat.

Adam Food Centre

$ | SINGAPOREAN | A bustling, palm-lined hawker center on the edge of the Botanic Gardens, Adam Food Center has a high hit rate of great stalls to choose from. Highlights include Warong Pak Sapari (stand 9) for fragrant *mee soto* (Indonesian noodles in chicken broth); and Noo Cheng Adam Road Big Prawn Noodles (stand 27) for juicy prawns served with pork ribs and noodles. **Known for:** tree-lined, cool dining space; Michelin-rated cheap eats; range of international food. ⑤ *Average main: S$6* ⊠ *2 Adam Rd., Bukit Timah* ⊕ *www.facebook.com/adamfoodcentre* ☱ *No credit cards* Ⓜ *Botanic Gardens.*

Al-Azhar

$ | INTERNATIONAL | This hugely popular Muslim eatery serves a dizzying array of dishes and cuisines, including Thai, Indian, Malay, Western, and Mediterranean. Despite the ambitious menu, the quality is unmatched for a place this size, with quick, friendly service and a great selection of (non-alcoholic) drinks. **Known for:** huge menu of local and international dishes; 24/7 dining; long evening and weekend queues. $ *Average main: S$7* ✉ *11 Cheong Chin Nam Rd., Bukit Timah* ☎ *6466–5052* ⊕ *www.al-azhar.com.*

Bukit Timah Food Centre

$ | ASIAN | This bustling food center is a true local's haunt, with more than 80 hawker stalls selling everything from succulent Hainanese chicken rice to tangy satay. When it comes to picking where to eat, use the golden rule of every hawker center in Singapore: choose the stalls with the longest lines. **Known for:** cheap eats; huge variety of hawker stalls; delicious fish soup. $ *Average main: S$5* ✉ *Bukit Timah Market & Food Centre, 51 Upper Bukit Timah Rd., Bukit Timah* Ⓜ *Beauty World.*

Greenwood Fish Market

$$ | SEAFOOD | This neighborhood favorite may be in a quiet residential area, but it's almost always packed at night. As you may expect, fish is the order of the day, with an all-encompassing menu that ranges from freshly-sliced sashimi to whole dover sole. **Known for:** neighborhood fish restaurant; lobster bisque and whole dover sole; $2 Oyster Tuesdays. $ *Average main: S$40* ✉ *34 and 38 Greenwood Ave., Bukit Timah* ☎ *6467–4950* ⊕ *www.greenwoodfishmarket.com* Ⓜ *Tan Kah Kee.*

★ iO Italian Osteria

$$ | ITALIAN | This busy neighborhood trattoria is off the beaten track in Hillview, a hidden gem were it not for the local residents packing the place each evening. The food is (unlike some other Italian spots on the island) genuinely authentic, with a decent selection of pizza, pasta, meats, and seafood, as well as regional chef's specials each weekend. **Known for:** buzzy neighborhood Italian; crisp pizzas and hearty pasta; chef's weekend specials. $ *Average main: S$30* ✉ *HillV2, 4 Hillview Rise, #02–01, Bukit Panjang* ☎ *6710–7150* ⊕ *io-osteria.com* Ⓜ *Hillview.*

★ Springleaf Prata Place

$ | INDIAN | An extensive menu of *prata* (Indian flatbread), *murtabak* (thick, stuffed pancakes) and *thosai* (thin, crepe-like pancakes) make this an island favorite. This branch in The Rail Mall is the perfect place to grab lunch or a snack at the end of a hike on the Rail Corridor, which tracks north to south just past the mall. **Known for:** fast, cheap Indian eats; chicken floss prata; fruit lassi. $ *Average main: S$7* ✉ *The Rail Mall, 396 Upper Bukit Timah Rd., Bukit Panjang* ☎ *6219–2540* ⊕ *spplace.com* Ⓜ *Hillview.*

☕ Coffee and Quick Bites

1932 Story

$ | CAFÉ | FAMILY | Located opposite the historic Bukit Timah Railway Station—and named after the year in which it was built—this bright, open café was once the railway staff quarters. It's a great spot to stop for a quick coffee or ice cream from the all-day menu, particularly if you're planning on walking another section of the Rail Corridor. **Known for:** ice cream and coffee; quiet outdoor space; historic setting. $ Average main: S$12 ✉ Bukit Timah Railway Station, 1005 Bukit Timah Rd., Bukit Timah ☎ 9427–7177 Ⓜ King Albert Park.

Salted Caramel

$ | ICE CREAM | A true hidden gem, this artisan ice cream shop serves Bukit Timah locals on a sleepy side street near Beauty World. Flavors range from classic (hazelnut, rum and raisin) to the more local (blue milk, milo crunch). **Known for:** handcrafted ice cream with local flavors; waffle cones and bowls; dark chocolate sorbet. $ Average main: S$8 ✉ Kilat Court, 17 Lor Kilat, #01–08, Bukit Timah ☎ 6235–0863 ⊕ www.saltedcaramel.sg Ⓜ Beauty World.

★ Woodlands Sourdough

$ | BAKERY | This hole-in-the-wall bakery serves some of the best baked goods in Singapore. Despite the name, it's not quite as out in the sticks as Woodlands, but you'll need to go a little farther north than usual to reach these goodies. **Known for:** popular Muslim-owned bakery; takeaway baked goods and sweet treats; artisanal sourdough bread. $ Average main: S$8 ✉ 183 Longhaus, 183 Upper Thomson Rd., #01–03, Central Water Catchment, Singapore ⊕ www.facebook.com/WoodlandsSD ⊘ Closed Mon. and Tues. Ⓜ Marymount.

🍸 Nightlife

Bar Bar Black Sheep

BEER GARDENS | This laid-back pub and beer garden on Cherry Avenue is a popular meeting spot for locals and expats in the Bukit Timah area, mainly because the drink prices are reasonable and the atmosphere is lively. There's a market-style set up for the food, with a mix of cuisines to order, including Indian and Thai stalls. ✉ 879/881 Bukit Timah Rd., Bukit Timah ☎ 8020–1586 ⊕ www.bbbs.com.sg Ⓜ Sixth Avenue.

★ Orh Gao Taproom

BARS | This hip hangout on the edge of the Botanic Garden bills itself as a craft beer bar and place to get no-frills Asian food, and it delivers. The beer choice is comprehensive, and there's a great menu for cocktails and interesting, approachable wines. If you're eating, the OG sambal curry mussels are a must. The team regularly hosts pop-ups with local businesses, so watch out for everything from bagel menus to "meet the brewers" sessions. On the weekends, things can get pretty busy, but there's a chill garden space to escape to. ⊠ *Serene Centre, 10 Jln Serene, #01–03, Bukit Timah* ☎ *8749–2755* ⊕ *www.orhgao.sg* Ⓜ *Botanic Gardens.*

Sixteen Ounces

BARS | This craft beer bar and bistro at The Rail Mall has a punky, underground vibe with a great selection of Singaporean and International craft ales. The menu offers a decent range for snacking, including wings, tacos, and burgers, and there are live music and trivia weekly. ⊠ *The Rail Mall, 398 Upper Bukit Timah Rd., Bukit Panjang* ☎ *6219–9304* ⊕ *www.sixteenouncesbistro.com* Ⓜ *Hillview.*

★ Wiped Out

BEER GARDENS | Occupying a small stall at the top of the aging Beauty World Food Centre, this bar may look like any other ordinary drink hawker, but it's not. Pints on tap are cold, there's a well-stocked fridge full of craft beer and cider, and there's a generous happy hour. The real draw, though, is the view from the roof-edge seating area (located 20 meters away—if you can't see it, ask their staff). Sit back and watch the sunset extend over the city, but just know that when you're finished, there will be someone in line to take your seat. ⊠ *Beauty World Food Centre, 144 Upper Bukit Timah Rd, #04–61, Bukit Timah* ⊹ *Top floor of the food center on the side looking out of the front of the building.* ⊕ *www.facebook. com/wipedout.bar* Ⓜ *Beauty World.*

Yeast Side

BARS | Craft beer spots like this are unusual to find on the west side of Singapore, so when this bar popped up it quickly became a hit with the locals. Part craft beer bar, part bakery, part pizza slinger, it has a decent enough menu that you can enjoy a full evening here. The real draws are the drinks, though, with beer fans choosing from a selection of exciting international craft ales. The space has a set of outside seats that are great for sipping a beer and watching the evening rush go past. ⊠ *9 King Albert Park, #01–09, Bukit Timah* ⊕ *www.yeastside.sg* Ⓜ *King Albert Park.*

🛍 Shopping

ANTIQUES

Junkie's Corner

ANTIQUES & COLLECTIBLES | Everything from intricately carved wooden figurines to shiny marble tables and 1970s jukeboxes can be discovered in this dilapidated Asian antiques warehouse (or Aladdin's cave of collectibles, depending on your view). It's not easy to comb through the slightly claustrophobic shop, but it is fun, especially when you unearth a bargain. ⊠ *2 Turf Club Rd., Bukit Timah* ☎ *9791–2607* Ⓜ *Sixth Avenue.*

SHOPPING CENTERS AND MALLS

★ Cluny Court

MALL | This boutique two-story mall is housed in a historic shop-house, just next to the Botanic Gardens' Bukit Timah gate. It's a great place to shop for gifts and keepsakes, with local artisans and lifestyle brands on the second floor. There's also a supermarket, eco-grocer, and collection of eateries on the first floor—or head around the corner (away from the park) to Micro Bakery to stock up on cakes and pastries. ⊠ *501 Bukit Timah Rd., Bukit Timah* ☎ *6467–6077* ⊕ *www.clunycourt.com* Ⓜ *Botanic Gardens.*

🏃 Activities

SPAS

Ikeda Spa

SPAS | There's no better place to de-stress in Singapore than this spa outside the city center and in the midst of calming nature reserves. The Japanese-style spa is known for its customized treatments, VIP couples suite, Japanese Zen Garden, and outdoor *onsen* (hot tub). ⊠ *787 Bukit Timah Rd., Bukit Timah* ☎ *6388–8080* ⊕ *www.ikedaspa.com* 🎟 *Facials and massages from S$190 (60 minutes)* Ⓜ *Sixth Avenue.*

Chapter 10

SIDE TRIPS

Updated by
Charlene Fang

⊙ Sights	🍴 Restaurants	🛏 Hotels	🛍 Shopping	🍸 Nightlife
★★★★☆	★★★★☆	★★★★☆	★☆☆☆☆	★☆☆☆☆

NEIGHBORHOOD SNAPSHOT

TOP EXPERIENCES

■ **Sentosa Island:** This beachy wonderland just south of Singapore is the perfect escape for lying on the sand in front of a resort (or going on a beach-bar crawl).

■ **Theme parks:** Get your scream on at Universal Studios Singapore, an outpost of the famous thrill-seeker's theme park.

■ **Fine dining:** Make a reservation at one of Sentosa Island's high-end eateries.

■ **Pulau Ubin:** Hop on a bumboat to this island and spend a day experiencing old-school Singapore.

■ **Indonesia's Bintan:** Catch a ferry to this island for an action-packed or utterly indulgent weekend.

GETTING HERE

Sentosa Island is connected to mainland Singapore by a causeway bridge that takes less than 3 minutes to cross. To get here for free, you can walk or bike across the 765-yard-long Sentosa Boardwalk. Otherwise, you can take a cable car or taxi, or use the Sentosa Express, a form of public transportation from VivoCity (MRT: Harbourfront). A selection of small "bumboats" and ferries will take you to Singapore's other islands.

PLANNING YOUR TIME

Set aside at least one day for Sentosa Island or two if you're combining it with an excursion to Universal Studios Singapore, S.E.A. Aquarium, or Adventure Cove. A visit to one of Singapore's smaller islands will likely take a full day given travel time.

VIEWFINDER

■ Time your visit right to Sentosa Island's Palawan Beach to catch a sunset photo from the southernmost point of continental Asia. Climb the viewing towers and position yourself as the sun sets over the South China Sea. Located at: Palawan Beach. Beach Shuttle: Palawan Beach.

Though it's small, Singapore is actually made up of 63 different islands. Although the bulk of sights and attractions are on the mainland, other islands like Sentosa (incidentally the largest island of the 62 other islands) and smaller ones like Pulau Ubin and Kusu Island are well worth a visit. If time permits, consider venturing a bit farther to Bintan Island, which is just a 75-minute ferry ride away.

Proving a respite from Singapore's hustle and bustle, the nearby islands like Pulau Ubin and Kusu Island are examples of Singapore's rich biodiversity and also serve as a gentle reminder that this city-state wasn't always a bustling metropolis.

If there is one spot in Singapore that has undergone a major transformation, it is Sentosa Island. What was once a British military base and a Japanese prisoner-of-war camp during World War II has evolved into an island focused on fun. Located just off Singapore's southern coast, Sentosa draws visitors eager to soak up the sun on one of its many beaches. Along with a string of high-end hotels, a world-class golf course and marina, numerous restaurants, and more than a few lively beach bars, sights, and attractions, it's an ideal outing for all ages, whether you stay for a half day or an extended weekend.

Sentosa Island

Sentosa, which means "peace and tranquility" in Malay, is far from tranquil these days. Located to the south of the main island, and connected to it via a causeway, this former fishing village was converted into a vacation resort back in 1968. Today, it's filled with pristine artificial beaches, golf courses, the hotel-and-casino hub Resorts World, and various other hotels, bars, and restaurants.

Sentosa can take up anywhere from the time it takes for a few afternoon cocktails on the beach to a long weekend devoted to Universal Studios, the S.E.A. Aquarium, and one of its five-star hotels. HarbourFront MRT station is on the North East (purple)

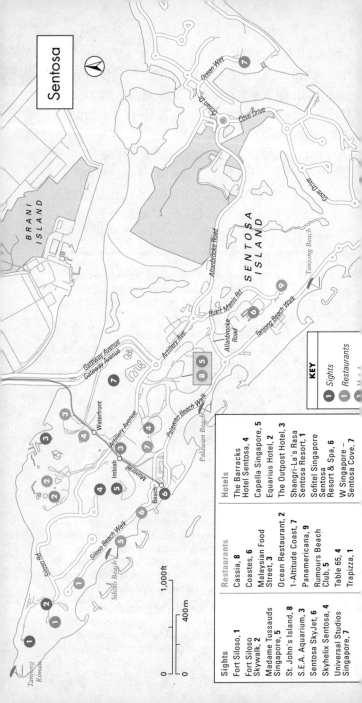

Sentosa

BRANI ISLAND

SENTOSA ISLAND

Tanjong Rimah

Tanjong Beach

Siloso Rd

Siloso Beach

Gateway Avenue

Artillery Ave.

Artillery Avenue

Waterfront

Imbiah

Beach

Monorail

Siloso Beach Walk

Palawan Beach Walk

Palawan Beach

Bukit Manis Rd.

Allanbrooke Road

Tanjong Beach Walk

Atlanbrooke Road

Cove Drive

Ocean Way

Imbiah Rd.

KEY

1 Sights

1 Restaurants

1 Hotel

Sights

Fort Siloso, **1**
Fort Siloso
Skywalk, **2**
Madame Tussauds
Singapore, **5**
St. John's Island, **8**
S.E.A. Aquarium, **3**
Sentosa SkyJet, **6**
Skyhelix Sentosa, **4**
Universal Studios
Singapore, **7**

Restaurants

Cassia, **8**
Coastes, **6**
Malaysian Food
Street, **3**
Ocean Restaurant, **2**
1-Altitude Coast, **7**
Panamericana, **9**
Rumours Beach
Club, **5**
Table 65, **4**
Trapizza, **1**

Hotels

The Barracks
Hotel Sentosa, **4**
Capella Singapore, **5**
Equarius Hotel, **2**
The Outpost Hotel, **3**
Shangri-La's Rasa
Sentosa Resort, **1**
Sofitel Singapore
Sentosa
Resort & Spa, **6**
W Singapore –
Sentosa Cove, **7**

0   400m
0   1,000ft

and Circle (yellow) lines. From here Sentosa is accessible via the Sentosa Express Monorail, cable cars, buses, and on foot by way of the outdoor Sentosa Boardwalk.

GETTING HERE AND AROUND
HarbourFront MRT station is on the North East (purple) and Circle (yellow) lines. From here Sentosa is accessible via the Sentosa Express Monorail, cable cars, buses, and on foot by way of the outdoor Sentosa Boardwalk. Extra surcharges are added to taxi fares when driving onto the island. Several bus services are available to navigate around the island as well.

A selection of boat services, ranging from the small "bumboats" to larger ferries, is available to explore Singapore's other islands from various ports.

◉ Sights

Fort Siloso
MILITARY SIGHT | FAMILY | This well-preserved fort covers 10 acres of gun emplacements and tunnels created by the British to fend off the Japanese. Unfortunately, the Japanese arrived by land (through Malaysia) instead of by sea, so the huge guns were pointed in the wrong direction. Fort Siloso is now home to a treasure trove of World War II memorabilia, including coastal guns and the remains of fortified structures. The displays have been successfully revamped with lots of interactive high-tech audiovisual and animatronic effects. Photographs document the war in the Pacific, and dioramas depict the life of POWs during the Japanese occupation. Free guided tours are available every second and third Saturday of the month from 3 pm to 4:30 pm, but you must register online in advance as limited slots are available. ⊠ Siloso Point, 33 Allanbrooke Rd., Sentosa Island ☎ 6736–8672 ⊕ www. sentosa.com.sg/explore/attractions/fort-siloso ≅ Free.

Fort Siloso Skywalk
VIEWPOINT | Singapore loves treating visitors to sky-high views. This one on Sentosa Island might not be the tallest at just 11 stories, but it is free to enter, and there's a short, scenic treetop walkway leading to Fort Siloso. To gain access, climb the staircase, or ride the elevator. Either way, the view of Keppel Harbour and the Southern Islands in the distance is pretty rewarding. ⊠ Siloso Rd., Sentosa Island ☎ 6736–8672 ⊕ www.sentosa.com. sg/en ≅ Free.

Madame Tussauds Singapore
OTHER ATTRACTION | FAMILY | Harry Styles, Taylor Swift, and local footballer Fandi Ahmad are just some of the realistic wax figures

to admire and strike a pose with at Madame Tussauds Singapore. Included with the standard ticket is "Images of Singapore," a 45-minute show about Singapore's history, and the *Spirit of Singapore* boat ride, in which iconic landmarks and Sir Stamford Raffles (the founder of modern Singapore) make an appearance. The entry fee also includes admission to the Ultimate Film Star Experience and one souvenir digital photo. There are additional combination packages for access to Marvel Universe 4D and VR Racing experience. ⊠ *Imbiah Lookout, 40 Imbiah Rd., Sentosa Island* ☎ *6715–4000* ⊕ *www.imagesofsingaporelive.com* 💲 *S$42.*

St. John's Island

ISLAND | St. John's was first a leper colony, then a prison camp, and then a place to intern political enemies of the republic. Today it's a great place for picnics and camping. You can stay overnight at St John's Island Lodge, and there are camping facilities as well. The island is also home to a Marine Aquaculture Centre and Tropical Marine Science Institute. Visit the 2.8-km (1.7-mile) St John's Island Trail marked by 15 stations and signboards detailing the island's history and diversity of flora and fauna. You can get to St. John's via the ferries at Marina South Pier with Marina South Ferries and Singapore Island Cruise. ⊠ *St. John's Island, Sentosa Island* ☎ *6534–9339* ⊕ *www.islandcruise.com.sg* 💲 *S$15.*

★ S.E.A. Aquarium

AQUARIUM | **FAMILY** | One of the world's largest aquariums, this underwater wonderland with seven themed zones provides views of more than 1,000 species from around the world. Gaze into a shipwreck habitat; walk through a tunnel surrounded by various shark species; and gape at goliath groupers, Napoleon wrasses, and a squadron of magnificent manta rays. There are educational shows on dive feeding and understanding dolphin behavior scheduled throughout the day. VIP tours can be organized. ⊠ *Resorts World, 8 Sentosa Gateway, Sentosa Island* ☎ *6577–8888* ⊕ *www.rwsentosa.com/en/attractions/sea-aquarium* 💲 *S$32.*

Sentosa SkyJet

FOUNTAIN | **FAMILY** | This refresh of the famed Sentosa Musical Fountain from the 1980s is also the tallest fountain in Southeast Asia, standing at 80 meters tall. A spectacular water show runs at various times of the day between 10 am and 10 pm (last show at 9 pm); it is at its most visually enticing at night when illuminated by full-color LED lights. ⊠ *Beach Station, Sentosa Island* ⊕ *www.sentosa.com.sg* 💲 *Free.*

Skyhelix Sentosa

AMUSEMENT RIDE | If sky-high views are your thing, this gentle, spiraling open-air ride that hovers 35 meters in the sky, affording

Cable cars connect mainland Singapore to Sentosa, a resort-filled island just offshore.

a panoramic view of the Keppel Bay area and the nearby Southern Islands, is one to make time for. If you're planning to travel over or back from the island via the cable car, you can slot in this ride as one of the bonuses for your combo pass. It's located at the Sentosa cable-car station. ✉ *109 Mount Faber Rd., Sentosa Island* ☎ *6361–0088* ⊕ *www.mountfaberleisure.com* ✉ *S$20 (included in some cable-car combo passes).*

★ Universal Studios Singapore

THEME PARK | FAMILY | Packed with cutting-edge rides, shows, and movie-themed attractions, this theme park inside Resorts World Sentosa is a family favorite. Eighteen of the 24 movie-themed rides were designed or adapted especially for the Singapore park, including the world's first *Puss in Boots' Giant Journey* and the dueling *Battlestar Galactica: Human vs Cyclone* roller-coaster. Spread across seven themed sections, the park has a number of kid-friendly rides and shows, including Shrek 4-D Adventure, Dino-Soarin', and Donkey-Live as well as the Hello Kitty Studio Store and Minion Mart. The five-hour guided VIP tour includes priority access to eight popular rides like *TRANSFORMERS* The Ride: The Ultimate 3D Battle and photo-ops with characters. Popular dining spots like Mel's Drive-In, Fossil Fuel, and Fairy Godmother's Juice Bar provide fuel for what will be a busy day. ✉ *8 Sentosa Gateway, Sentosa Island* ⊕ *www.rwsentosa.com* ✉ *S$61* Ⓜ *Harbourfront.*

🏖 Beaches

Sentosa may be a small island but it has a 1.2-mile stretch of white sand separated into a few small beaches. Each has its own distinct character and attractions.

Palawan Beach

BEACH | FAMILY | The most family-friendly beach in Sentosa, Palawan has fine sand and waves so gentle the little ones can frolic freely. There's also a small island reachable via a short swim or a walk across a photo-worthy suspension rope bridge. The reward at the end of it? Reaching what's allegedly the southernmost point of continental Asia. **Amenities:** food and drink; showers; toilets. **Best for:** sunset; swimming. ⊠ *Sentosa Island.*

Siloso Beach

BEACH | This wide, sandy beach is a hive of activity thanks to the concentration of beach clubs, water-sports centers, and nearby attractions such as the Mega Adventure Park. There are a number of casual eateries along the stretch of sand, and in-line skaters zoom up and down the promenade. For swimmers, there are red and yellow flag markers (swim here), as well as beach patrol officers if help is required. **Amenities:** food and drink; showers; toilets; water sports. **Best for:** partiers; sunset; swimming. ⊠ *Sentosa Island* ⊕ *www.sentosa.com.sg.*

Tanjong Beach

BEACH | Shaped like a numeral three from above, this stretch of beach is busy on weekends thanks to the always vibing beachfront Tanjong Beach Club. It's also popular with dog owners and their water-trained pooches. Come on a weekday if you fancy having the beach all to yourself. **Amenities:** food and drink; showers; toilets. **Best for:** sunset; swimming solitude. ⊠ *Sentosa Island* ⊕ *www.sentosa.com.sg.*

Tanjong Rimau

BEACH | Sentosa Island isn't all fancy hotels and beach bars—there's also the natural, biodiverse area of Tanjong Rimau. Located at the far end of Siloso Beach, it is home to many creatures like red egg crabs, hairy crabs, sea snails, and occasionally, octopuses that can be spotted at low tide. For an experiential journey led by volunteer guides, join the Siloso Headland Intertidal Programme. The closest amenities are at Fort Siloso Skywalk or Silver Shell Cafe. **Amenities:** none. **Best for:** solitude; walking. ⊠ *Tanjong Rimau, Sentosa Island* ⊕ *www.sentosa.com.sg/en/things-to-do/events/siloso-headland-intertidal-programme.*

 Restaurants

Cassia

$$ | **CHINESE** | Traditional Cantonese dishes are presented with modern flair in an understated setting at this award-winning Chinese restaurant. Plush banquettes and elegant wallpaper by designer Andre Fu grace the dining room, and an outdoor seating area overlooks lush grounds. **Known for:** Peking duck; modern twists on traditional Cantonese dishes; elegant setting. *$ Average main: S$24* ⊠ *Capella Singapore, 1 The Knolls, Sentosa Island* ☎ *6591–5045* ⊕ *www.capellahotels.com/en* ☺ *Closed Mon.–Thurs.*

Coastes

$$ | **INTERNATIONAL** | **FAMILY** | At this kid-friendly hangout, adults can unwind over pizza and watch the little ones take a dip in the shallow water or play with the restaurant's sand toys. Expect a laid-back vibe here with sunbeds and deck chairs for customers. **Known for:** laid-back beachfront setting; family-friendly atmosphere; curry laska and chicken wings. *$ Average main: S$16* ⊠ *50 Siloso Beach Walk, #01–05, Sentosa Island* ⊕ *www.coastes.com.*

★ Malaysian Food Street

$ | **MALAYSIAN** | Who wins the great debate over which country has the best hawker food, Singapore or Malaysia? Judge for yourself without crossing the causeway at this cluster of hawker stalls (thankfully air-conditioned), which has all the signature Malaysian hawker noshes in one spot. The variety (and aromas) can prove overwhelming, so your best (and safest) bet is opting for the places with the longest lines. **Known for:** authentic Malaysian hawker food such as clay pot chicken rice; affordable prices; wide variety. *$ Average main: S$8* ⊠ *8 Sentosa Gateway, Waterfront Level 1, Sentosa Island* ⊕ *www.rwsentosa.com/en/restaurants/malaysian-food-street/overview* ▭ *No credit cards.*

Ocean Restaurant

$$$$ | **MEDITERRANEAN** | The sight of sharks and manta rays swimming past your dinner table at this elegant restaurant in the S.E.A. Aquarium makes for quite the memory. **Known for:** romantic atmosphere (no kids under 8); fresh Mediterranean-California creations; unusual destination dining experience. *$ Average main: S$148* ⊠ *S.E.A. Aquarium, 22 Sentosa Gateway, #B1–455 and 456, Sentosa Island* ⊹ *West zone carpark B1M* ☎ *6577–6688* ⊕ *www.rwsentosa.com.*

1-Altitude Coast

$$ | ASIAN FUSION | Perched at the top of The Outpost Hotel, this rooftop bar, day club, and restaurant serves up crowd-pleasing modern Asian dishes like soft shell crab pasta and platters like the "Taste of Archipelago" (including tasting portions of nasi biru, tempeh goreng, and papa gulai chicken) offer a sampling of Southeast Asian flavors. Sundown sessions are particularly popular (weekdays 5–8 pm) for unobstructed views of the Singapore Straits; at the Sunday pool parties, DJs spin from 3 to 10 pm. **Known for:** shareable platters; sunset drinks; per-person minimum spend. $ *Average main: S$24* ⊠ *The Outpost Hotel Sentosa, 10 Artillery Ave., Level 7, Sentosa Island* ☎ *8879–8765* ⊕ *www.1-altitudecoast.sg.*

Panamericana

$$ | SOUTH AMERICAN | Come for the view, stay for the food and laid-back vibes. The menu of farm-to-fire dishes spans the Americas with standouts like the slow-cooked lamb charred on the asador, Argentinian empanadas, and market-fresh ceviche swimming in coconut milk. **Known for:** lamb cooked over an asador; large platters and cocktails; view of the South China Sea. $ *Average main: S$32* ⊠ *Sentosa Golf Club, 27 Bukit Manis Rd., Sentosa Island* ☎ *6253–8182* ⊕ *www.panamericana.sg.*

Rumours Beach Club

$$ | INDONESIAN | Bringing a bit of Bali's beach swagger to Singapore, this beach club's Jimbaran seafood grill station (from 12 pm onwards) is a big draw for its smoky, charred dishes like ikan bakar (grilled whole fish) and lobster bakar (grilled whole lobster). The menu also has a selection of Indonesian dishes and an extensive selection of bar-friendly food and drinks to enjoy for something more casual. **Known for:** Indonesian-style grilled dishes; seafood platters; three swimming pools. $ *Average main: S$30* ⊠ *40 Siloso Beach Walk, Sentosa Island* ☎ *6970–0625* ⊕ *www.rumours.com.sg.*

★ Table 65

$$$$ | MODERN EUROPEAN | For a really special treat, this celebrated eatery by chef Richard van Oostenbrugge of Amsterdam's Restaurant 212 will do the trick, offering pricey but precise and elegant tasting menus. In the convivial, communal setting, you might sit next to strangers. **Known for:** theatrical presentations; communal fine-dining experience; no kids under 12 allowed. $ *Average main: S$118* ⊠ *Hotel Michael, 26 Sentosa Gateway, #01–104 and 10, Sentosa Island* ☎ *6577–7939* ⊕ *www.rwsentosa.com/en* ⊗ *Closed Sun. and Mon.*

Trapizza

$$ | **ITALIAN** | **FAMILY** | Channeling a Palm Springs vibe with cacti and palm-tree landscaping, this family-friendly Italian eatery on Siloso Beach has a dedicated children's water play area and coloring corner. Order the thin-crust, wood-fired pizzas—including a shareable 16-inch pie—or a hearty burger. **Known for:** family-sized 16-inch pizza; chill beachfront setting; kid-friendly facilities. $ *Average main: S$28* ⊠ *Shangri-La Rasa Sentosa, 10 Siloso Beach Walk, Sentosa Island* ☎ *6376–2662* ⊕ *www.shangri-la.com.*

🛏 Hotels

The Barracks Hotel Sentosa

$$$$ | **HOTEL** | For those who appreciate luxe heritage spaces, the Barracks Hotel provides an intimate setting on the premises of an old British artillery outpost. **Pros:** extras like the heritage tour; ground-floor rooms have direct pool access; nightly happy hour. **Cons:** pricier than other nearby hotels; shared gym facilities; expensive in-room dining. $ *Rooms from: S$586* ⊠ *2 Gunner La., Sentosa Island* ☎ *6722–0802* ⊕ *www.thebarrackshotel.com.sg* ⇴ *40 rooms* ⫟ *Free Breakfast.*

★ Capella Singapore

$$$$ | **HOTEL** | Situated on a lush 30-acre property, this word-class hotel is made up of a pair of restored colonial bungalows from the 1880s and a modern wing designed by Foster + Partners. **Pros:** direct access to Palawan Beach; triple-tier infinity pool; several award-winning restaurants. **Cons:** small spa (advanced booking recommended); pricey; breakfast not included. $ *Rooms from: S$780* ⊠ *1 The Knolls, Sentosa Island* ☎ *6377–8888* ⊕ *www. capellahotels.com* ⇴ *112 rooms* ⫟ *No Meals.*

Equarius Hotel

$$$$ | **RESORT** | **FAMILY** | This hotel feels less like a family theme park than the five other hotels that make up Resorts World Sentosa. **Pros:** some rooms have direct pool access; a tranquil escape; access to amenities at other Resorts World hotels. **Cons:** not centrally located; could use more character; very expensive. $ *Rooms from: S$800* ⊠ *Resorts World, 8 Sentosa Gateway, Sentosa Island* ☎ *6577–8899* ⊕ *www.rwsentosa.com* ⇴ *172 rooms* ⫟ *No Meals.*

The Outpost Hotel

$$$$ | **HOTEL** | With a spectacular sky pool complete with a swim-up cocktail bar and complimentary partner yoga and gin-making workshops, this Sentosa hotel is geared more for couples and travel groups looking to let loose on vacation than the typical family contingent the island is famous for. **Pros:** adults-only sky pool; interactive guest activities; adults-only property. **Cons:** shared pool with Village Hotel Sentosa; rooms on the smaller side; some rooms do not include closets, just clothing racks. $ *Rooms from: S$559* ⊠ *10 Artillery Ave, #03–01, Sentosa Island* ☎ *67220–0801* ⊕ *www.theoutposthotel.com.sg* ☞ *193 rooms* ⦿ *No Meals.*

Shangri-La's Rasa Sentosa Resort

$$$ | RESORT | FAMILY | The rooms in this vast, arc-shaped building all have balconies; ask for ones facing the sea, or else your view will be of a grassy knoll. **Pros:** family-friendly; beachfront location; complimentary shuttle bus service to and from VivoCity. **Cons:** isolated; lots of kids; conference-center feel. $ *Rooms from: S$500* ⊠ *101 Siloso Rd., Sentosa Island* ☎ *6275–0100, 020/8747–8485 for reservations in the U.K., 800/942–5050 for reservations in Canada and the U.S.* ⊕ *www.shangri-la.com* ☞ *454 rooms* ⦿ *No Meals.*

Sofitel Singapore Sentosa Resort & Spa

$$ | RESORT | The remote location of this resort made it good for business seminars and those looking for a real escape. **Pros:** pet-friendly; large pool; resort-style setting. **Cons:** away from city center; unimpressive lobby; lots of steps to the beach. $ *Rooms from: S$325* ⊠ *2 Bukit Manis Rd., Sentosa Island* ☎ *6708–8310, 800/637–7200 for reservations in the U.S.* ⊕ *www.sofitel-singapore-sentosa.com* ☞ *213 rooms* ⦿ *No Meals.*

★ W Singapore – Sentosa Cove

$$$$ | RESORT | At this, another of the Starwood chain's trendy W brand hotels, works by Andy Warhol and Damien Hirst are mixed in with unique art installations, and the glam-rock atmosphere starts in the lobby with an illuminated wall and fountain at WOO-BAR, where a DJ often spins. **Pros:** seaside city escape; huge pool with underwater speakers; stylish rooms. **Cons:** no beach; not centrally located; doesn't feel local, despite the lush surroundings. $ *Rooms from: S$528* ⊠ *Sentosa Cove, 21 Ocean Way, Sentosa Island* ☎ *6808–7288* ⊕ *www.marriott.com* ☞ *240 rooms* ⦿ *No Meals.*

🍸 Nightlife

There isn't much real "nightlife" per se on Sentosa, but you can still find rather lively hangouts after sunset. Bob's is the most tranquil; Tanjong Beach Club and Rumours Beach Club are good afternoon-sunset spots.

Bob's Bar

BARS | Sentosa's resident blue-and-green peafowls are regularly sighted at this unforgettable spot—the perfect place for sunset drinks. The cocktail menu is extensive with libations like the tropical rum-based Palawan Fizz and the gin and prosecco-based Pandan Spritz. To try something uniquely theirs, order a drink containing Navegante, a rum made exclusively for the bar. Time your session to coincide with the daily "Bosum's Call" at 6 pm, when the staff hand out tasting portions of rum and canapes. ✉ *Capella Singapore, 1 The Knolls, Sentosa Island* ☎ *6591–5047* ⊕ *www. capellahotels.com.*

★ Tanjong Beach Club

GATHERING PLACES | For those looking to lounge in the sun among the palms or play outdoor games, this trendy beach bar often tops world's-best lists and has pretty good food as well. Daybeds are available (they can also be reserved) as well as lounge chairs, a swimming pool, and DJs that are often on deck. The weekend crowd is typically young professionals looking to let loose over a game of beach volleyball or beer pong. This stretch of sand, shaped like a numeral three from above, is also popular with dog owners and their water-trained pooches. To avoid the crowds; come on a weekday, then linger for the sunset, which is especially pretty here. ✉ *120 Tanjong Beach Walk, Sentosa Island* ☎ *9750– 5323* ⊕ *www.tanjongbeachclub.com.*

🎭 Performing Arts

SOUND AND LIGHT SHOWS

Magical Shores at Siloso

SOUND/LIGHT SHOW | **FAMILY** | This immersive light-and-sound show is staged along a stretch of Siloso Beach, including two sections where you can interact with the light art on the sand. The 15-minute show runs from 7:30 pm to 9:30 pm on weekdays, till 10:30 pm on Friday, Saturday, and Sunday. ✉ *Siloso Beach Walk, Sentosa Island* ⊕ *www.sentosa.com.sg* 🎟 *Free* Ⓜ *Harbourfront.*

Wings of Time

SOUND/LIGHT SHOW | **FAMILY** | A crowd-pleasing multisensory night show about two cranes that journey together through time, this story is told via a larger-than-life water screen programmed with 3-D effects, lasers, robotic water fountains, and spectacular pyrotechnics. For a good view of the stage, dole out extra for the premium seats. Shows take place at 7:40 pm and 8:40 pm nightly. Discounted tickets are available online. ✉ *Beach View, Sentosa Island* ☎ *6736–8672* ⊕ *www.mountfaberleisure.com* 🎟 *S$19 (standard), S$24 (premium)* Ⓜ *Beach Station.*

🛍 Shopping

Unlike other parts of Singapore, Sentosa is not known for its retail stores. However, there are a decent number of luxury brands available at Resorts World Sentosa, as well as gift shops and souvenir kiosks scattered across the island. The bulk of the 45 retail outlets at Resorts World Sentosa are high-end luxury brands like Cartier, Tiffany & Co., Rolex, and Bulgari. For the little ones, there are shops like Hershey's Chocolate World and a LEGO Certified Store.

🏃 Activities

Sentosa Island packs a punch with high-octane sports like bungee jumping and zip-lining, but it also offers the chance to be pampered in spa heaven and some idyllic beach club chill time.

ADVENTURE SPORTS

AJ Hackett Sentosa

LOCAL SPORTS | The bungee jump at AJ Hackett Sentosa offers a rather compelling 155-foot plunge above the palm tree–lined Siloso Beach. If that's too much of a daredevil activity for you, alternatives include the 130-foot-long Skybridge, the 138-foot Vertical Skywalk, and a group-friendly Giant Swing ride. ⊠ *30 Siloso Beach Walk, Sentosa Island* ☎ *6736–8672* ⊕ *www.sentosa.com.sg* 🖃 *S$129 (Bungee Jump), S$69 (Giant Swing), S$15 (Skybridge).*

Mega Adventure Park

LOCAL SPORTS | **FAMILY** | The 1,475-foot-long MegaZip Sentosa, the steepest zip-line in Southeast Asia, is just one of the attractions at this adventure park. There's also the MegaBounce, a bungee-assisted trampoline; the free-fall MegaJump; and the kid-friendly 36-obstacle treetop MegaClimb. Combination packages are sold online. Activities are weather dependent, so check the forecast before booking. ⊠ *10A Siloso Beach Walk, Sentosa Island* ☎ *6736–8672* ⊕ *www.sentosa.com.sg* 🖃 *Individual attractions from S$20.*

Skyline Luge

AMUSEMENT RIDE | **FAMILY** | Embrace the irony of luging—a winter sport that involves sledding down an ice track feet first—in perennially hot and humid Singapore. Here, however, you twist and turn down one of four paved tracks while seated on a luge with handlebars. If day luging is too tame, night rides are also available at no additional cost. The four-seater Skyride chairlift offers a more leisurely way to take in the view. ✉ *45 Siloso Beach Walk, Sentosa Island* ☎ *6274–0472* ⊕ *www.skylineluge.com* 🚇 *From S$29 (Luge, 2 rides), S$12 (Skyride).*

GOLF

Sentosa Golf Club

GOLF | Members and guests can play two 18-hole courses at this award-winning eco-friendly golf club with rolling greens, large bunkers, mangrove swamps, and stunning city and ocean views. ✉ *27 Bukit Manis Rd., Sentosa Island* ☎ *6275–0022* ⊕ *www. sentosagolf.com* 🚇 *From S$370 weekdays; from S$500 weekends* 🏌 *Serapong course: 18 holes, 6,675 m, par 72; New Tanjong course: 18 holes, 6,210 m, par 72.*

GUIDED TOURS

Gogreen Segway Eco Adventure

GUIDED TOURS | **FAMILY** | This outfit's fun 30-minute Eco Adventure rides scoots past Palawan and Siloso beach. Instructions are provided beforehand, and helmets are mandatory. Call for tour times, only available on Friday, Saturday, and Sunday ✉ *51 Siloso Beach Walk, #01–01 Sentosa, Sentosa Island* ☎ *9825–4066* ⊕ *www. segwaytours.com.sg* 🚇 *S$49.90.*

SPAS

★ Auriga Spa

SPAS | In this traquil cocoon, treatments take place in spacious spa suites, each with its own private garden. There are just nine suites, so pre-booking is recommended. The Waning Moon (60 or 90 minutes) employs a detoxing lymphatic massage technique that corresponds to the different phases of the moon. Block time to have a 90-minute massage, which includes facial cleansing and a nourishing scalp massage. Pre- or post-treatment, linger in the vitality pool, herbal steam room, or ice fountain. ✉ *Capella Singapore, 1 The Knolls, Sentosa Island* ☎ *6377–8888* ⊕ *www. capellahotels.com* 🚇 *Treatments from S$295.*

CHI, The Spa

SPAS | This intimate spa offers a tranquil escape after a long travel day with treatments based on Asian wellness remedies. Try the Singapore massage which combines Chinese, Malay, and Indian therapies using bamboo sticks, an abdomen massage, and Kansu bowl to fully relax and unwind the body. For an extra special experience, book your treatment to take place at the outdoor Thai Pavilion perched over a fish pond and gentle waterfall. ✉ *Shangri-La Rasa Sentosa, 101 Siloso Rd., Sentosa Island* ☎ *6371–1027* ⊕ *www.shangri-la.com/singapore/rasasentosaresort/chi-the-spa/.*

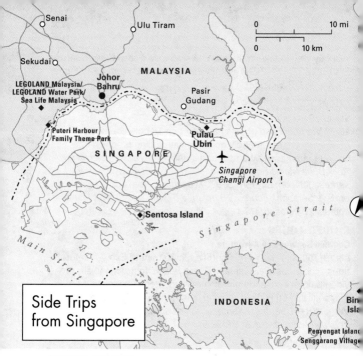

WATER SPORTS

Ola Beach Club

WATER SPORTS | There's no shortage of beach clubs on Sentosa Island, but pet-friendly Ola Beach Club stands out for its water sports activities (everything from hydrofoils to banana boats), Hawaiian-themed food (order the Lomi Lomi Salmon), tiki cocktails, and private pool tailored to active sun seekers. Come here to try your hand at hydro-flight with a water jet pack, a donut ride, or stand-up paddleboarding. There are also beach-facing cabanas in which to lounge for a minimum spend of $50/adult on Friday, Saturday and Sunday. ⊠ *46 Siloso Beach Walk, Sentosa Island* ☏ *6250–6978* ⊕ *www.olabeachclub.com* ☜ *Experiences from S$25.*

Pulau Ubin

Singapore is made up of 63 islands, so it would be a shame to explore only the mainland when several other spots are also worth a visit. A trip to Pulau Ubin offers a glimpse of what Singapore was like before modernization; ferries can also get you to to Kusu and St. John's, two of the Southern Islands, both of which have some especially good sights on offer.

Sights

★ Pulau Ubin

ISLAND | FAMILY | Take a 10-minute ride on a bumboat (a small launch) from Changi Point Ferry Terminal to be transported back in time on this boomerang-shaped island. It's best explored by bicycle, which can be rented on the island. There are three trails that lead past old plantations, mangrove swamps, forests, the occasional wild boar, and abandoned granite quarries that look surprisingly picturesque. You should also consider a visit to the Chek Jawa Wetlands, one of Singapore's richest ecosystems, to wander the 1-km (0.62-mile) boardwalk (Mangrove and Coastal Loops) and take in views from the 66-foot Jejawi Tower. There's also the Ketam Mountain Bike Park, a 10-km (6.2-mile) park around the Ketam Quarry. Before heading back, cool off with a fresh coconut drink or order a kampong-style meal from one of the small seafood restaurants near the jetty. ⊠ *Pulau Ubin* ⊕ *www.nparks.gov.sg* 🚢 *Boat ride from S$4 per person; bicycle rentals from S$10.*

🍴 Restaurants

Pulau Ubin's food options are casual and affordable, and, as there are no restrictions on what you can bring on the island, you can also pack your own food and drink. If you don't have access to a kitchen, swing by the Changi Village Hawker Center near the jetty and pick up some takeout. Otherwise, make sure you have some cash on hand, as at some of the island's simple eateries, cash is the payment of choice.

Cheong Lian Yuen

$ | ASIAN | Simple and unassuming, this spot close to the jetty and near the bicycle rental shops is a good place to have a cold drink after exploring the island. You can't go wrong with any of the wok-fried dishes or the chilli crab. **Known for:** affordable food; cash only; chilli crab. ⑤ *Average main: S$5* ⊠ *20 Pulau Ubin, Pulau Ubin* 🕿 *6542–1147* ▭ *No credit cards.*

Season Live Seafood

$ | ASIAN | This restaurant is located close to the jetty and has a laid-back island vibe, like all the other places. It's a good place to grab a fresh, cold coconut drink, but if you're hungry, the dishes to try include the not-too-spicy *sambal kangkong* (stir-fried water spinach with chili) and the black-pepper crab. **Known for:** black-pepper crab; simple home-cooked food; cash only. ⑤ *Average main: S$10* ⊠ *59E Pulau Ubin, Pulau Ubin* 🕿 *6542–7627* ▭ *No credit cards.*

🏃 Activities

Exploring Pulau Ubin is easily done. Whether you join a guided expedition or plan your own itinerary, resources like⊕ *www. wildsingapore.com* (a blog dedicated to Singapore's outdoors) can come in handy.

★ Adventures by Asian Detours

KAYAKING | Join this group's six-hour Ubin Bisect Kayaking tour to kayak through the mangroves of Pulau Ubin. Four hours will be spent on the water. The eight-hour Paddle to Pedal includes kayaking the backwaters of the Sungei Jelutong and cycling along Ubin's trails. ⊠ *34 Pulau Ubin, Pulau Ubin* ☎ *9772–2071* ⊕ *www. adventures.network* ▦ *From S$138.*

National Parks Board

GUIDED TOURS | For a guided tour (60 minutes) of the intertidal flats of Chek Jawa and its rich marine life, check in with the National Parks Board, which runs regular group tours (max 15 participants) of the area. Booking ahead is recommended as spots fill up fast. The parks board has also mapped out two self-guided walking tours of the island for those who prefer to explore independently. ⊠ *Pulau Ubin* ⊕ *www.nparks.gov.sg* ▦ *From S$60 per group.*

Bintan Island

Just a short ferry ride from Singapore, the Indonesian island of Bintan is a peaceful retreat from the bustling city. This leisure-focused island offers pristine beaches, luxurious day spas, championship golf courses, and a number of high-end resorts. It's an easy add-on to any stay in Singapore—one that does not require flying.

GETTING HERE AND AROUND

The best way to get to Bintan is via a fast ferry operated by Bintan Resort Ferries (⊕ *www.brf.com.sg*). It departs daily from Singapore's Tanah Merah Ferry Terminal to Bintan's Bandar Bentan Telani Ferry Terminal. Once on the island, make use of complimentary shuttle bus services (⊕ *www.bintan-resorts.com*) that run between the resorts, Bandar Bentan Telani (BBT) Ferry Terminal, Plaza Lagoi, and Safari Lagoi. Taxi and car rental services are also available and can be booked at the Ferry Terminal. Look for Wira Taxi Service (☎ *+62 821/12000998*) and Global Bintan Transportation (☎ *+62 770/691–818*).

TIMING

Depending on how long you plan to stay in Singapore, Bintan Island can be done as a day-trip, an overnight, or even extended weekend excursion. As the island is a popular weekend spot for both Singaporeans and Indonesians, avoid the crowds and snag better accommodation and activity deals by visiting on a weekday.

Like Singapore, Bintan is humid, with a monsoon season that runs from early November to around late March. Singapore is also one hour ahead of Bintan.

MONEY

Although Bintan is in Indonesia, some hotels charge in Singapore or U.S. dollars, but it's advisable to have some Indonesia rupiah on you. Most resorts accept American Express, Visa, and Mastercard.

VISAS

Although Bintan is just a ferry ride from Singapore, it is part of Indonesia, and you'll need to get the necessary visas. U.S. citizens don't need a visa for visits under 30 days but otherwise can purchase one on arrival.

⊙ Sights

Penyengat Island

RUINS | Located 15 minutes by water taxi from Bintan's Tanjung Pinang district lies Penyengat Island, once the epicenter of the Malay Riau-Lingga empire. It offers a peek into Malay cultural heritage and has been nominated as a UNESCO World Heritage Site. The main landmark is the Sultan's Palace, rumored to be built from a mixture of egg white and lime. Inside the grounds, there's a restored fort, tombs, and a handwritten and illustrated Qur'an that's more than 150 years old. To get here, hire a speed boat at Tanjung Pinang jetty (US$7). ✉ *South China Sea, Tanjungpinang Kota* ⊕ *www.indonesia.travel/gb/en.*

Senggarang Village

TOWN | The first settlement for ethnic Chinese immigrants who arrived in Bintan sometime in the 1700s, this rustic village is home to some of Bintan's oldest temples: the complex of Lau Ya Keng and the unusual Banyan Tree Temple, a 200-year-old structure that's become intertwined with the trunk of an ancient banyan tree. The village is best reached via a 15-minute water taxi ride from Tanjung Pinang and can be combined with a visit to Penyengat Island.

⚓ Beaches

Lagoi Beach
BEACH | A public beach situated near the Plaza Lagoi shopping area, this pristine coastal stretch has crystal clear water and a wide variety of water sports such as kayaking, jet-skiing, and snorkeling, plus the odd game of beach volleyball. **Amenities:** food and drink; toilets; water sports. **Best for:** sunset; swimming; windsurfing. ⊠ *Lagoi Beach, Bintan Island.*

Trikora Beach
BEACH | Although Bintan has many swanky beach resorts, the coastline toward the east is worth a trek if you prefer to enjoy white-sand beaches without paying five-star resort prices. Located an hour's car ride from Bintan Resorts—where the ferries arrive and depart—Trikora Coast has a number of modest accommodations and eateries and is a popular spot for weekend kite surfers. There are four beaches in total and basic sheltered beach huts for rent. To get around, bring or hire a bicycle, or employ the services of a driver. **Amenities:** showers; toilets; water sports. **Best for:** sunset; swimming; snorkeling.

🍴 Restaurants

The Kelong Seafood Restaurant
$$ | SEAFOOD | Traditional *kelongs* (floating platforms built on stilts used for fishing) were once off limits to women but those that remain have mostly discarded the superstition. This one at Nirwana Gardens was transformed into a seafood restaurant and now serves fresh catches in a rustic setting overlooking the ocean. **Known for:** black-pepper crab, sea snails, and catch of the day; laidback atompshere; scenic setting overlooking the ocean. $ *Average main: S$16* ⊠ *Jalan Panglima Pantar, Lagoi* ☎ *811/691–8277* ⊕ *www.nirwanagardens.com* ☉ *Closed Mon.*

Warung Yeah!
$ | INDONESIAN | For a taste of authentic Indonesian cuisine in a casual, café setting, this local favorite situated beachfront of Lagoi Bay is popular for traditional Javanese dishes such as smoke-kissed *ayam bakar* (grilled chicken) and signature *nasi goreng Yeah* (Indonesian-style fried rice). **Known for:** ayam bakar (Indonesian grilled chicken); nasi goreng Yeah (special fried rice); affordable prices. $ *Average main: S$4* ⊠ *Jl. Gurindam Duabelas, Teluk Sebong Lagoi Bintan Utara* ☎ *813/1311–1128* ⊕ *www.yeahbintan. com.*

🛏 Hotels

Natra Bintan, A Tribute Portfolio Resort

$ | HOTEL | Ditch the cookie-cutter hotel room for a glamping-style stay in one of these stylish, circular tents that come kitted out with king-size canopy beds, and some with private patios and whirlpool tubs. **Pros:** novel luxury camping set-up; easy access to watersports; proximity to Crystal Lagoon. **Cons:** rooms could do with more lighting; no direct food and drink service by the lagoon; limited dining options on-site. ⑤ *Rooms from: S$154* ✉ *Jalan Raya Haji KM 01 Kawasan Pariwisata, Teluk Sebong Lagoi, Bintan* ☎ *7706–92252* ⊕ *www.marriott.com* ⤏ *100 rooms* ⦿ *Free Breakfast.*

The Sanchaya

$$$$ | RESORT | It's safe to say that your privacy is assured at The Sanchaya, which encompasses a 25-acre beachfront estate with just 29 villas and suites, each with deluxe chaise longues on private verandas that offer lagoon, pool, or ocean views, and one private residence. **Pros:** unbeatable beachfront location; charming colonial architecture; spacious, luxurious rooms. **Cons:** small spa; expensive activities; pricey food and drink. ⑤ *Rooms from: S$574* ✉ *Lagoi Bay, Bintan* ☎ *770/692–200* ⊕ *www.thesanchaya.com* ⤏ *29 rooms, 1 villa* ⦿ *Free Breakfast.*

🏃 Activities

Mangrove Discovery Tour

BOAT TOURS | FAMILY | This 60-minute tour of the mangrove forests in Bintan's Sebung River—there are four kinds of forest to explore here—can be done either during the day or night. By day, expect to see some of the river's wildlife: snakes, lizards, monkeys, and even the occasional crocodile. By night, the fireflies come out in full force, magically lighting the route down the river. The tour departs at 9 am during the day and 7 pm at night. There's a minimum of two people per tour. ✉ *48WJ+PH Teluk Sebong, Bintan* ☎ *852/7114–2660* ⊕ *www.bintan-resorts.com* 🎫 *From IDR 380,000.*

Ria Bintan

GOLF | On weekends, many Singapore-based golfers play on this championship course, one of Asia's best. Its 18-hole Ocean Course and 9-hole Forest Course cut through the island's natural junglescape and feature challenging ocean-facing holes, including a par 3 on the 9th hole (Ocean Course) that plays across the South China Sea. There's a hotel attached, the Ria Bintan Golf Lodge, for overnight or longer stays, and day-trips can be

organized with a transfer from the ferry terminal. ✉ *Jl Perigi Raja.
Lagoi, Bintan* ☎ *770/692–839* ⊕ *www.riabintan.com* 🛏 *From Rs.
1,575,000 (S$150)* 🍴 *Weekdays S$147; weekends and holidays
S$199* ⛳ *Ocean Course:18 holes, 7,075 yards, par 72; Forest
Course: 9 holes, 3,266 yards, par 36.*

Johor Bahru

Just a short drive (one hour) from Singapore, this vibrant city in
Malaysia is actually connected to Singapore by two causeways
(Woodlands and Tuas). A bustling city, it's a favorite weekend
destination for locals who are drawn by the attractive exchange
rate, delicious street food, and attractions such as LEGOLAND
in the Iskandar Puteri area. It's also an easy add-on to any stay in
Singapore—one that does not require a flight.

GETTING HERE AND AROUND

The most popular way is to cross the Johor-Singapore Causeway
by private car, taxi (from S$100, one-way), or bus (170X from Kranji
MRT, or Bus 950 from Woodlands; both go to JB Sentral).

You can also take the Shuttle Tebrau train from Woodlands Train
Checkpoint in Singapore to JB Sentral in Johor Bahru.

CONTACTS Singapore-Malaysia Private Car Service. ⊕ *www.
sgmytaxi.com.* **SBS Transit.** ⊕ *www.sbstransit.com.sg.* **Shuttle
Tebrau.** ⊕ *shuttleonline.ktmb.com.my.*

👁 Sights

Arulmigu Sri Rajakaliamman Glass Temple

TEMPLE | Known for its exquisite glass artwork and elaborate
designs, this unique Hindu temple is the only one of its kind
with 500,000 pieces of colored glass lining the walls and ceiling.
Dedicated to the goddess Kali, it is open for tourists daily in the
afternoons (between 1 and 5 pm). ✉ *Jalan Tun Abdul Razak 1/1,
Wadi Hana* ☎ *7224–5152* 🛏 *RM10.*

★ LEGOLAND Malaysia

THEME PARK | **FAMILY** | Packed with all things LEGO, the park offers
40 rides across 8 themed areas (LEGO City, LEGO Technic, LEGO
Kingdom) including Miniland, where Asia's landmarks (the Taj
Mahal, Merlion, Forbidden City) are re-imagined in a 1:20 scale
using over 30 million LEGO bricks. The park caters to both the
younger and older kids with interactive attractions like DUP-
LO Playtown, the VR roller coaster Great LEGO ride, hands-on

workshops, 4D movies, as well as nine retail concepts like The Brick Shop and Sensei's World. Tickets can be combined with entry to Sea Life and the attached LEGOLAND Water Park. For food, the Asian Deli, Burger Junction and Fire Rescue Bistro will keep everyone fed and energized throughout the day. ✉ *LEGOLAND Malaysia Resort, 7 Persiaran Medini Utara 3, Iskandar Puteri* ☎ *7597–8888* ⊕ *www.legoland.com.my* ✆ *RM199 (LEGOLAND only), RM 279 (with Sea Life), RM 339 (with Sea Life & LEGOLAND Water Park)* ⊙ *Closed Wed.*

★ LEGOLAND Water Park
WATER PARK | FAMILY | Over 20 water slides, attractions, and rides such as the Build-A-Raft lazy river, DUPLO Splash Safari, and LEGO Slide Racers make up the fun at this LEGO-themed water park. There are rides for young (min. 91 cm) and older kids (min. 107 cm) with a couple of non-height restricted attractions like the Build-A-Boat and Imagination Station. You can rent towels, cabanas, and gazebos for a full or half-day. Children under 3 must wear a swim diaper. ✉ *LEGOLAND Malaysia Resort, 7 Persiaran Medini Utara 3, Iskandar Puteri* ☎ *7597–8888* ⊕ *www.legoland.com.my* ✆ *RM149* ⊙ *Closed Tues.*

Puteri Harbour Family Theme Park
AMUSEMENT PARK/CARNIVAL | FAMILY | This four-story indoor theme park is geared more for younger kids who will appreciate Sanrio Hello Kitty Town and Thomas Town. Highlights include The Little Big Club, where tots can meet Barney and Bob the Builder, go on an interactive Black Wonder hunt o find Hello Kitty and Dear Daniel, and get on toddler-friendly Thomas-themed rides such as the Windmill, Colin Crane Drop, and Harold Helicopter. There is also an indoor playground and a live stage for character shows. ✉ *Puteri Harbour, G-07C level GF Marina Walk, Iskandar Puteri* ☎ *1092–43404* ⊕ *www.amitravel.my/package-pakej/puteri-harbour-family-theme-park-johor-bahru* ✆ *RM81.*

Sea Life Malaysia
AQUARIUM | FAMILY | Take a break from all things LEGO and wander the 11 habitat zones at this aquarium. Some 25 display tanks hold more than 13,000 sea creatures; you can discover a Portuguese Wanli shipwreck; immerse your hand in a live rockpool; walk through a tunnel with 180-degree views and black-tip reef sharks swimming about. There are also educational shows run by SEA LIFE rangers daily. ✉ *LEGOLAND Malaysia Resort, 7 Persiaran Medini Utara 3, Iskandar Puteri* ☎ *7597–8888* ⊕ *www.legoland.com.my* ✆ *RM89.*

Sultan Abu Bakar Royal Palace Museum

HISTORY MUSEUM | Once the Grand Palace of the Sultan of Johor, this 1886 building has aspects of both colonial and Islamic architecture. Now a museum, it showcases the history and opulence of the Johor royal family through historic artifacts, royal regalia, and pieces of art including traditional Malay weapons. Don't leave without catching the panoramic view of the city from the palace's hilltop location. ☒ *Jalan Seri Belukar, Kebun Merah* ☎ *7223–0555* 🎫 *RM32* 🕐 *Closed Fri.*

 Restaurants

Merah Kitchen & Bar Cafe

$$ | CAFÉ | The neon-lit restaurant off Jalan Wong Ah Fook is a popular choice for causeway-crossing Singaporeans. With all the Japanese vending machines and arcade game machines, you'll almost forget you're there to fuel up. **Known for:** colorful, fruity mocktails; rice-based bowls; trendy café vibe with arcade game machines. ⑤ *Average main: RM29* ☒ *17, Jalan Ibrahim,, Bandar Johor Bahru* ☎ *5135–9434* ⊕ *www.facebook.com/merahkitchennbar/.*

★ Shun Fa Bak Kut Teh Restaurant Eco Botanic

$$ | ASIAN | FAMILY | This Malaysian chain is known for serving some of the best-tasting *bak kut teh* (pork ribs cooked in herbs and spices) in Johor thanks to its mild, sweet herbaceous broth. Presented in a clay pot with side dishes like crispy tofu skin and liver, it's best enjoyed with some fried dough fritters or a plain bowl of white rice. **Known for:** sesame oil chicken; pig trotters; bak kut teh (braised pork ribs). ⑤ *Average main: RM15* ☒ *55, Jalan Eko Botani 3/5, Taman Eko Botani, Gelang Patah* ☎ *6712–2100* ⊕ *www.facebook.com/ShunFaBakkuttehEcoBotanic/.*

Yi Jia Taste

$ | ASIAN | FAMILY | Sitting down for a seafood meal is a must-do when in Johor Bahru, and this air-conditioned option is located close to LEGOLAND in Iskandar Puteri. Check for their specials, but failsafe orders include the seafood porridge, curry fish fillet, and Nanyang-style crab with glass noodles. **Known for:** affordable seafood dishes; Nanyang-style crab with glass noodles; seafood porridge. ⑤ *Average main: RM48* ☒ *5 and 7, Jln Eko Botani 3/4, Taman Eko Botani, Nusajaya* ☎ *10760–1177* ⊕ *www.facebook. com/YiJiaTaste/.*

Hotels

★ LEGOLAND Hotel

$$$ | **HOTEL** | **FAMILY** | In addition to being right next to the theme park, this whimsical property with LEGO-themed elevators, a LEGO castle centerpiece, and live character appearances offers the opportunity to live and breathe all things LEGO. **Pros:** LEGO-themed rooms; unique LEGO decor and themed areas; adjacent to LEGOLAND theme park. **Cons:** suitable only if you are visiting LEGOLAND; theme park tickets not included; no fitness center or spa. ⑤ *Rooms from: RM1070* ⊠ *7 Jalan Legoland, Medini, Iskandar Puteri* ☎ *7597–8888* ⊕ *www.legoland.com.my* ⤵ *263 rooms* ⦿I *Free Breakfast.*

Somerset Medini Iskandar Puteri

$$ | **HOTEL** | **FAMILY** | Close to LEGOLAND, this serviced apartment hotel is suitable for families looking to stay somewhere with a fully-equipped kitchen. **Pros:** walking distance to LEGOLAND and Mall of Medini; rooms have kitchens; large rooms. **Cons:** messy check-in process; mediocre breakfast; no daily room cleaning. ⑤ *Rooms from: RM203* ⊠ *Lot 5 Jalan Medini Utara 4, Medini Iskandar, Iskandar Puteri* ☎ *7560–5555* ⊕ *www.discoverasr.com* ⤵ *310 rooms* ⦿I *Free Breakfast.*

⬤ Shopping

Johor Premium Outlets

OUTLET | Located close to LEGOLAND, the mall has about 150 retail outlets, most of which are familiar, high-end brands like Jimmy Choo, Gucci, Balenciaga, and Valentino. For non-shoppers, there's a food court and local Malaysian chains like OldTown White Coffee and The Chicken Rice Shop. ⊠ *Jalan Premium Outlets, Indahpura* ☎ *7661–8888* ⊕ *www.premiumoutlets.com.my/ johor-premium-outlets.*

Pasar Karat

MARKET | This nightly flea market behind the City Square Mall and JB Sentral is a hive of activity thanks to the rows of affordable clothing (with the odd hip, streetwear find) and ample street food offerings—donuts, local milk tea, dragon beard candy. It's open until 2 am nightly except Friday, it's worth a visit for the people-watching alone. ⊠ *26/20 Jalan Segget, Bandar, Johor Bahru.*

Index

Photo Credits

Front Cover: Gavin Hellier/Alamy Stock Photo [D9WN9K Southeast Asia, Singapore, Elevated view over the Entertainment district of Clarke Quay, the Singapore river and City Skyline]. **Back cover, from left to right:** Vichy Deal/Shutterstock. Luciano Mortula/Shutterstock. Marcin Stolarek_Shutterstock. **Spine:** Zhukova Valentyna/Shutterstock. **Interior, from left to right:** Noppanun Lerdwattanapaisan/iStockphoto (1). Hel080808/Dreamstime (2-3). **Chapter 1: Experience Singapore:** Lena_serditova/iStockphoto (6-7). Supertree Grove/National Parks Board, Singapore (8-9). Efired/Dreamstime (9). Singapore Tourism Board (9). Raffles Singapore (10). Singapore Tourism Board (10). Courtesy of Marina Bay Sands (10). Singapore Tourism Board (11). Singapore Tourism Board (12). Singapore Tourism Board (12). Janelle Lugge/Shutterstock (12). Singapore Tourism Board (13). Zhnger/iStockphoto (13). Plain Vanilla Bakery (14). Euriico/Dreamstime (14). CharlieTong/iStockphoto (15). Pipop_Boosarakumwadi/iStockphoto (20). ThamKC/iStockphoto (21). Bennymarty/iStockphoto (22). Courtesy of Shangri-La Singapore (22). Daniel Koh/Village Hotel Sentose (22). Conrad Centennial Singapore (22). Sebastien Nagy/Park Royal Hotels (23). Courtesy of Native (24). Tawan C. Photography (24). Tom White (24). Nutmeg & Clove (24). EK Yap and Atlas (25). Singapore Tourism Board (26). Bobby Oh/National Parks Board, Singapore (26). National Parks Board, Singapore (26). Richie Chan/Shutterstock (26). Blue Planet Studio/Shutterstock (27). Miew S/Shutterstock (27). Singapore Tourism Board (27). Mega Adventure (27). **Chapter 3: Civic District and Marina Bay:** Molpix/Shutterstock (49). Casper1774 Studio/Shutterstock (52). Akekalak/iStockphoto (57). Courtesy of Gardens by the Bay (71). **Chapter 4: Chinatown the CBD, and Tanjong Pagar:** Badahos/iStockphoto (81). Nikolaj Alexander/iStockphoto (84). Pablo Hidalgo/Dreamstime (99). **Chapter 5:Tiong Bahru, Singapore River, and River Valley:** Joyfull/Dreamstime (117). James Davies/Alamy Stock Photo (123). Freedomz/Shutterstock (138). N8Allen/Shutterstock (142). **Chapter 6: Little India and Kampong Glam:** Ronnie Chua/Shutterstock (147). Filipe.Lopes/Shutterstock (153). Tang Yan Song/Shutterstock (159). **Chapter 7: Orchard:** LeeYiuTung/iStockphoto (169). Marek Poplawski/Shutterstock (176). **Chapter 8: Eastern Districts:** Bennymarty/iStockphoto (191). Mehdi33300/Shutterstock (205). **Chapter 9: Western Districts:** Qiongna Liao/Shutterstock (213). Xuefeng Nong/Dreamstime (227). Uraiwons/Shutterstock (237). Tristan Tan/Shutterstock (245). **Chapter 10: Side Trips:** AliB_Photography/iStockphoto (251). Photon-Photos/iStockphoto (257). **About Our Writers:** All photos are courtesy of the writers except for the following. Charlene Fang Courtesy of Claire van der Lee (288). Olivia Lee Courtesy of Claire van der Lee (288).

*Every effort has been made to trace the copyright holders, and we apologize in advance for any accidental errors. We would be happy to apply the corrections in the following edition of this publication.

Notes

Fodor's InFocus SINGAPORE

Publisher: Stephen Horowitz, *General Manager*

Editorial: Douglas Stallings, *Editorial Director;* Jill Fergus, Amanda Sadlowski, *Senior Editors;* Brian Eschrich, Alexis Kelly, *Editors;* Angelique Kennedy-Chavannes, *Assistant Editor;* Yoojin Shin, *Associate Editor*

Design: Tina Malaney, *Director of Design and Production;* Jessica Gonzalez, *Senior Designer;* Jaimee Shaye, *Graphic Design Associate*

Production: Jennifer DePrima, *Editorial Production Manager;* Elyse Rozelle, *Senior Production Editor;* Monica White, *Production Editor*

Maps: Rebecca Baer, *Senior Map Editor;* Mark Stroud (Moon Street Cartography), *Cartographer*

Photography: Viviane Teles, *Director of Photography;* Namrata Aggarwal, Neha Gupta, Payal Gupta, Ashok Kumar, *Photo Editors;* Jade Rodgers, *Photo Production Intern*

Business and Operations: Chuck Hoover, *Chief Marketing Officer;* Robert Ames, *Group General Manager*

Public Relations and Marketing: Joe Ewaskiw, *Senior Director of Communications and Public Relations*

Fodors.com: Jeremy Tarr, *Editorial Director;* Rachael Levitt, *Managing Editor*

Technology: Jon Atkinson, *Executive Director of Technology;* Rudresh Teotia, *Associate Director of Technology;* Alison Lieu, *Project Manager*

Writers: Charlene Fang, Marco Ferrarese, Olivia Lee

Editor: Douglas Stallings

Production Editor: Jennifer DePrima

2nd Edition

ISBN 978-1-64097-662-7

ISSN 2690-4365

All details in this book are based on information supplied to us at press time. Always confirm information when it matters, especially if you're making a detour to visit a specific place. Fodor's expressly disclaims any liability, loss, or risk, personal or otherwise, that is incurred as a consequence of the use of any of the contents of this book.

SPECIAL SALES

This book is available at special discounts for bulk purchases for sales promotions or premiums. For more information, e-mail SpecialMarkets@fodors.com.

PRINTED IN CANADA

10 9 8 7 6 5 4 3 2 1

About Our Writers

 Charlene Fang, a Singapore native, is a freelance writer who splits her time between Singapore and California. She writes for a number of lifestyle and travel publications, including *Condé Nast Traveler*, *AFAR*, *Time Out*, and *SilverKris*. Charlene updated the Little India and Kampong Glam and Side Trips chapters for this edition.

 Marco Ferrarese, a freelance travel and culture writer based in Penang, is an expert on Malaysia and Borneo and has written for *Travel + Leisure Southeast Asia*, *CNN Travel*, *BBC Travel*, *The Guardian*, and *National Geographic Traveller* (UK), among others. Marco updated the Travel Smart, Experience, Civic District and Marina Bay, and Eastern Districts chapters for this edition.

 Olivia Lee is a freelance writer and recent transplant to Singapore, where she writes about travel and hospitality. In the past she has contributed to *The Guardian*, *The Wall Street Journal Magazine*, *Wanderlust*, and *Adventure Travel*, as well as Fodor's *Portugal*. For this edition, Olivia updated the Chinatown, Tanjong Pagar, and CBD; Tiong Bahru, River Valley, and Singapore River; Orchard Road; and Western Districts chapters.